PRACTICAL

Cisco Routers

Joe Habraken

Contents
at a Glance

W9-COR-058

A Division of Macmillan Computer Publishing, USA
201 W. 103rd Street
Indianapolis, Indiana 46290

Practical Cisco Routers

Copyright © 1999 by Que Corporation

International Standard Book Number: 0-7897-2103-1

Library of Congress Catalog Card Number: 99-63284

Printed in the United States of America

First Printing: September 1999

01   00   4   3

Trademarks

Warning and Disclaimer

Acquisitions Editor
Jenny Watson

Development Editor
Rick Kughen

Managing Editor
Lisa Wilson

Project Editor
Tonya Simpson

Copy Editor
Kate Givens

Indexer
Rebecca Salerno

Proofreader
Andy Beaster

Technical Editor
Ariel Silverstone

Interior Design
Anne Jones

Cover Design
Radar Design

Copy Writer
Eric Borgert

Layout Technicians
Stacey DeRome
Ayanna Lacey
Heather Miller

Contents

About the Author

Joe Habraken is an information technology consultant and best-selling author whose publications include *The Complete Idiot's Guide to Microsoft Access 2000*, *Microsoft Office 2000 8-in-1*, *Easy Publisher 2000*, and *Sams Teach Yourself Microsoft Outlook 2000 in 10 Minutes*. Joe has a Masters degree from the American University in Washington, D.C. and over 12 years of experience as an educator, author, and consultant in the information technology field. Joe is a Microsoft Certified Professional and currently provides consulting services in the NT Server and internetworking arenas to companies and organizations. He also currently serves as the lead instructor for the Networking Technologies program at Globe College in St. Paul, Minnesota.

Dedication

To all the NSS students at Globe College.

Good luck with your careers, and thanks for staying awake in my Cisco class (even when I babbled excitedly about internetworking and routing technology).

Acknowledgments

Creating a book like this takes a real team effort, and this particular book was created by a team of incredibly dedicated professionals. I would like to thank Jenny Watson, our acquisitions editor, who worked very hard to assemble the team that made this book a reality and always made sure the right pieces ended up in the right places.

I would also like to thank Rick Kughen, who served as the development editor for this book and who came up with many great ideas for improving its content. He always asked the right questions and wasn't afraid to burn the midnight oil to get the job done.

Also a tip of the hat and a thanks to Ariel Silverstone, who as the technical editor for the project did a fantastic job making sure that everything was correct and suggested several additions that made the book even more technically sound. Finally, a great big thanks to our production editor, Tonya Simpson, who ran the last leg of the race and made sure the book made it to press on time—what a great team of professionals.

Tell Us What You Think!

As the reader of this book, *you* are our most important critic and commentator. We value your opinion and want to know what we're doing right, what we could do better, what areas you'd like to see us publish in, and any other words of wisdom you're willing to pass our way.

As an Associate Publisher for Que Corporation, I welcome your comments. You can fax, email, or write me directly to let me know what you did or didn't like about this book—as well as what we can do to make our books stronger.

Please note that I cannot help you with technical problems related to the topic of this book, and that due to the high volume of mail I receive, I might not be able to reply to every message.

When you write, please be sure to include this book's title and author as well as your name and phone or fax number. I will carefully review your comments and share them with the author and editors who worked on the book.

Fax: 317-581-4666

Email: hardware@mcp.com

Mail: Jim Minatel
        Associate Publisher
        Que Corporation
        201 West 103rd Street
        Indianapolis, IN 46290 USA

introduction

I find it amazing how rapidly computer technology has changed over the last 10 years. Technology once considered too costly or too complex for small or medium-sized companies is now being embraced at breakneck speed. Internetworking devices, and routers in particular, are some of the former "big-company" technologies now being used by even the smallest companies.

Inexpensive, low-end routers provide the connection to service providers and the public switched telephone network for small companies (and even individuals) who are looking for more bandwidth as they increasingly use the Internet as a communication and marketing tool. And as companies grow, they also look for strategies to conserve the bandwidth on their company-owned LANs; LAN segmentation with routers has become a viable and cost-effective solution.

With this explosion of internetworking technology hitting the business world, there has been a growing need for professionals to configure, manage, and troubleshoot routers and other internetworking devices. And although several excellent books and training materials that relate to internetworking and Cisco products are available, most of these materials have been written for IT professionals with many years of experience or training already under their belts. A basic primer and entry-level book on the subject really hasn't been available—until now.

About This Book

When I sat down to write this book, I wanted to do two things: share my excitement about internetworking and Cisco router configuration and provide a book that someone new to this technology could use to explore the incredible possibilities this technology offers. I also wanted to create a solid learning tool and make the book useful as a reference for someone with little internetworking background, who suddenly found working with Cisco routers part of their job description. And although that sounds like somewhat of a tall order, I knew that I would have help.

Skilled designers and editors at Macmillan Publishing have worked very hard to create a book design that embraces fresh ideas and approaches that will provide an environment in which you can get the information you need quickly and efficiently. You will find that this book embraces a streamlined, conversational approach to the subject matter that will help you learn the concepts and become familiar with the hardware and software facts that you need to get the job done.

How This Book Is Organized

- Part I, "Networking Overview"—This section of the book helps you get up to speed or review several networking technologies. Information is provided on LANs, WANs, and internetworking. A chapter also provides information on the Open System Interconnection reference model and how it relates to real-world network protocols. The basics on how routers work is also included in this section.

- Part II, "Router Design and Basic Configuration"—This section walks you through the hardware components of a typical Cisco router. You are also introduced to the basic configuration of routers and learn an overview of the Cisco Internetwork Operating System.

- Part III, "Routing LAN Protocols"—This section provides information about popular LAN protocols, such as TCP/IP, IPX/SPX, and AppleTalk. You learn conceptual information on each of these protocol stacks. You also walk through the steps of configuring a Cisco router for each of these protocols.

- Part IV, "Advanced Configuration and Configuration Tools"—This section helps you become familiar with several WAN technologies available and how they are configured on a Cisco router. Restricting access to your routers and troubleshooting routers are also covered to give you a complete picture of working with internetworking devices. Information on using Cisco's ConfigMaker router configuration software is also included in this section. It provides someone who must get a router connected and configured in a hurry, a step-by-step look at how to use the ConfigMaker software.

Who Should Use This Book

This book is for anyone who needs a primer on internetworking and the configuration of Cisco routers. And whether you work for a big company, small company, or are just beginning your education to become a network professional, this book is an excellent first step as you build your knowledge base.

Conventions Used In This Book

Commands, directions, and explanations in this book are presented in the clearest format possible. The following items are some of the features that will make this book easier for you to use:

- Commands that you must enter—Router commands that you'll need to type are easily identified by a monospace font. For example, if I direct you to get the encapsulation (the WAN protocol set) for a serial interface, I'll display the command like this: `show interface serial 0`. This tells you that you'll need to enter this command exactly as it is shown.

- Combination and shortcut keystrokes—Text that directs you to hold down several keys simultaneously is connected with a plus sign (+), such as Ctrl+P.

- Cross references—If there's a related topic that is prerequisite to the section or steps you are reading, or a topic that builds further on what you are reading, you'll find the cross reference to it at the end of the section, like this:

SEE ALSO

➤ *To see how to create newspaper columns, see page xx.*

- Glossary terms—For all the terms that appear in the glossary, you'll find the first appearance of that term in the text in *italic* along with its definition.

- Sidenotes—Information related to the task at hand, or "inside" information from the author, is offset in sidebars that don't interfere with the task at hand. This valuable information is also easier to find. Each of these sidebars has a short title to help you quickly identify the information you'll find there. You'll find the same kind of information in these that you might find in notes, tips, or warnings in other books but here, the titles should be more informative.

part

1

NETWORKING OVERVIEW

chapter 1

LAN Review

The Advent of the PC

How and where people use computer technology has changed dramatically over the past 30 years. In the 1960s, computing revolved around large mainframe computers. In the early days, users typically interfaced with this highly centralized computer through an intermediary: an IS administrator or programmer. As computer technology evolved further, mainframe users were able to directly communicate with the computer using a dumb terminal (basically, a monitor and a keyboard hard-wired to the mainframe). In the 1970s, the miniframe gained dominance in the computing world, making computer technology accessible to a larger number of companies and organizations (even though these companies paid a premium for their ability to compute). All storage and computing power was still centralized, however, much the same as in the mainframe environment.

In the 1980s the personal computer (particularly the IBM Personal Computer) revolutionized the way you compute. Computing power was brought to the individual desktop. Not only was this new type of computer relatively easy to use (when compared to mainframes and miniframes) but also it was very affordable. The only flaw in this computing renaissance was the inability of users to collaborate and share resources. The individuality of the PC isolated its users.

Networking PCs

To overcome this decentralized computing model offered by the PC, software and hardware were developed in the 1980s and 1990s to connect PCs into networks that could share resources (such as printers and files). Networked PCs made it easy to design a collaborative computing environment for any business situation. Networked computers can share a variety of resources, including hardware (printers, modems), software (application software), and user-created files.

Different networking models arose to fit different types of networking needs. In situations where a few computers needed to share a particular hardware device, such as a printer, but did not require centralized file storage, the *peer-to-peer network* evolved. The only time individual users interfaced with this type of network was when they printed. The alternative to the peer-to-peer network was a network with more centralized control of resources and better security. This type of network—a *server-based network*—uses a server computer (the central controller of the network) to authenticate users on the network and provide central file storage (as well as access to a number of different hardware and software resources). How these two networking models differ deserves some additional discussion.

Peer-to-Peer Networks

Peer-to-peer networks provide an easy way to share resources, such as files and printers, without the need for an actual server computer. Peer computers act as both *clients* (the users of resources) and *servers* (the providers of resources). The only real requirements for building a peer-to-peer network are installing an operating system on the PCs that supports peer-to-peer networking and physically connecting the PCs.

Several operating systems, such as Microsoft Windows 3.11, Microsoft Windows 95/98, and Microsoft Windows NT Workstation, have peer-to-peer networking capabilities built in. Local drives, folders, and printers can be shared with others on the peer-to-peer network (see Figure 1.1).

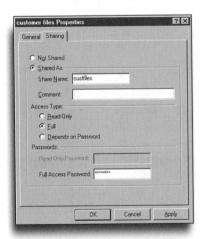

FIGURE 1.1
Operating systems such as Windows 98 make it easy for you to share resources on a peer-to-peer network.

Each resource that is shared (such as a drive or printer) potentially will have a different share password. This is one of the downsides of peer-to-peer networking—every resource is capable of having a separate password. If many resources are shared across the network, you will have to remember the password for each resource. This type of security is referred to as *share-level security*.

Peer-to-peer networks also don't require a great deal of additional administration because each user can manage resources on his own peer computer. Peer networks, however, do have their downsides:

- Increased performance hit on computers because of resource sharing
- No centralized location of shared files makes it difficult to back up data
- Security must be handled on a resource-by-resource level
- Decentralization of resources makes it difficult for users to locate particular resources
- Users might have to keep track of numerous passwords

Although peer-to-peer networking may seem like a fast and cheap way to connect a group of computers, the biggest drawback in using this type of networking is that only a small number of users can be accommodated. Peer networking isn't scalable (meaning expandable, because most peer networks are limited to 10 peer computers) and so is certainly not the appropriate choice for a growing company.

It is pretty much a consensus among IS managers that peer-to-peer networking works ideally with five or fewer peer machines.

SEE ALSO

➤ *For more information on the physical connections, see page 12.*

Server-Based Networks

Server-based networks provide greater centralized control of resources and expandability if required. A server computer is basically a special-purpose machine that logs in users and "serves" up resources to them. Because the server verifies users, this type of network makes it easier to manage your resources by providing different access levels to the various users in your user pool. A username and one password puts users onto the network and gives them access to any resource for which they have the appropriate permissions.

A server-based network typically employs a more powerful (in terms of processor speed, RAM, and hard-drive capacity) computer to act as the server. In addition to hardware that can handle a large number of user requests for services, the server computer must run special software—a network operating system (NOS). Two commonly used network operating systems are Microsoft Windows NT Server and Novell NetWare.

Server-based networks, as mentioned before, are scalable. This means that the network can grow along with your company. Servers can be added to your network that take on specialized duties. For example, one server may handle user login and verification (a primary domain controller on a Windows NT network would be an example), while another server on the network may handle the email system (a communications server). Table 1.1 lists some of the specialized servers you might use on a local area network.

Table 1.1 LAN Server Types

Server Type	Use
File server	Stores shared user files and provides home directory space for users (such as a Novell NetWare server)
Communication server	Provides communication services such as email (such as an NT Server running Microsoft Exchange Server)
Application server	Provides access to a database or other application (such as an SQL server database)
Print server	Provides the print queue and other services related to a network printer

A server-based network of computers that is limited to a fairly small geographical area such as a particular building is described as a local area network (LAN). LANs are found in small, medium, and large companies. When several LANs are connected, you are dealing with an *internetwork*, which is a network of networks (this type of network can also be referred to as a *campus*). When you start connected campuses and create networks that span large geographical areas, you are working in the realm of the Wide Area Network (WAN).

Server-based networks are really the standard for even small local area networks; these types of networks do have their downside, however. Much of the downside, at least for the small company wanting to set up a PC network, is cost—the cost of at least one server PC and the cost of the network operating system. Server-based networks also typically require the hiring of a full-time administrator to maintain and manage the network (and whereas management sees this as an additional cost, the network administrator sees it as money well spent).

Other negatives associated with the server-based network revolve around server failures, *broadcast storms* (tons of broadcast traffic from devices on the network), and other hardware- and software-related disasters that are too numerous to mention in this book. Networks are by nature challenging, and that is why a good network administrator is worth his or her weight in gold.

SEE ALSO

➤ *For more information on internetworking, see page 67.*

SEE ALSO

➤ *For more information on wide area networking see page 53.*

Making the Connection

To create a computer network, you must use some type of connective medium that allows the transfer of your data. This medium can range from copper cable to microwave transmissions to a beam of infrared light (our discussion of network media will be restricted to copper and fiber-optic cables, with the understanding that there are a lot of possibilities for moving data from one point to another).

After you choose a connective medium, such as copper cable, you also need a device that can prepare the data on the computer so that it can travel along your network cabling. This data restructuring is handled by a network interface card (NIC). A NIC is typically placed in one of the computer's bus expansion slots and then the network cable is attached to a port on the NIC. Understanding how the NIC works, and your options as far as copper and fiber-optic cabling, will go a long way when you have to sit down and design even the smallest networks.

Network Interface Cards

The network interface card (NIC) provides the connection between the PC and the network's physical medium (such as copper or fiber-optic cable). Data travels in parallel on the PC's bus system; the network medium demands a serial transmission. The transceiver (a transmitter and receiver) on the NIC card is able to move data from parallel to serial and vice versa.

Network interface cards each have a unique address that is burned onto a ROM chip on each NIC. This addressing system is used to move data from one physical connection to another (and you will find that resolving logical addresses such as IP addresses to NIC hardware addresses is really what networking is all about).

NICs are available for a number of bus types (Figure 1.2 shows a PCI Ethernet NIC), so make it a point to open up the PC or PCs that you are going to network and check to see what type of bus slots are available. Newer PCs will typically have PCI slots available. Older computers mean that you will have to deal with ISA and possibility EISA slots. Obviously, purchasing the appropriate card is extremely important in making the computer network-ready. The remainder of the battle is installing the network card and the appropriate software drivers for the NIC and getting the computer to recognize both.

FIGURE 1.2
Network interface cards provide the physical connection between a computer and the network.

Match the NIC to the network architecture

If you are putting together an IBM Token Ring network, you need to purchase Token Ring network cards. Although this may be one of those things that goes without saying, acquiring the hardware (NICs and cabling) that is appropriate to the type of network you are building (say Ethernet versus Token Ring) is a complete and utter necessity.

Make sure you have the CD or disk set for the operating system running on the computer (such as Windows 98) and that you have any disks or CDs that came with the network card. Implement the following steps to get the PC up and running on the network:

Setting up the PC on the network

1. Open the case on the computer and install the NIC in an open expansion slot.

2. Close the case and attach the network medium (typically twisted-pair cabling).

3. Boot up the computer. If you purchased a plug-and-play network card and are using Windows 95/98, the card will be detected and the appropriate software drivers installed. You may be prompted to provide the drivers during this process (these drivers are on a disk or CD that came with the network card).

4. If you are using an operating system that doesn't detect new hardware devices, you will have to manually install the NIC. If the card came with installation software, use that software to install the necessary drivers.

5. Some operating systems will require that you select an IRQ and I/O port for the new NIC (this is the case with Windows NT 4—both the server and workstation OS; select an open IRQ and I/O port and then complete the installation of the card as required by your operating system.

After you physically install the card and add the appropriate driver to your software operating system, you should be up and running on the network (you might have to reboot the machine after installing any drivers for the NIC). Problems associated with NICs usually revolve around improper installation (press the card firmly into the expansion slot) and IRQ conflicts. The latter is discussed in the next section.

Dealing with IRQs and I/O Ports

One of the most common pitfalls when installing any new device into one of the expansion slots on a PC is an IRQ conflict. IRQ stands for *Interrupt ReQuest*. Each device in your computer, such as the mouse, keyboard, and NIC, are assigned an Interrupt Request line that the device uses to alert the microprocessor (CPU) that the device needs data processed. Each device must be assigned a unique IRQ or you have (yes, you guessed it) an IRQ conflict. Neither device will probably operate correctly if two devices are vying for the same IRQ. Knowing which IRQs are already spoken for on your system will make it easier for you to assign an IRQ to a new device such as an NIC.

Finding the available IRQs isn't that difficult, and each operating system (both PC operating systems and network operating systems) provides you with a tool to view both the used and available IRQs on a system.

For DOS clients, you can use the executable file MSD.EXE, which runs the Microsoft System Diagnostics program. This program is also available for Windows 3.11 clients.

For Windows 95 and 98, open the Control Panel (double-click My Computer and then double-click the Control Panel icon). In the Control Panel, double-click the System icon. On the System Properties dialog box, click the Computer icon, and then click Properties. A list of the IRQs on the system will appear (see Figure 1.3).

The latest operating systems make it easier to install NICs

Windows NT 2000 Server and Windows NT 2000 Professional both embrace Microsoft's Plug and Play scheme for plug-and-play hardware devices. This means that both of these operating systems in most cases will identify and install the appropriate drivers for a number of the network interface cards available on the market. And although you can't call what they do "plug and play," Novell NetWare 4.2 and Novell NetWare 5 both do a pretty good job of helping you set up the appropriate network card in your network server when you install either of these Novell network operating systems.

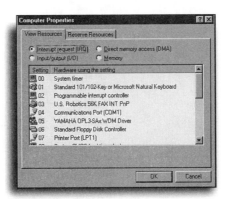

FIGURE 1.3
Operating systems like Windows 95 typically provide a tool that you can use to determine the available IRQs on a system.

In Windows NT Workstation 4.0 and Windows NT Server 4.0, you can check the available IRQs by clicking the Start menu, and then pointing at Programs. Point at Administrative Tools (Common), and then click Windows NT Diagnostics. On the Windows NT Diagnostics dialog box, click the Resources tab to view the IRQ assignments on the system.

Table 1.2 shows the standard IRQ settings for a PC. As you can see, several IRQs are reserved for particular system devices.

Table 1.2 IRQ Settings

IRQ	Use
0	System Timer
1	Keyboard
2	Cascade to secondary IRQ controller
3	COM Port 2 and 4 (serial port)
4	COM Port 1 and 3 (serial port)
5	LPT2 (printer port)
6	Floppy disk controller
7	LPT1 (printer port)
8	Real-time clock
9	Free
10	Primary SCSI adapter (or free)
11	Secondary SCSI adapter (or free)
12	PS/2 Mouse
13	Floating-point math coprocessor
14	Primary hard disk controller
15	Secondary hard disk controller (or free)

Obviously, in cases where the computer doesn't have a second COM port or an LTP2, these IRQs will be available. Each computer will vary, so use the tools mentioned earlier in this section to determine how your IRQs have been assigned.

Not only do devices need a unique IRQ to communicate with the processor, they also need a communication line that the microprocessor can use to route processed information to the device. The base I/O port for a device essentially serves as the address that the processor uses when sending and receiving data from that device. As with IRQs, each device needs a unique base I/O port. Typically, I/O ports 280h, 300h, 320h, and 360h are available for your NIC (I/O port addresses are written in hexadecimal, or base-16, format accounting for the h). The same tools for finding available IRQs on a system can also be used to determine the available base I/O ports.

Network Cabling

Copper cable is the most frequently employed network medium for local area networks. Fiber-optic cable is being increasingly employed because of its higher potential bandwidth and cable run. Fiber-optic cable is used in a number of high-speed networking implementations such as FDDI and SONET (Synchronous Optical Network, which delivers voice video and data over a high-speed fiber-optic network).

As already mentioned, copper cable is the most commonly used medium for LANs. And although copper cable comes in several different types, the most commonly used copper cable is now category 5 unshielded twisted pair (twisted-pair cable comes in 5 categories, with categories 3 to 5 being data grade cable).

Category 5 twisted pair allows Ethernet implementations of 10Mbps, 1000Mbps (Fast Ethernet), and 1Gbps (Gigabit Ethernet). Unshielded twisted pair can also be used in IBM Token Ring networks. IBM has its own defining system for twisted-pair cable (both shielded and unshielded); Type 1 is the twisted-pair cable used most commonly in Token Ring installations. Twisted-pair cable typically uses an RJ-45 connector to hook to network cards, hubs, and other connectivity devices.

Although it's becoming less popular, installations of thicknet (RG-58 or RG-11 coaxial cable) can still be found in certain settings such as manufacturing companies. Thicknet is characterized by a cable backbone that is tied to servers and workstations on the network by vampire taps (the taps actually pierce the cable). The transceiver is actually attached to the tap, and then the computer is connected to the transceiver/tap by a drop cable.

Thinnet (RG-58 coaxial cable) was the cable of choice at one time because of its relative ease of installation and lower cost. Thinnet LANs employ a bus topology where a T-connector is connected to each computer's network card. The computers are then chained together using appropriate lengths of cable. Thinnet installations require that each end of the network be terminated, and terminators are placed on the downside T-connector of the computers that reside on either end of the network.

Although copper wire is an inexpensive and easy-to-install network medium, it does have some inherent limitations. First, it can be highly susceptible to electromagnetic interference (EMI). Attenuation (the weakening of the signal over the length of the cable) also limits the length of copper cable that can be used. Copper wire can also be tapped, which may be an issue depending on the proprietary nature of the information that is being moved on the network.

Fiber-optic cable is a high-speed alternative to copper wire and is often employed as the backbone of larger corporate networks. Fiber-optic cable uses glass or plastic filaments to move data and provides greater bandwidth, longer cable runs, and is impervious to tapping. With the need for network speed seemingly on the rise, fiber installations are becoming commonplace.

Fiber-optic cable uses pulses of light as its data-transfer method. This means a light source is required and lasers and light emitting diodes (LEDs) are used. Fiber-optic cable is more expensive and more difficult to install than copper cable installations, but fiber's capability to move data faster and farther makes it an excellent alternative to copper.

Table 1.3 provides a quick summary of the various cable types. Figure 1.4 provides a look at each of the cable types listed in the table.

Choosing cable

When selecting cable for a network, a number of factors are important, including cost, cable bandwidth (the amount of information you can cram through the cable), the cable's susceptibility to EMI, attenuation (which affects the maximum cable length possible), and ease of installation. Choose the cable type that best suits your needs and budget.

Table 1.3	Network Cable Comparison		
Cable Type	Bandwidth	Maximum Length	Cost
CAT 5 UTP	10Mbps to 100Mbps	100 meters	Inexpensive
Thinnet	10Mbps	185 meters	Inexpensive
Thicknet	10Mbps	500 meters	Expensive
Fiber optic	100Mbps to 2Gbps+	2 kilometers	Expensive

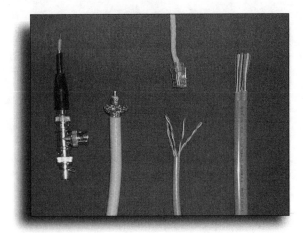

FIGURE 1.4
Thinnet, thicknet, twisted-pair, and fiber-optic cables are commonly used network media.

SEE ALSO
➤ *For more information on the bus topology, see page 21.*

Hubs, Repeaters, and MAUs

Depending on the type of cable you use and the topology of your network, you may need to use connectivity devices to connect the nodes or expand the number of nodes on your network. The type of connective device used will also depend on the type of network architecture you are using (Ethernet versus Token Ring), which is discussed later in this chapter.

Hubs are used in twisted-pair deployments and serve as the central connection point for the network. A basic hub contains no active electronics and so cannot be used to extend the network. It basically organizes your cables and relays signals to all the connective devices (see Figure 1.5).

When is a hub no longer a hub?

Hub technology is evolving very quickly. Active hubs not only serve as the physical connection for your network nodes, but they can also serve as a repeater, allowing you to extend the size of a network. New hubs with switching capabilities are also available that can help you maximize the bandwidth on your network. Intelligent hubs are even available—they can actually help you troubleshoot connectivity problems with your network.

Physical medium equals OSI Physical layer

The actual physical medium such as the cable, hubs, and connectors operate at the Physical layer of the OSI networking model.

In cases where the network needs to be extended beyond the maximum length of the particular cable type that you are using, a repeater can be used. Repeaters take the signal that they receive and regenerate it.

In IBM Token Ring networks, the device that serves as the central connecting point is a multistation access unit, or MAU. These units actually contain active electronics and while serving as the physical connection for the devices on the network, they also provide the logical ring that is used to circulate network traffic. Multistation access units will be discussed further in the "IBM Token Ring" section of this chapter.

SEE ALSO

➤ *For more information about the Physical layer, see page 43.*

Understanding Network Topologies

A convenient way to discuss local area networks is by their physical layout, or *topology*. To a certain extent, the topology of a certain network will reflect the cable type used and the actual architecture of the network (such as Ethernet or IBM Token Ring). And although the different types of topologies have been assigned particular characteristics (a bus topology, for instance, is considered to be a passive, contention-based network), the actual behavior of a particular network is better defined by the architecture used for the network. A short description of each basic network topology and a diagram of that topology type follow.

SEE ALSO

➤ *For more information on network architectures, see page 25.*

Bus Network

A *bus network* is characterized by a main trunk or backbone line with the networked computers attached at intervals along the trunk line (see Figure 1.6). Bus networks are considered a passive topology. Computers on the bus sit and listen. When they are ready to transmit, they make sure that no one else on the bus is transmitting, and then they send their packets of information. Passive, contention-based bus networks (contention-based because each computer must contend for transmission time) would typically employ the Ethernet network architecture.

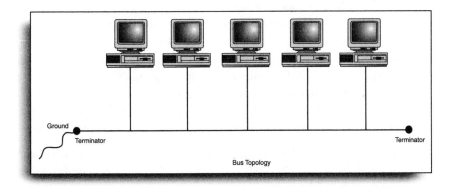

FIGURE 1.6
A bus topology provides a passive network layout.

Bus networks typically use coaxial networking cable hooked to each computer using a T-connector. Each end of the network is terminated using a terminator specific to the cable type (if you use 50 Ohm cable, you use 50 Ohm terminators). Because the bus network is really just a collection of cable, connectors, and terminators, there is no amplification of the signal as it travels on the wire.

That bus has bounce!

When bus topology networks aren't terminated properly, the network will experience signal bounce; packets sent over the wire will actually bounce back up the line and cause collisions on the network and bring the network down. If you use the bus topology, always check the physical aspects of the network first when you are having problems. These types of networks are notorious for connector, cable, and termination problems.

Bus networks are easy to assemble and extend. They require a fairly limited amount of cabling when compared to other topologies. Bus networks are prone to cable breaks, loose connectors, and cable shorts that can be very difficult to troubleshoot. One physical problem on the network, such as a detached connector, can actually bring down the entire bus network.

SEE ALSO

➤ *For more information on wide area networking, see page 25.*

Star Network

In a *star topology*, the computers on the network connect to a centralized connectivity device called a *hub*. Each computer is connected with its own cable (typically twisted-pair cable) to a port on the hub (see Figure 1.7). Even though the star topology uses a hub (special hubs—multiport repeaters—can actually enhance the packet signals before passing them onto the network), this type of network still employs the passive, contention-based method of moving information on the wire that is embraced by the bus topology. Computers listen to the wire and then contend for transmission time.

Because the star topology uses a separate cable connection for each computer on the network, stars are easily expandable, with the main limiting factor being the number of ports available on the hub (although hubs can be daisy-chained together to increase the number of ports available). Expanding a star topology network is also very unobtrusive; adding a computer to the network is just a matter of running a wire between the computer and the hub. Users on the network will be pretty much unaware that the expansion is taking place.

Disadvantages of the star topology revolve around cabling needs and the hub itself. Because each computer on the network requires a separate cable, cable costs will be higher than a bus topology network (although twisted pair, the cable type used for stars, is the least expensive cable). Purchasing a hub or hubs for your network does add additional costs when you are building a network based on the star topology, but considering the benefits of this type of topology in terms of managing the physical aspects of your network, it is probably well worth it. (Hub prices have fallen to a point where even computer users with a small home network will probably want to use a hub to connect computers.)

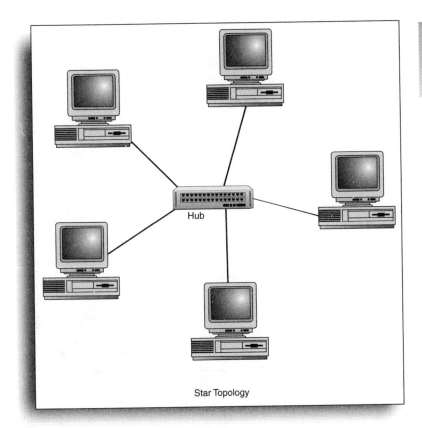

FIGURE 1.7
A star topology is easily expandable.

Star Topology

The most negative aspect of the star topology is related to the central hub. If the hub fails, so does the network. You will find that many network administrators who don't like crisis management keep an extra hub squirreled away just in case.

Ring Topology

A *ring topology* connects the networked computers one after the other on the wire in a physical circle (see Figure 1.8). The ring topology (an example of an architecture that uses a ring topology is Fiber Distributed Data Interface—*FDDI*) moves information on the wire in one direction and is considered an active topology. Computers on the network actually retransmit the packets they receive and then send them on to the next computer in the ring.

FIGURE 1.8
The ring topology uses a token-passing strategy to provide equal access to all the computers on the network.

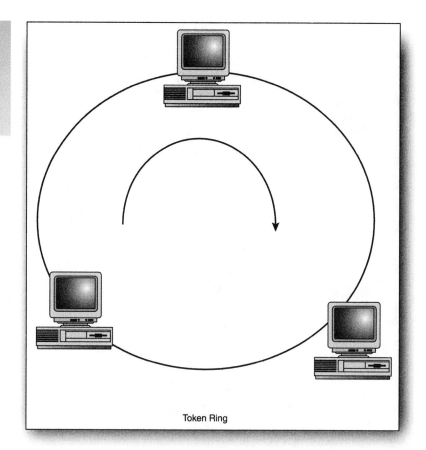

FIGURE 1.8
The ring topology uses a token-passing strategy to provide equal access to all the computers on the network.

Token Ring

Access to the network media is granted to a particular computer on the network by a token. The token circulates around the ring and when a computer wants to send data, it waits for the token to come around and then takes possession of it. The computer then sends its data onto the wire. After the computer that sent the data receives verification from the destination computer that the message was received, the sending computer creates a new token and passes it onto the next computer in the ring, beginning the token passing ritual again.

The fact that a computer must have the token to send data means that all the computers on the network have equal access to the network media. Token passing rings provide a more timely transmission of data (because of the level playing field provided by the token passing strategy) when compared to contention-based networks like the bus or star. Token Rings actually degrade more gracefully (in terms of performance) during times of high traffic when compared to passive topologies, which can go down quickly in very high traffic situations due to increased packet collisions.

True ring topologies can be difficult to troubleshoot, and the failure of one computer on the ring can disrupt the data flow because data circulates around the ring in one direction. Adding or removing computers from this type of topology also can disrupt the operation of the network.

SEE ALSO

➤ *For more information on FDDI see page 29.*

Mesh Topology

The *mesh topology* uses redundant connections between computers on the network as a fault tolerance strategy. Each device on the network is connected to every other device. In short, this type of topology requires a lot of cable (see Figure 1.9). This type of topology also can weather a broken segment or two and still continue to operate as a network because of all the redundant lines.

Mesh networks, obviously, would be more difficult and expensive to install than other network topologies because of the large number of connections required. In most cases, networks that use this redundant connection strategy will actually be comprised of a hybrid mesh. In a hybrid mesh only highly important servers and mission-critical computers are configured with redundant connections. This protects the most important parts of the companywide network but doesn't require multiple lines to every computer.

Understanding Network Architectures

Network architectures provide different ways to solve a common problem—moving data quickly and efficiently on the network medium. The particular network architecture that you use, such as Ethernet, not only will define the topology for your network but also defines how the network media is accessed by the nodes on the network. There are several network architectures available, all with a different strategy for moving information on the network.

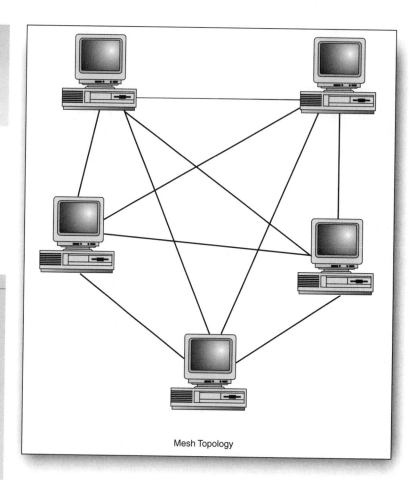

Mesh Topology

Hybrid topologies

As already mentioned,
topologies are a convenient
way to categorize the physical layout of a particular
network and the strategy
that it uses to move data
on the wire. A number of
hybrid topologies that combine the topologies dis-
cussed can exist. For
example, you may chain a
number of hubs together in
a line, which would create
a star bus topology. Or a
ring network may use a
connective device much
like a hub that contains a
logical ring (an example of
a device that contains a
logical ring is a
Multistation Access Unit
used as the central hub in
an IBM Token Ring net-
work). Computers are then
connected in a star topology to this central device.
This gives you a star ring
configuration.

Ethernet

Ethernet is the most commonly deployed network architecture in the
world. Ethernet provides access to the network using CSMA/CD
(carrier sense multiple access with collision detection). This strategy
of network access basically means that the nodes on the network listen (sense) to the network and wait until the line is clear. The computer then sends its packets out onto the line. If there is more than
one computer transmitting, collisions result. Sensing the collisions,
the computer stops transmitting and waits until the line is free. One
of the computers will then transmit, gaining control of the line and
completing the transmission of packets.

Ethernet is a passive, wait-and-listen architecture. Collisions are common on the network and computers are required to contend for transmission time. Ethernet networks typically will be found in a bus or star bus configuration depending on the type of network media used. One of the common implementations (on several different media types) of Ethernet runs at 10Mbps. This 10 Megabit Ethernet run over twisted pair would be designated as 10BaseT (the 10 stands for the Megabits per second, the Base means a baseband transmission (*baseband* simply means a single bit stream, or a digital flow of information), and the T stands for twisted pair). Table 1.4 lists some of the Ethernet implementations available.

The IEEE 802.3 specification

The specifications for running the Ethernet architecture have been defined by the Institute of Electrical and Electronic Engineers. Its designation is IEEE 802.3. Ethernet runs at the media access control sublayer of the OSI model's Data-link layer. The OSI model and the various MAC specifications are discussed in Chapter 2, "The OSI Model and Network Protocols."

Table 1.4   Ethernet Implementations

Ethernet Designation	Cable Type	Maximum Cable Length	Connector Types
10BaseT	CAT 5 UTP	100 meters	Hub
10Base2	Thinnet	185 meters	T connectors, barrel connectors, terminators
10Base5	Thicknet	500 meters	Vampire taps, transceiver drop cables, terminators
10BaseFL	Fiber optic	2 kilometers	Repeaters, terminators

When packets of information are prepared for transmission over the wire, their final form is called a frame. Ethernet actually embraces more than one frame type, which can cause problems on a network if you don't have all the nodes configured to use the same frame type. The various Ethernet frame types are as follows:

- Ethernet 802.3—Although this frame has the appropriate IEEE number, it is actually not completely in compliance with the specifications for Ethernet. This frame type is used by Novel NetWare 2.2 and 3.1 networks.

- Ethernet 802.2—This is the frame type that is in full compliance with the IEEE specifications. It is used by later versions of Novell NetWare, including NetWare 3.12, 4.x, and 5.x.

- Ethernet SNAP—This Ethernet frame type is used in AppleTalk networks.

- Ethernet II—Networks running multiple protocols such as the Internet generate Ethernet II frames.

Although the 10 Megabit installations of Ethernet have been common, they are rapidly being replaced by Fast Ethernet (100 Mbps) and Gigabit Ethernet (1000Mbps or 1Gbps). Both of these versions of Ethernet require CAT 5 cabling and special network cards and hubs (Gigabit Ethernet in many cases uses CAT 6 twisted pair).

The main advantage of Ethernet is that it is one of the cheaper network architectures to implement. NICs, cabling, and hubs are fairly inexpensive when compared to the hardware required for other architectures such as Token Ring. A major disadvantage of Ethernet relates to the number of collisions on the network. The more collisions, the slower the network will run, and excessive collisions can even bring down the network.

SEE ALSO

➤ *Segmenting a network with a bridge or dividing a network into subnets with a router are two strategies for overcoming traffic problems on Ethernet networks. For more information, see page 67.*

IBM Token Ring

The IEEE 802.5 specification

The specifications for running IBM Token Ring architecture have been defined by the Institute of Electrical and Electronic Engineers. Its designation is IEEE 802.5. Token Ring runs at the media access control sublayer of the OSI model's Data-link layer. The OSI model and the various MAC specifications will be discussed in Chapter 2, "The OSI Model and Network Protocols."

IBM Token Ring is characterized as a fast and reliable network that uses token passing as its media access strategy. Token Ring networks are wired in a star configuration with a *Multistation Access Unit* (MAU) providing the central connection for the nodes. The actual ring on which the token is circulated (the token moves in one direction as characterized by the ring topology) is a logical ring inside the MAU.

The token is passed around the ring until a computer wanting to send information out onto the network takes possession of the token. A computer that passes the token to the next computer on the logical ring would be called the nearest active upstream neighbor (*NAUN*). The computer being passed the token is the nearest active downstream neighbor (*NADN*).

After a computer takes possession of the token and transmits data, it then passes a new token to its NADN and the token makes its way around the ring until a node on the network takes possession to transmit.

Token Ring is characterized by no collisions and equal access to the network media by all the nodes on the network. It is slower than some implementations of Ethernet (Token Ring can run at 4 and 16Mbps) but the network degrades more gracefully during times of high traffic. (A gigabit implementation of Token Ring will soon be a reality.)

Token Ring also provides some fault tolerance to the network with its error detection strategy, *beaconing*. When the computers on the network are first brought online, the first computer powered on is designated as the Active Monitor. The Active Monitor sends out a data packet every seven seconds that travels around the ring to help determine if any of the nodes on the network are done. For example, if a particular computer doesn't receive the packet from its NAUN, it creates a packet containing its address and the NAUN's address and sends the packet onto the network. This packet provides information that the Token Ring can actually use to automatically reconfigure the ring and maintain network traffic.

FDDI

The Fiber Distributed Data Interface (*FDDI*) is an architecture that provides high-speed network backbones that can be used to connect a number of different network types. FDDI uses fiber-optic cable and is wired in a ring topology. FDDI uses token passing as its media access method and can operate at high speeds (most implementations are 100Mbps but faster data transfer rates are possible).

Because FDDI uses a token-passing media access strategy, it is reliable and provides equal access to all the nodes on the network. With FDDI you can set priority levels, however, servers on the network could be allowed to send more data frames onto the network than client computers.

Because FDDI uses a true ring topology, breaks in the cable system can be a problem. To build fault tolerance into the FDDI network, a secondary ring is used. When a computer cannot communicate with its downstream neighbor, it sends its data to the second ring (which circulates the data in the opposite direction from the one the primary ring uses).

Obviously, a special NIC is required to implement FDDI. Dual attachment stations (computers connected to both rings on the network) will use a special card that connects to both ring backbones. In place of hubs, concentrators are used on the FDDI network for the connection of LAN nodes. Because these computers don't sit directly on the FDDI ring, they only require a single attachment NIC for connection to the concentrator.

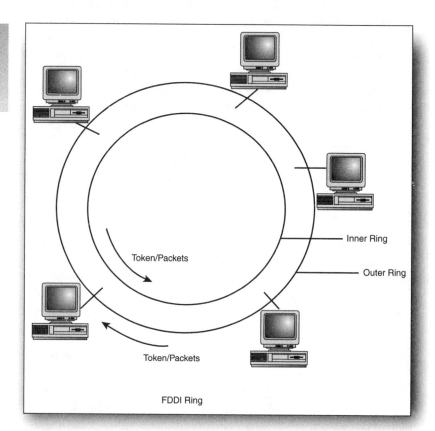

Token/Packets

Inner Ring

Outer Ring

Token/Packets

FDDI Ring

AppleTalk

AppleTalk is the networking architecture used by Apple Macintosh computers. The networking hardware required is already built into each Macintosh (although if you want to connect Macs to an Ethernet network, you need a Mac Ethernet NIC). The cabling system used to connect Macintosh computers is called *LocalTalk* and uses shielded twisted-pair cables with a special Macintosh adapter.

AppleTalk uses a special dynamic addressing system to determine the address of the nodes on the network. When a Macintosh is powered up on the network, the computer generates a random address and broadcasts it out onto the network. This random address becomes its network address (if another Macintosh isn't already using that address; if so, the newly powered on Mac will continue to generate random addresses until it finds one that is unused).

AppleTalk is similar to Ethernet in that it is a passive network architecture. AppleTalk uses Carrier Sense multiple access with collision detection—*CSMA/CA*. Basically the computers sit on the network and listen to determine whether the wire is clear. After making sure the network is clear, the computer will send a packet onto the network letting all the other computers know that it intends to transmit data. The computer then sends out its data.

The fact that a computer that intends to send data out onto the network notifies the other network nodes as to its intentions greatly reduces the number of collisions on a CSMA/CA network (especially when compared to Ethernet).

These announcement packets, however, do have a tendency to slow down the network and Macintosh networks only have a transmission speed of 230.4 Kbps. The fact that the hardware and software needed to network a group of Macintosh computers comes with each Macintosh (other than the LocalTalk cable) makes it an easy and inexpensive way to network several workstations to share a printer or files.

chapter

2

The OSI Model and Network Protocols

OSI—The Theoretical Networking Protocol Stack

Conceptual models are something that you run into no matter what discipline you tackle. Art embraces color and design theories; physics embraces nearly every theoretical model that Einstein scrawled on a napkin. Computer networking is no different and it also uses a conceptual model or framework that allows us to discuss a complex chain of events—data movement on a network.

ISO seems to ring a bell

The International Standards Organization (ISO) is involved in developing sets of rules and models for everything from technical standards for networking to how companies do business in the new global market. You've probably seen banners on businesses announcing that they are ISO 9002 certified. This means that they are in compliance with the set of rules and protocols that have been developed by the ISO for doing business in the world marketplace. Another common ISO certification—ISO 9660—defines file systems for CD-ROMs.

In the late 1970s the International Standards Organization (ISO) began to develop a conceptual model for networking called the *Open Systems Interconnection Reference Model*. Networking folk more commonly refer to it as the OSI model (and I'm sure a number of them have forgotten what the OSI stands for). In 1984, the model became the international standard for network communications, providing a conceptual framework that helps explain how data gets from one place to another on a network.

The OSI model describes network communication as a series of seven layers that operate in a stack; each layer is responsible for a different part of the overall process of moving data. This framework of a layered stack, while conceptual, can then be used to discuss and understand actual protocol stacks that we see used for networking. For example, TCP/IP and AppleTalk are two real-world network protocol stacks; protocols that actually serve as layers in a protocol suite like TCP/IP can then be discussed in terms of how they relate to and serve at various levels of the OSI model's stack.

SEE ALSO

➤ *To learn more about several of the commonly used network protocol suites, see page 44.*

The OSI model provides the model for a number of important events that take place during network communication. It provides basic rules of thumb for a number of different networking processes:

- How data is translated into a format appropriate for your network architecture. When you send an email or a file to another computer, you are working with a certain application such as an email client or an FTP client. The data you transmit using this application must be placed in a more generic format if it is going to move out onto the network and to the intended recipient.

- How PCs or other devices on the network establish communications. When you send data from your PC, there must be some mechanism that supplies a communication channel between sender and receiver. It's not unlike picking up a telephone and making a call.

- How data is sent between devices and how sequencing and error checking is handled. After a communications session has been established between computers, there must be a set of rules that controls how the data passes between them.

- How logical addressing of packets is converted to the actual physical addressing provided by the network. Computer networks use logical addressing schemes such as IP addresses. There must be a conversion of these logical addresses to the actual hardware addresses found on the NICs in the computers.

The OSI model provides the mechanisms and rules that make the handling of the issues discussed in the bulleted list possible. Understanding the various layers of the OSI model not only provides insight into actual network protocol suites, but it also provides you with a conceptual framework that can be used to better understand complex networking devices like switches, bridges and routers. (Much of this book is devoted to a discussion of routers and routing.)

The OSI Layers

The layers of the OSI model explain the process of moving data on a network. As a computer user, the only two layers of the model that you actually interface with are the first layer—the Physical layer—and the last layer—the Applications layer.

- The *Physical layer* constitutes the physical aspects of the network (the network cabling, hubs, and so on). You've probably interfaced with the physical layer at least once, when you tripped over a poorly situated cable.

- The *Application layer* provides the interface that you use on your computer to send email or place a file on the network.

Obviously, this would be a very short chapter if we only discussed these two layers, but you will find each and every layer of the OSI model plays an important part in the networking of information.

So, what's a protocol stack?

Protocol stacks or suites (or layers) are a group of small protocols that work together to accomplish the movement of data from one node on a network to another. Protocol stacks are not unlike relay-race runners, although packets of data rather than a baton are handed off to each subsequent protocol until the packets of data are in a form (a single bit stream) that can be placed on the network medium.

The ISO/OSI protocol stack exists!

While network protocol stacks like NetWare's IPX/SPX and TCP/IP are something with which most network administrators are quite familiar, there is actually a real protocol suite based on the OSI model; it's called the OSI protocol stack. Unfortunately, it is not embraced by any of the network operating systems (such as Novell NetWare or Windows NT) with which you will actually work.

Figure 2.1 provides a list of the OSI model layers from the top of the stack to the bottom. An upside-down pyramid is also an apt representation of the model because data is taken in a fairly complex form and eventually converted to a simple bit stream that can be placed on the network wire. You will notice that the layers are numbered, however, from top to bottom. For instance, in a discussion of the Network layer, you may hear the layer described as Layer 3. Whether you use the name or number is unimportant; you just need to make sure that you understand the role of each layer in the overall process of data communications.

FIGURE 2.1
The OSI model provides a conceptual basis for how data moves from a sending computer to a receiving computer.

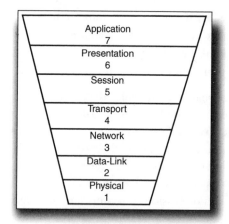

A good way to remember the network layers from bottom to top is the following mnemonic: **P**lease **D**o **N**ot **T**hrow **S**ausage **P**izza **A**way. And (unfortunately, you may be thinking), you really do need to remember the OSI model; it is important to any discussion of networking technology from the very simple to the very complex. Every book or article you pick up on networking will make some reference to the model.

Before we discuss each of the layers in the stack, it makes sense to get a general idea of what takes place when data moves through the OSI model. Let's say that a user decides to send an email message to another user on a network. The user sending the email will take advantage of an email client or program (such as Outlook or Eudora) that serves as the interface tool where the message is composed and then sent. This user activity takes place at the Application layer.

After the data leaves the Application layer (the layer will affix an Application layer header to the data packet) it moves down through the other layers of the OSI stack. Each layer in turn does its part by providing specific services related to the communication link that must be established, or by formatting the data a particular way.

No matter what the function of a particular layer is, it adds header information (the headers are represented as small boxes on Figure 2.2) to the data. (The Physical layer is hardware—a cable, for instance—so it doesn't add a header to the data.)

The data eventually reaches the Physical layer (the actual network medium such as twisted pair cable and the hubs connecting the computer) of the email sender's computer and moves out onto the network media and to its final destination—the intended recipient of the email.

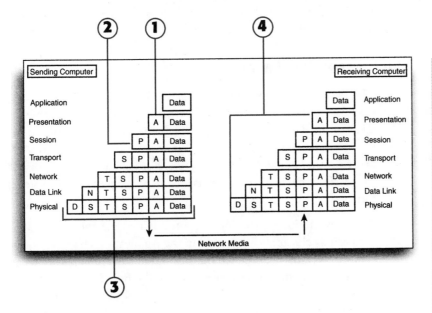

FIGURE 2.2
Data moves down through the OSI stack of the sending computer and moves up through the OSI stack on the receiving computer.

① Application layer header

② Presentation layer header

③ Packet with full complement of OSI layer headers

④ Headers are removed as the data moves up the OSI stack

The data is received at the Physical layer of the recipient's computer and moves back up through the OSI stack. As the data moves through each layer, the appropriate header is stripped from the data. When the data finally reaches the Application layer, the recipient can use his or her email client to read the received message.

The following discussion of the OSI layers will discuss the layers in the stack from top to bottom (Application layer to Physical layer).

The Application Layer

The Application layer provides the interface and services that support user applications. It is also responsible for general access to the network.

FTP, Message Handling, DB, HTTP, SMTP

This layer provides the tools that the user actually sees. It also provides network services related to these user applications such as message handling, file transfer, and database queries. Each of these services are supplied by the Application layer to the various applications available to the user. Examples of information exchange services handled by the Application layer would include the World Wide Web, email services (such as the Simple Mail Transfer Protocol—more commonly referred to as SMTP—found in TCP/IP), and special client/server database applications.

The Presentation Layer *- Encryption, Compression/decompression*

The Presentation layer can be considered the translator of the OSI model. This layer takes the packets (packet creation for the movement of the data to the network actually begins in the Application layer) from the Application layer and converts it into a generic format that can be read by all computers. For instance, data represented by ASCII characters will be translated to an even more basic, generic format.

The Presentation layer is also responsible for data encryption (if required by the application used in the Application layer) and data compression that will reduce the size of the data. The packet created by the Presentation layer is pretty much the final form that the data will take as it travels down through the rest of the OSI stack (although there will be some additions to the packets by subsequent layers and data may be broken into smaller packet sizes).

The Session Layer *- comm -checkpoints in stream, fault tolerance, connection/connectionless*

The Session layer is responsible for setting up the communication link or *session* between the sending and receiving computers. This layer also manages the session that is set up between these nodes (see Figure 2.3).

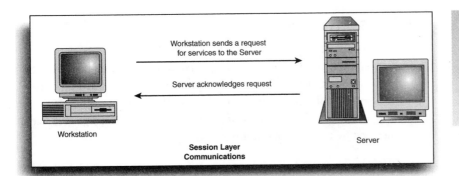

FIGURE 2.3
The Session layer pro-
vides the communication
link between the two
communicating
computers.

After the session is set up between the participating nodes, the Session layer is also responsible for placing checkpoints in the data stream. This provides some fault tolerance to the communication session. If a session fails and communication is lost between the nodes, once the session is reestablished only the data after the most recently received checkpoint will need to be resent. This negates the need to tie up the network by resending all the packets involved in the session.

Actual protocols that operate at the Session layer can provide two different types of approaches to getting the data from sender to receiver: connection-oriented communication and connectionless communication.

Connection-oriented protocols that operate at the Session layer provide a session environment where communicating computers agree upon parameters related to the creation of checkpoints in the data, maintain a dialogue during data transfer, and then simultaneously end the transfer session.

Connection-oriented protocols operate much like a telephone call: You establish a session with the person you are calling. A direct connection is maintained between you and the party on the other end of the line. And when the discussion concludes both parties typically agree to end the session.

Connectionless protocols operate more like the regular mail system. They provide appropriate addressing for the packets that must be sent and then the packets are sent off much like a letter dropped in the mailbox. It is assumed that the addressing on the letter will get it to its final destination, but no acknowledgment is required from the computer that is the intended destination.

Users must run the same protocol stack to communicate

In the previous example of an email message being sent and received, it was assumed that both the sender and receiver of the data involved were running the same protocol stack (the theoretical OSI stack) on their client computers. Very different computers running very different operating systems can still communicate if they embrace a common network protocol stack. This is why a UNIX machine, an Apple Macintosh, or a PC running Windows all use TCP/IP to communicate on the Internet. A case where two computers could not communicate would be where a computer running TCP/IP is trying to communicate with a computer that is only running IPX/SPX. Both of these real-world protocols use different rules and data formats, making communication impossible.

39

The Transport Layer *- sizing packets*

The Transport layer is responsible for the flow control of data between the communicating nodes; data must not only be delivered error-free but also in the proper sequence. The Transport layer is also responsible for sizing the packets so that they are in a size required by the lower layers of the protocol stack. This packet size is dictated by the network architecture.

SEE ALSO

> *For more about network architectures such as Ethernet and Token Ring, see page 25.*

Communication also takes place between peer computers (the sender and receiver); acknowledgements are received from the destination node when an agreed upon number of data packets have been sent by the sending node. For example, the sending node may send three bursts of packets to the receiving node and then receive an acknowledgement from the receiver. The sender can then send another three bursts of data.

This communication at the Transport layer is also useful in cases where the sending computer may flood the receiving computer with data. The receiving node will take as much data as it can hold and then send a "not ready" signal if additional data is sent. After the receiving computer has processed the data and is able to receive additional packets, it will supply the sending computer with a "go-ahead" message.

The Network Layer *Layer 3 - IP Logical Mac - Hardware Address*

The Network layer addresses packets for delivery and is also responsible for their delivery. Route determination takes place at this layer, as does the actual switching of packets onto that route. Layer 3 is where logical addresses (such as the IP address of a network computer) are translated to physical addresses (the hardware address of the NIC—Network Interface Card—on that particular computer).

Routers operate at the Network layer and use Layer 3 routing protocols to determine the path for data packets.

How routes are determined and how routers convert logical addresses to physical addresses are subjects that we will look at in much more detail throughout this book.

Application layer services make user applications work over the network

When a user working in a particular application (Excel, for example) decides to save a worksheet file to his or her home directory on the network file server, the Application layer of the OSI model provides the appropriate service that allows the file to be moved from the client machine to the appropriate network volume. This transaction is transparent to the user.

Each layer performs functions on outgoing and incoming data

Remember that each layer in the OSI model (or in an actual network protocol stack such as IPX/SPX or TCP/IP) have responsibilities related to outgoing and incoming information. When data is moving down the stack on a sending computer, the Presentation layer converts information from a particular application to a generic format. On the receiving computer the Presentation layer would take generic information moving up the OSI stack and convert it into a format usable by the appropriate Application layer program on the receiving computer.

SEE ALSO
➤ *Our discussion of the Network layer will be greatly expanded in later chapters. To begin an exploration of how routers operate at the Network layer see page 77.*

The Data-Link Layer

When the data packets reach the Data-Link layer, they are placed in data frames defined by the network architecture embraced by your network (such as Ethernet, Token Ring, and so on). The Data-Link layer is responsible for data movement across the actual physical link to the receiving node and so uniquely identifies each computer on the network based on its hardware address that is encoded into the NIC (Network Interface Card). Figure 2.4 shows the hardware address for the network interface card used in a networked computer running Windows 98.

Movem of dat over NIC

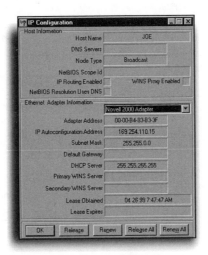

FIGURE 2.4
Each node on the network will have a unique physical address.

Real-world protocols use a combination of connection-oriented and connectionless communication

You will find that in network protocol stacks—such as TCP/IP and IPX/SPX—both connection-oriented and connectionless communication strategies are used to move data on the network. Typically, more than one protocol will operate at the Session layer to handle these different communication strategies.

Header information is added to each frame containing the sending address and the destination address. The Data Link layer is also responsible for making sure that the frames sent over the physical link are received error-free. So, protocols operating at this layer will add a *Cyclical Redundancy check* (CRC) as a trailer on each frame. The CRC is basically a mathematical calculation that takes place on the sending computer and then on the receiving computer. If the two CRCs match up, the frame was received in total and its integrity was maintained during transfer.

Again, as mentioned earlier, the frame type produced by the Data Link layer will depend on the network architecture that your network embraces, such as Ethernet, IBM Token Ring, or FDDI. Figure 2.5 shows an Ethernet 802.2 frame. Table 2.2 lists and describes each of the frame components. While you may not fully understand all the parts of the frame shown, note that the makeup of the frame is basically header information that describes the frame, the actual data in the frame, and then Data-link layer information (such as Destination Service Access Points and Service Access Points) that not only define the Frame type (in this case Ethernet) but also serve to help get the frame to the receiving computer. (For more about the IEEE 802 specifications, see the "Ethernet Frame Trivia" sidebar.)

FIGURE 2.5
The Ethernet frame is created at the Data Link layer of the OSI model.

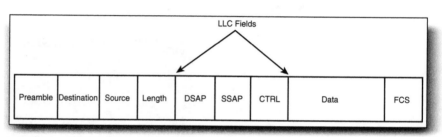

Table 2.2 Ethernet Frame Segments

Segment	Purpose
Preamble	Alternating bits (1s and 0s) that announces that a frame has been sent
Destination	The destination address
Source	The source address
Length	Specifies the number of bytes of data in the frame
DSAP	Destination Service Access Point—this tells the receiving network card where to place the frame in buffer memory
SSAP	Provides the Service Access Point information for the frame (Service Access points are discussed in the "Data-Link section later in this chapter)
CTRL	A Logical Link control field (Logical Link control is discussed in the "Data-Link Sublayers" section later in this chapter).
Data	This part of the frame holds the actual data being sent
FCS	Frame Check Sequence field contains the CRC value for the frame

The Data Link layer also controls how computers access the physical network connections. This aspect of Layer 2 will be discussed more fully in the "Data Link Sublayers" section that follows this discussion of the OSI layers.

The Physical Layer

At the Physical layer the frames passed down from the Data Link layer are converted into a single bit stream that can then be sent out onto the network media. The Physical layer also defines the actual physical aspects of how the cabling is hooked to the computer's NIC. On a computer that is receiving data, the Physical layer receives the bit stream (information consisting of 1s and 0s).

SEE ALSO

➤ *To learn more about the commonly used network media and cable types, see page 17.*

The Data-Link Sublayers

Before we end our discussion of the OSI networking model, we need to back track a little and discuss additional specifications that were developed for the Data Link layer of the OSI model by the IEEE. The IEEE 802 specifications divided the Data Link layer into two sublayers: Logical Link Control (LLC) and Media Access Control (MAC).

The Logical Link Control sublayer establishes and maintains the link between the sending and receiving computer as data moves across the network's physical media. The LLC sublayer also provides Service Access Points (SAPs), which are reference points that other computers sending information can refer to and use to communicate with the upper layers of the OSI stack on a particular receiving node. The IEEE specification that defines the LLC layer is 802.2 (see IEEE specifications sidebar for more information on the categories).

Finding MAC addresses on Windows computers

To find the address of a network card running on a Windows 95/98 computer, click the **Start** menu, and then click **Run**. In the Run dialog box, type **winipcfg**, and then click **OK**. The IP Configuration dialog box will appear for the computer and provide the address for the Network card. On a Windows NT computer, right-click on the Network Neighborhood icon and then select the **Adapters** tab on the Network dialog box. Select your network adapter and then click the **Properties** button. The MAC address of the NIC should be provided.

43

The Media Access Control sublayer determines how computers communicate on the network and how and when a computer can actually access the network media and send data. The 802 specifications actually break the MAC sublayer down into a list of categories (ways of accessing the network media) that directly relate to specific network architectures such as Ethernet and Token Ring (see Figure 2.6).

SEE ALSO

➤ *For more information on some of the common network architectures like Ethernet and Token Ring, see page 25.*

FIGURE 2.6
The Data Link Layer consists of two sublayers: the LLC and the MAC.

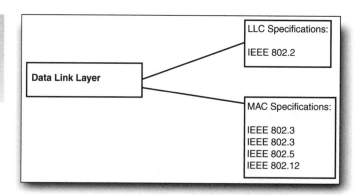

Real-World Network Protocols

Now that we've taken a look at the theoretical model for how data moves from one computer to another on a network, as seen in the different layers of the OSI model, we can take a look at some of the most commonly used network protocol stacks and map their different layers to the OSI model. This will provide you with a good understanding of how these real-world protocol stacks operate and provide data transport on the network.

You will also see which protocols in a particular protocol stack are involved at the Network layer of the OSI model. These protocols will become important as we discuss the routing of packets on an Internetwork (something that we will do for much of the book).

NetBEUI

NetBEUI (NetBIOS Extended User Interface) is a simple and fast network protocol that was designed to be used with Microsoft's and IBM's NetBIOS (Network Basic Input Output System) protocol in small networks. NetBEUI operates at the Transport and Network layers of the OSI model.

Because NetBEUI provides only the services needed at the Transport and Network layers of the OSI stack, it needs NetBIOS, which operates at the Session layer of the OSI stack, and is responsible for setting up the communication session between two computers on the network. Two other networking components found in Microsoft networks are the Redirector and the Server Message Block. The Redirector operates at the Application layer and makes a client computer perceive all the network resources as if they were local. Server Message Block (SMB) provides peer-to-peer communication between the Redirectors on client and network server machines. The Server Message Block operates at the Presentation layer of the OSI model.

While an excellent transport protocol with very low overhead, NetBEUI is not a routable protocol, so it cannot be used on Internetworks where routing takes place. This means that while you should remember NetBEUI as a network protocol possibility for small, simple networks, it is not an option for larger networks that make use of routers (and so this is the last time you will hear about NetBEUI in this book).

TCP/IP

Often referred to as the "protocol of low bid" (see the TCP/IP Trivia sidebar for more information on TCP/IP's interesting genesis), TCP/IP has become the de-facto standard for enterprise networking. TCP/IP networks are highly scalable, so TCP/IP can be used for small or large networks.

A word about hardware addresses

NIC hardware addresses are also called *MAC Addresses*. MAC stands for Media Access Control and it is one of the sublayers of the Data-Link layer (the MAC sublayer will be discussed in the "Data-Link Sublayers" section later in this chapter). Hardware addresses are burned onto ROM chips on network interface cards, giving each of them a unique address. The addressing scheme was developed by the Institute for Electrical and Electronic Engineers (IEEE). The actual address takes the form of a 48-bit address that is written in hexadecimal format. An example of a MAC address is 00-00-B3-83-B3-3F.

Ethernet frame trivia

The Ethernet frame used by early versions of Novell NetWare (NetWare 2.x and 3.x) was created before the IEEE specifications were completed. This means that The Ethernet 802.3 frame type is actually not to specifications as outlined by the IEEE. New versions of NetWare and other Ethernet network operating systems now use the 802.2 Ethernet frame, which is completely compliant with the IEEE specifications (the IEEE specifications are listed later in this chapter).

TCP/IP is a routable protocol stack that can be run on a number of different software platforms (Windows, UNIX, and so on) and it is embraced by most network operating systems as the default network protocol. TCP/IP contains a number of "member" protocols that make up the actual TCP/IP stack. And because the TCP/IP protocol stack was developed before the completion of the OSI reference model, these protocols do not map perfectly to the various layers of the model. Figure 2.7 shows the TCP/IP stack mapped to the OSI layers (the figure provides a general overview of TCP/IP and is not an exhaustive list of all the protocols in the stack). Table 2.3 describes the protocols listed in the figure. More information will be provided on all the protocols in the TCP/IP stack in Chapter 10, "TCP/IP Primer."

FIGURE 2.7
TCP/IP is a large protocol stack using a number of member protocols at various layers of the OSI model.

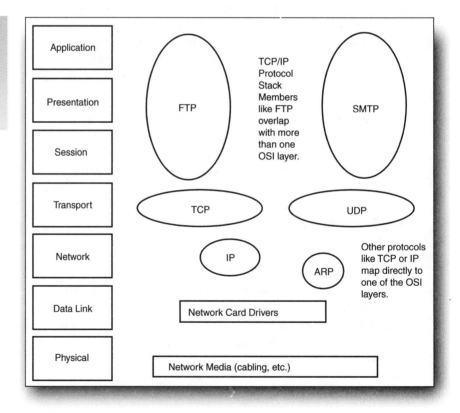

Table 2.3 TCP/IP Protocol Stack Members

Protocol	Role
FTP	File Transfer Protocol provides an interface and services for file transfer on the network.
SMTP	The Simple Mail Transport Protocol provides email services on the Internet and IP networks.
TCP	The Transport Control Protocol is a connection-oriented transport protocol. TCP handles a connection between sending and receiving computers much like a phone conversation.
UDP	User Datagram Protocol is a connectionless transport protocol that provides transport services in conjunction with TCP.
IP	The Internet Protocol is the basis for all addressing on TCP/IP networks and it provides a connectionless oriented Network layer protocol. Works much like an addressed letter that is dropped in a mail box and then delivered to the intended destination.
ARP	Address Resolution Protocol maps IP addresses to MAC hardware addresses. ARP will be discussed in greater detail in Chapter 10.

The IEEE 802 specifications

The IEEE 802 specifications provide categories that define the Logical Link Layer and the different network architectures that can be embraced by the MAC layer. A complete list of the 802 categories is provided:

- 802.1 Internetworking
- 802.2 Logical Link Control
- 802.3 Ethernet(CSMA/CD) LAN
- 802.4 Token Bus LAN
- 802.5 Token Ring LAN
- 802.6 Metropolitan Area Network
- 802.7 Broadband Technical Advisory Group
- 802.8 Fiber Optic Technical Advisory Group
- 802.9 Integrated Voice and Data Networks
- 802.10 Network Security
- 802.11 Wireless Networks
- 802.12 Demand Priority LAN

TCP/IP not only provides a very rich set of network-related features (which means that TCP/IP requires a fair amount of overhead to run) but also provides a unique logical addressing system. Anyone connected to the Internet is familiar with the 32-bit IP address, which is commonly written as 4 octets (an *octet* being 8 bits of information). The typical IP address is written in the format 129.30.20.4, where each of the four dotted decimal values actually represent 8 bits of binary information. Much more information concerning IP addressing will be discussed in Chapter 10.

Because of TCP/IP's importance in Internetworks and the complexities related to routing TCP/IP networks, an entire chapter of this book has been provided reviewing all the aspects of TCP/IP addressing. A great deal of information will also be provided on the commands related to routing TCP/IP on a campus or enterprise network.

SEE ALSO

➤ *The best place to start in on TCP/IP and routing is Chapter 10, "TCP/IP Primer," beginning on page 167.*

IPX/SPX

IPX/SPX (Internetwork Packet Exchange/Sequenced Packet Exchange) is a network protocol stack developed by Novell for use in the Novell NetWare network operating system. IPX/SPX is a leaner stack than TCP/IP and does not require the overhead needed by TCP/IP. IPX/SPX is suitable for small and large networks and is a routable network protocol suite.

Figure 2.8 maps protocols in the IPX/SPX stack to the OSI Layers. Table 2.4 gives a brief description of each of the protocols.

FIGURE 2.8
IPX/SPX is an efficient network protocol stack used on large and small networks.

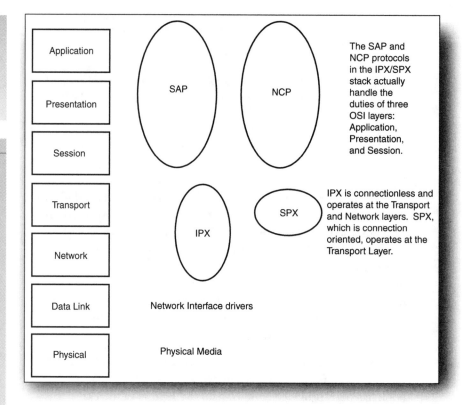

The SAP and NCP protocols in the IPX/SPX stack actually handle the duties of three OSI layers: Application, Presentation, and Session.

IPX is connectionless and operates at the Transport and Network layers. SPX, which is connection oriented, operates at the Transport Layer.

TCP/IP trivia

TCP/IP was developed by Defense Advanced Research Projects Agency (DARPA). The Department of Defense needed a protocol stack that could communicate across unlike networks. The unlike networks existed because the government uses a bidding system and suddenly found itself with different computer systems at various branches of the Defense Department: the Army, Navy, and so on. So, TCP/IP is jokingly called the protocol of low bid because it was in part developed to fix a problem that arose because of the way the government takes bids for procuring technology and other goods.

Table 2.4 IPX/SPX Protocol Stack Members

Protocol	Role
SAP	The Service Advertising Protocol is used by NetWare File Servers and Print Servers to announce the address of the server.
NCP	The NetWare Core Protocol handles network functions at the Application, Presentation, and Session layers. It handles packet creation and is responsible for providing connection services between clients and servers.
SPX	Sequenced Packet Exchange Protocol is a connection-oriented transport protocol
IPX	Internetwork Packet Exchange Protocol is a connectionless transport protocol that handles addressing and routing on the network.

Our major concern with IPX/SPX is routing this protocol suite on an Internetwork. More information on routing IPX/SPX and how the IPX/SPX stack moves data on the network is provided later in this book.

SEE ALSO

➤ *Routing IPX/SPX is discussed in Chapter 12, "Routing Novell IPX," which begins on page 211.*

AppleTalk

While many network administrators would not consider AppleTalk an Internetworking or enterprise network protocol, AppleTalk is routable. And with the appropriate type of NIC (Apple Macintoshes can participate on an Ethernet network if they are outfitted with EtherTalk cards or other adapters) it can support Ethernet, Token Ring, and FDDI architectures. It is not uncommon to have Macintosh computers in the Enterprise to support graphic manipulation and other multimedia duties and so it makes sense to include AppleTalk as another key routable protocol stack on the corporate network.

Earlier, in Chapter 1, we discussed AppleTalk as architecture, but it is also a network protocol stack. Figure 2.9 maps the protocols in the AppleTalk stack to the layers of the OSI model. Table 2.5 gives a brief description of each protocol.

Figure alert!

Figures 2.7 through 2.9 map real-world protocols to the OSI model. To understand these figures, think back to how the OSI model describes in seven layers how data moves from one computer to another and the transformation that it must undergo. Real-world stacks like TCP/IP perform all the tasks described in the OSI model; they just do it with fewer protocols. Rather than having seven protocols (one for each of the OSI layers) TCP/IP has certain protocols that handle the duties of more than one OSI layer. For example, FTP handles Application, Presentation and Session layer duties. The circle around FTP spans all three of the layers on the OSI model (the layers are the boxes).

FIGURE 2.9
AppleTalk is a routable protocol stack for Macintosh networks that can communicate with Ethernet, Token Ring, and FDDI networks.

Terminology alert!

Before we go too much farther, we should sort out some terms that you will find throughout this book:

Internetwork: a network of networks. Local Area Networks connected by an Internetwork device such as a bridge or router. Internetworking is discussed in detail in Chapter 4, "Internetworking Basics."

Internet: The global network of networks. TCP/IP is the de-facto standard for this global collection of heterogeneous computers.

Intranet: A corporate network that is internal to the enterprise (not connected to the global Internet) but uses Internet protocols such as Simple Mail Transport Protocol and Hypertext Transport Protocol (the protocol used by Web Browsers) to share information among corporate users. An *extranet* is an intranet that provides corporate network access to specified users outside the company.

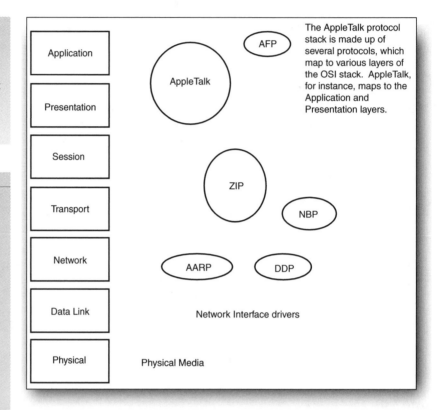

The AppleTalk protocol stack is made up of several protocols, which map to various layers of the OSI stack. AppleTalk, for instance, maps to the Application and Presentation layers.

Table 2.5 AppleTalk Protocol Stack Members

Protocol	Role
AppleShare	AppleShare provides services at the Application layer
AFP	The AppleTalk Filing Protocol provides and managing file sharing among nodes on the network
ATP	The AppleTalk Transaction protocol provides the Transport layer connection between computers
NBP	The Name Binding Protocol maps computer hostnames to Network layer addresses
ZIP	The Zone Information Protocol controls AppleTalk zones and maps zone names to network addresses
AARP	The AppleTalk Address Resolution Protocol maps logical Network layer addresses to Data Link hardware addresses

Protocol	Role
DDP	The Datagram Delivery Protocol provides the addressing system for the AppleTalk network and provides connectionless transport of datagrams between computers

As with IPX/SPX, our interest in the AppleTalk network protocol stack relates to routing AppleTalk. More information on how AppleTalk networks are configured and how AppleTalk is routed on a Cisco router is provided later in this book (see Chapter 13, "Routing Apple Talk.")

SEE ALSO

➤ *More information on how AppleTalk networks are configured and how AppleTalk is routed on a Cisco router is provided on page 227.*

Where are the routing protocols?

You might have noticed that the diagrams that map various protocol stacks to the OSI model did not include routing protocols. Obviously, each protocol stack has a default routing protocol; for example, RIP is the default routing protocol for TCP/IP and the Routing Table Maintenance Protocol is the routing protocol for the AppleTalk stack. These protocols will be discussed in greater detail when routing of these protocol stacks is discussed later in this book.

Wide Area Networking

Understanding Wide Area Connectivity

As the PC local area network became more and more important to businesses, corporations, and institutions, the need to expand and then connect LANs became a necessity. Expanding or connecting LANs locally (in a fairly limited geographic area) was taken care of by internetworking devices such as repeaters, bridges, switches, and routers. However, when connecting LANs over large distances, other technology must come into play.

A need for technology that provided network administrators with the ability to connect LANs over greater geographic areas became extremely important as networking the enterprise (the enterprise is the entire corporation—which in many cases can be a worldwide operation) became an imperative.

Expanding a network across great distances can be accomplished by taking advantage of several different wide area networking technologies. Networks can be connected with services provided by the public switched telephone network (PSTN) or private carrier companies. Extremely large companies can invest in their own WAN infrastructure and invest in microwave and satellite transmission equipment.

WAN technology can be used to connect networks between two cities, across the country, or around the world. As with LANs and internetworks, after the Physical layer aspects have been taken care of, various protocols are used to move the data on the WAN. On a LAN, the cable and the hubs provide the Physical layer, while on a WAN, the Physical layer can be a T1 leased line or a satellite dish.

SEE ALSO
➤ *For more information on internetworking, see page 67.*

Getting Connected

While the actual physical infrastructure (the cabling and networking devices such as hubs, repeaters, and so on) of a LAN will be owned by a company, most businesses and institutions find it too costly to own the physical WAN connections that they use.

WANs take advantage of wireless technologies

Although LANs typically use some sort of physical wiring (copper or fiber-optic cable), WANs can take advantage of several wireless technologies, including microwave transmissions, satellite links, infrared light, and network communications via radio signals (both single-frequency and spread-spectrum radio transmissions).

Three types of WAN connections are available: a connection over the Public Switched Telephone System via a modem, a dedicated connection such as a full-time leased line, or a switched connection that enables multiple users to take advantage of the same line.

Each of these WAN connection possibilities offers its own set of pros and cons and each embraces different hardware needs. The following sections discuss these three WAN connection alternatives.

Dial-Up Connections

The simplest and least expensive type of dial-up connection uses a modem to connect two computers over a regular analog voice-grade telephone line. The modem converts the digital information on the computer to an analog signal (modulation) and vice versa (demodulation). That's how the modem got its name. This conversion process allows computer data to be sent over the analog line. Modems are now available that have potential transmission speeds of up to 56Kbps, but line noise can limit the speed at which a connection over an analog line can run.

Routers can be outfitted with a modem connection (and then are often referred to access servers). This means that two LANs could be connected via a dial-up connection and packets routed (although this would provide a very slow connection between the networks). Figure 3.1 shows two LANs connected via a dial-up connection with routers serving as the connection point for the asynchronous connection over modems.

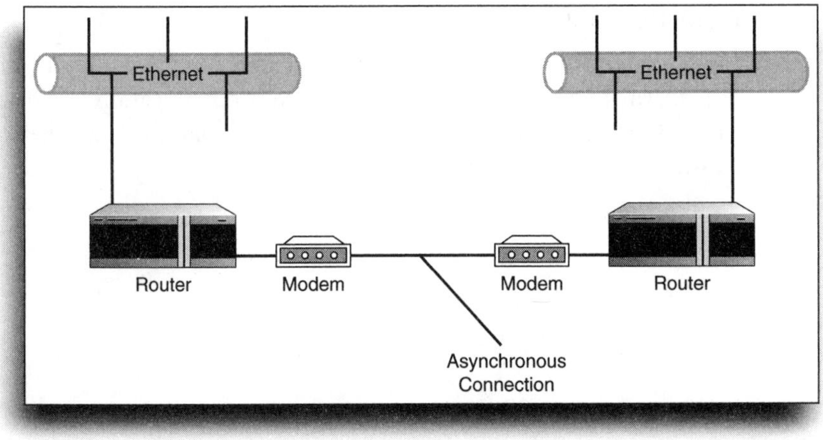

> **Keep the packets on the company-owned wire**
>
> One of the secrets of being a highly successful WAN or internetwork administrator is designing large networks and setting up the potential routing of packets so that traffic circulates on the company-owned networking infrastructure as much as possible. Running a cost-effective internetwork or WAN is the ultimate challenge when involving leased lines and connections for which you basically pay for the bandwidth.

FIGURE 3.1
LANs can be connected using dial-up connections via modems.

Leased Lines

56K modems don't give you 56Kbps

Although 56K modems greatly increase the speed of downloads and uploads from a home or office PC (when compared with the previously available 33.6 modems), you probably have found that you never get more than 53Kbps as your throughput. This is because it takes increased power to move data over regular phone lines at higher speeds (such as those supported by the 56K modem technologies) and the FCC has placed a limit on the power available. This is because increasing the power on the phone lines increases the amount of interference (or crosstalk) between the wires present in the twisted-pair copper wiring used for the phone system. Your connection speed will also be limited by the age and amount of interference on the lines. You might find that you never get more than 49Kbps at times, and this is directly related to the "dirty" phone lines that you are forced to use as your communication medium.

Dedicated leased lines provide a full-time connection between two networks through the PSTN or another service provider. Leased lines are typically digital lines. They provide much more bandwidth than analog lines and are less susceptible to the line noise and interference found on voice-grade connections.

Digital lines commonly used for data transfer are DDS (digital data service) lines and the T-carrier system, which provides a range of line types that provide different data rates.

DDS Lines

DDS lines, which are typically available from your local phone service provider, can provide bandwidth of up to 64Kbps and supply your network with a permanent, full-duplex connection (data can be sent and received at the same time). Because DDS lines are digital, they require a Channel Service Unit/Data Service Unit (CSU/DSU) as the connecting point between your LAN and the DDS line. The CSU/DSU converts the LAN data transmission into a digital signal on the DDS line.

The DSU side of the CSU/DSU is connected to your LAN and the leased digital line is connected to the CSU port of the device. Some sort of internetworking device such as a bridge or router will typically sit between your network and the CSU/DSU (on both ends of the DDS connection). Figure 3.2 shows two LANs connected by a DDS line.

T-Carrier Lines

The T-carrier system takes advantage of technology that allows several transmissions, which can include voice communication and data (divided onto several different channels), to be combined and then transmitted on a single high-speed line.

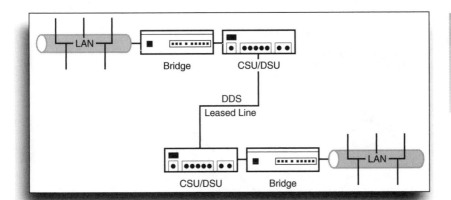

FIGURE 3.2
DDS lines provide a constant connection between local area networks.

The device that combines signals carried on these separate channels (when data must be sent over the digital line as a single data stream) and also has the capability to split a received data stream into the appropriate channels is called a multiplexor, or MUX. Figure 3.3 shows two different LANs connected by a T-carrier. Multiplexors are used at either end of the digital connection to assemble and disassemble different data channels, including data from any attached networks and the company's voice channel (used for their telephone system).

The T-1 line is the basic unit of the T-carrier system. It provides 24 64Kbps channels that can be combined to provide a total transmission bandwidth of 1.544Mbps. Several other T-carrier classes exist, which can provide a larger number of channels and extremely high data rates. A greater number of channels and a higher data throughput, however, relates directly to the cost for the carrier line. Table 3.1 provides a listing of the T-carriers.

Telephone trivia

The Public Switched Telephone Network (PSTN) is also often referred to as POTS. This stands for Plain Old Telephone System (you might also hear it referred by other names, especially when your leased lines are down).

DDS lines are not ISDN lines

DDS lines are digital lease lines. They are special lines to which the phone company provides access. ISDN is a digital technology designed to use digital technology over the existing phone lines.

Table 3.1 The T-Carrier Systems

Carrier Line	Channels	Total Data Rate
T1	24	1.544Mbps
T2	96	6.312Mbps
T3	672	44.736Mbps
T4	4032	274.760Mbps

FIGURE 3.3
Multiplexors can combine channels for transmission or disassemble a data stream into its channels when connected to T-carrier lines.

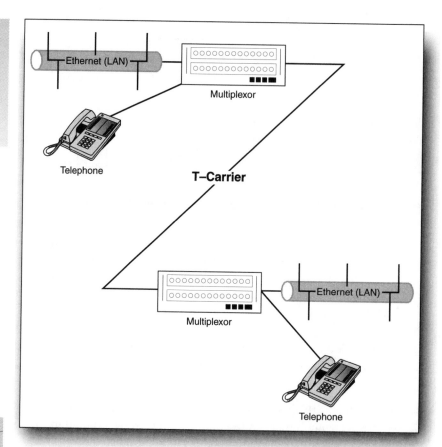

DDS line connections are being replaced by other WAN technologies

DDS line connections are becoming a thing of the past and are fast being replaced by other WAN technologies, specifically some of the packet-switching alternatives such as Frame-Relay. A drop in the price of T-carrier lines and the use of Fractional-T connections (a portion of a T1 line is leased) are giving network administrators more bandwidth for their buck in the WAN arena.

The T-1 line is the most affordable T-carrier (and the most leased of the T-carrier classes) and can be deployed on copper wire. And as mentioned earlier, smaller companies can lease a portion of a T-1 line, selecting to use only a certain number of channels. T-2 lines aren't available to the public and are used internally by the phone company.

T-carriers offering greater bandwidth such as T-3 and T-4 lines are employed by only very large corporations or government entities (in a large part because of cost). T-3 lines and T-4 lines also require fiber optic cabling.

When attaching a company to a T-carrier line, the equipment needed is the same as for a connection to any dedicated digital line. A CSU/DSU sits between the line connection and an internetworking device such as a bridge, switch, or router, which is attached to your computer network. And as mentioned before, if channels on the carrier line are going to be split between voice and data communications, a multiplexor is needed to combine and split the signals as needed (outgoing versus incoming in relation to the T-carrier line).

Switched Network Overview

The third alternative for WAN connections is the use of switched networks. Switched networks allow multiple users to take advantage of the same line. Switched networks offer a cheaper alternative to the cost of leasing dedicated lines.

Basically, your network is connected to the wide area network via a service provider or the phone company itself. Data leaving your network through the WAN connection then enters the switched network (which is often represented on diagrams as a cloud because the path of your switched data can potentially be different each time as it makes its way to the designated destination). See Figure 3.4.

The connection between your network and the switched network, or *PDN* (public data network), will be in the form of a digital terminal device (*DTE*) such as a router. (A *DCE*—data circuit terminating equipment—such as a DSU/CSU may sit between your router and the PDN; with the DCE providing the bandwidth and timing settings for the transfer of your data.) The PDN provides the lines and switching equipment that will move your data through the switched network cloud.

Two types of switched network possibilities exist for WAN connections: circuit switching and packet switching.

Cable television holds the key

The concept of what a multiplexor does (at least on the receiving end of a single bit stream from a T-carrier connection) isn't really new to anyone who has cable television in his or her home. A single data signal comes into the house, and your cable-ready television or VCR contains a multiplexor that breaks down the data feed into the 100+ television channels that you constantly are surfing through. That's what broadband transmission is all about—multiple channels on a single feed.

The T-carriers are multiples of T-1s

The T-1 line is the basic unit of the T-carrier system. All the other T-carriers available can actually be thought of as simply a particular multiple of T-1 lines. The T-2 line consists of 4 T-1s; T-3 consists of 28 T-1s; and T-4 consists of 168 T-1 lines.

FIGURE 3.4
Switched networks enable you to connect LANs at different sites so that they can share data over greater distances.

Public switched network versus private data networks

When you work with WAN technology, you basically have two types of networks that you can use as the carrier for your data. The public switched network—also known as the public data network and the plain old telephone system (POTS)—is one avenue for the movement of your data. You can also use private data networks as your carrier. These networks are owned by companies like GE, Sprint, and MCI and provide another avenue for WAN-switched technologies and leased lines.

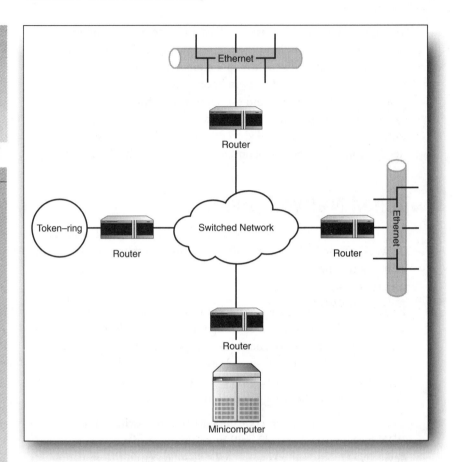

Circuit Switching

Circuit switching establishes a dedicated connection between the sender and receiver on the PDN. Data moves from the source to the destination along the circuit (the lines) that has been established for the particular session. When the data transfer is complete, the connection between the sender and receiver ends and the circuit is terminated.

An example of a circuit-switching WAN technology is *ISDN* (Integrated Services Digital Network). ISDN is available from local phone providers and takes advantage of digital phone switching systems. The cost of an ISDN connection will be dictated by how often the line is used for data transfer. Your usage charge is determined by the connection charge (and there is also often a recurring monthly charge for being connected to the service). ISDN comes in two flavors: basic rate ISDN (BRI) and primary rate ISDN (PRI).

Basic rate ISDN provides three channels: two B channels that each provide 64Kbps of bandwidth for data transfer and a D channel operating at 16Kbps that is used exclusively for setup and control information. BRI can be used for both voice and data communications by dedicating a B channel for each. Typically, however, the two B channels are combined in BRI to provide a data transfer speed of 128Kbps.

Primary rate ISDN—designed for larger businesses that require greater bandwidth—uses a T1 line and provides 23 B channels (each operating at 64Kbps). One D channel is also necessary (as with BRI) to handle setup and control of the connection).

SEE ALSO

➤ *Configuring ISDN on a router is discussed on page 268.*

Packet Switching

In WAN connections that use *packet switching*, the data is divided into packets. The small packet size used in packet-switching WANs provides fast and efficient delivery of data.

Each packet has its own control information and is switched through the network independently. This means that data packets can follow different routes through the WAN cloud and reach the destination out of sequence. However, sequencing information in the packet header can be used by the receiving device to reassemble the data in the appropriate order.

Packet switching networks can take advantage of virtual circuits when transferring data. A *virtual circuit* establishes a defined route across the WAN cloud so that all the data packets move to the destination along the same route (remember that this route is shared by packets from many other users because switched networks use shared lines). The use of virtual circuits in packet switching networks can improve the overall performance of your data transfers.

Basic rate ISDN a thing of the past?

Basic rate ISDN was designed for the small business and home users who required faster connections of very small networks or single workstations to WANs, specifically the Internet. A newer technology that provides faster connection speeds is digital subscriber line service (DSL). DSL offers voice and data communication over the digital line with speeds of up to 7Mbps. Again, handled by your local phone service provider, DSL costs can actually be cheaper than the sum of a home phone bill and the monthly cost for a 56K analog connection to an Internet service provider. This makes DSL a much cheaper alternative to BRI (DSL charges are typically flat rate, while BRI charges are based on the amount of time the connection is used).

Several packet switching technologies exist such as X.25, frame relay, and ATM. The next section of this chapter discusses these packet switching protocols.

WAN Packet Switching Protocols

Packet switching networks have been available since the late 1970s when X.25 became available. The lower cost of packet switching networks (when compared to dedicated leased lines) led to a fairly rapid evolution of packet switching protocols that now makes the movement of data over packet switching networks very fast and extremely efficient. The following sections discuss some of the popular packet switching protocols.

X.25

X.25 was designed for use over the PDNs that were operated by companies such as AT&T and General Electric. The X.25 protocol stack provides point-to-point communications between local area networks on the WAN using DTEs and DCEs (with the DCE providing the connection from a DTE, such as a router, to the actual WAN connection).

Because the purpose of any WAN is to connect geographically separated LANs, X.25 sessions consist of communications between two DTEs. For example, you might have a LAN in Chicago that is connected to a router that then provides a connection to a PDN. Likewise, you have a LAN in Minneapolis that is connected to a PDN via a router. The X.25 protocol can then handle a connection between these two DTE devices on the WAN, so that they can exchange data (see Figure 3.5).

The X.25 protocol stack consists of protocols that operate at the Network, Data Link, and Physical layers of the OSI model. These protocols are as follows:

- **Packet Layer Protocol (PLP)**—Operating at the Network layer, this protocol manages the exchange of packets between the connected LANs (such as the routers in Chicago and Minneapolis discussed earlier). PLP establishes the virtual circuit between the DTE devices and is also responsible for segmenting and reassembling the packets as they move from the sending to the receiving device. PLP also closes the virtual circuit when data transfer is complete.

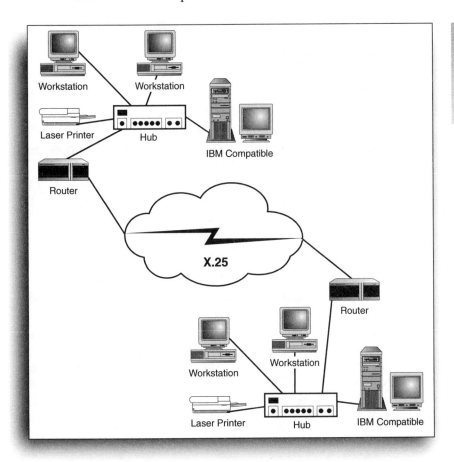

FIGURE 3.5
X.25 establishes a virtual circuit between two DTEs (routers) on the WAN.

- **Link Access Procedure/Balanced Protocol (LAP/B)**—Operates at the Data Link layer and makes sure the frames are delivered error free and in the proper sequence.

- **X.21bis**—This Physical layer protocol provides the activation and deactivation of the physical media that connects the DTE and DCE devices.

Two types of virtual circuits

Two different types of virtual circuits can be established using X.25 packet switching. Switched virtual circuits (SVC) are set up for a particular communication session and then torn down at its conclusion. A PVC (permanent virtual circuit) is established and used for recurring communication between two points, providing an active session for communication between networks.

Because X.25 was created for use on the public switched telephone network that typically consisted of noisy analog lines, X.25 is bogged down with a great deal of error-checking capabilities. Although still in use, X.25 is fast being replaced by speedier packet switching protocols such as frame relay and ATM.

SEE ALSO

➤ *Configuring X.25 on a router is discussed on page xxx.*

Frame Relay

Frame relay is the successor to the X.25 protocol. It is a layer 2 WAN protocol that provides high-speed connections between DTE devices (such as bridges and routers) that typically operate over fiber optic cable. DCE devices on frame relay networks consist of the carrier-owned switches. Frame relay is faster than X.25 because it has shed some of the control and error-checking functions that slowed the packet-switching capabilities of X.25.

Frame relay uses permanent virtual circuits for communication sessions between points on the WAN. These virtual circuits are identified by a DLCI (Data Link connection identifier)—a value provided by the frame relay service provider. Because several virtual circuits can exist on a frame relay interface, the DLCI for a particular virtual circuit (the one you are using to move your packets) can be used as a reference or pointing device that makes sure the packets end up at the proper destination. This is done by mapping the logical addresses (IP addresses, for example) of the sending and receiving DTEs to the DLCI of the virtual circuit that they use to communicate.

SEE ALSO

➤ *Configuring frame relay on a router is discussed on page 265.*

Asynchronous Transfer Mode (ATM)

Another packet switching WAN technology is asynchronous transfer mode (ATM). ATM is an advanced packet-switching protocol that uses fixed packet sizes (53 bytes) called *cells*. Using a fixed packet size (which X.25 and frame relay do not) actually increases the throughput speed of the data because the switching and routing equipment can move the consistently sized cells faster. ATM can move data at a theoretical speed of up to 2.4Gbps. Typically ATM WAN speeds fall between 45 and 622Mbps. The 622Mbps is achieved on the fastest WAN network medium available—ONET (synchronous optical network, a fiber optic network developed by Bell Communications Research that provides voice, data, and video at high speeds).

ATM is similar to frame relay in that it assumes that the lines it uses are noise-free; therefore, it doesn't require a great deal of overhead for error checking (which, as you remember, slowed X.25 packet switching down). ATM can be used over FDDI backbones on metropolitan area networks (at speeds of 100Mbps) and T-3 leased lines (at speeds of 45Mbps).

While they aren't one of the WAN technologies that we will look at in terms of router configurations, ATM networks take advantage of fast ATM switches that quickly move data from port to port as it travels from sending station to receiving station.

Other WAN Protocols

When you work with routers, two other WAN protocols become important: High-Level Data-Link Control (HDLC) and Point-to-Point Protocol (PPP). Each is commonly configured as the protocol for router serial interfaces.

- **HDLC**—HDLC is the default WAN protocol for Cisco Router serial interfaces and is used for synchronous serial connections (digital connections such as ISDN). Cisco's version of this Data Link layer WAN protocol is proprietary and unfortunately will not communicate with other HDLC implementations.

- **PPP**—PPP is widely used as the protocol for connecting dial-up connections to TCP/IP networks such as the Internet. PPP can be used over asynchronous (dial-up) or synchronous lines. PPP supports data compression and provides authentication using either the Password Authentication Protocol (PAP) or the Challenge Handshake Authentication Protocol (CHAP).

SEE ALSO

➤ *Configuring HDLC on a router is discussed on page 261.*

SEE ALSO

➤ *Configuring PPP on a router is discussed on page 262.*

chapter 4

Internetworking Basics

What Is Internetworking? •

Internetworking Devices •

Building a Campus Network •

What Is Internetworking?

Network growth means expansion and segmentation

As LANs grow, you will find that you must expand the number of workstations locally. In cases where the network expands beyond your local geography (from a building on one side of town to a building on the other side of town, for example) your expansion might require the use of WAN technology to connect the two networks. As localized networks grow (LANs in a large corporate office location), you will find that the more workstations and servers you add, the more burden you put on the network in terms of maintaining the bandwidth available. In this case you use segmentation as a strategy to break the larger network into segments that operate as separate units when communicating locally on the segment. This helps preserve bandwidth. This chapter discusses both of these situations in terms of internetworking strategies.

In its strictest sense, internetworking is the connecting of two or more LANs where the LANs still function as separate entities. In a broader sense, internetworking is a strategy for expanding, segmenting, and connecting LANs so that *bandwidth* on and between the networks is maximized. (Bandwidth in this case would be the potential throughput of the medium that you are using, for example a 10baseT LAN runs at a bandwidth of 10Mbps.)

Internetworking embraces both LAN and WAN technologies to move information between the networks. The great thing about internetworking is that it could be used as a strategy for connecting networks that embrace the same network architecture (such as two Ethernet LANs) or as a strategy for networks that use different network architectures (such as an Ethernet network and Token Ring network). An excellent example of a real-world internetwork is the Internet.

Figure 4.1 shows an internetwork that employs some of the internetworking strategies and devices that are typically used.

Internetworking Devices

As your company's network grows, you will need to deal with issues related to extending the network, conserving bandwidth on your network, and connecting your network across greater geographical distances (using WAN technology). Several different internetworking devices exist to fill network expansion needs. These devices are as follows:

- Repeaters
- Bridges
- Switches
- Routers
- Gateways

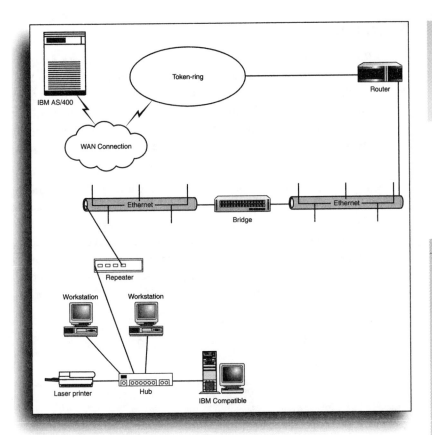

FIGURE 4.1
Internetworks embrace LAN and WAN technologies to expand and connect networks.

So, internetworking is...?

For purposes of discussion in this chapter, internetworking embraces the expansion, segmentation, and connection of LANs using LAN, internetworking, and WAN devices and protocols. This means that repeaters, bridges, switches, routers, and gateways will all be included in the list of internetworking devices (whereas in the very strictest definition of internetworking, only routers and gateways would qualify as internetworking devices).

LAN and WAN protocol reviews

Because internetworking uses both LAN and WAN protocols, you might want to review Chapters 1, "LAN Review" and 3, "Wide Area Networking" if you find this chapter difficult to follow.

The overall capabilities and duties of the device will be related to where the device operates in the OSI model. For example, repeaters work at the Physical layer boosting the data signal over a greater distance on your network (allowing you to beat *attenuation* on long cable runs—attenuation is the degradation of the data signal over the run of the cable). On the other end of the internetworking spectrum, gateways operate at the upper layers of the OSI model (such as the Application and Presentation layers) and provide a way to connect computer systems using unlike network protocols (such as connecting an Ethernet LAN to an IBM AS400 miniframe).

Repeaters are simple devices, whereas gateways require both hardware and software to accomplish the task of allowing very different kinds of networks to communicate. The other internetworking devices that will be discussed, bridges and routers, fall in complexity in between repeaters and gateways.

69

Repeaters

Repeaters take the signal that they receive from network devices and regenerate the signal so that it maintains its integrity along a longer media run than is normally possible. Because all media types (copper cable, fiber optic cable, and wireless media) must deal with attenuation limiting the possible distance between network nodes, repeaters are a great way to physically enlarge the network.

Because repeaters are Physical layer devices, they don't examine the data packets that they receive, nor are they aware of any of the logical or physical addressing relating to those packets. This means that placing a repeater on a network doesn't slow down the flow of information on the network to any great degree. The repeater just sits on the network boosting the data signals received on one particular segment and passing it back out to another segment on the network as the data makes its way to its final destination (see Figure 4.2).

FIGURE 4.2
Repeaters boost the data signal from one network segment and pass it on to another network segment, extending the size of the network.

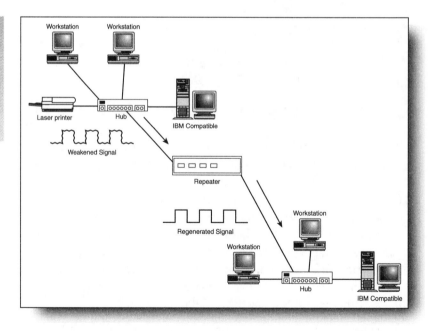

Bridges *(DLL) of OSE*

Bridges are internetworking devices that operate at the Data Link layer of the OSI model. This means that they have greater capabilities (networking-wise) than Layer 1 devices like repeaters and hubs. Bridges are used to segment networks that have grown to a point where the amount of data traffic on the network media is slowing the overall transfer of information.

Mac Addres

Bridges (which consist of the bridge hardware and some type of bridge operating system software) have the capability to examine the MAC address (also known as the hardware address; remember it's burned onto the NIC in each computer on the network) on each data packet that is circulating on the network segments that are connected to the bridge. By learning which MAC addresses are residents of the various segments on the overall network, the bridge can help keep data traffic that is local to a particular segment from spreading to the other network segments that are serviced by the bridge.

So basically bridges provide a segmentation strategy for recouping and preserving bandwidth on a larger homogenous network (homogenous meaning that the entire network consists of a particular architecture such as Ethernet). For example, you may segment a larger network using a bridge into three different segments as shown in Figure 4.3.

Let's say that a computer on segment A transmits data that is intended for another computer on segment A. The bridge will examine these data packets (checking out their source and destination MAC addresses), determine that they stay on segment A, and discard the packets. (It doesn't clear the packets from the network; remember that Ethernet is a passive architecture where all the nodes on the network sense the data on the carrier line.) The fact that the bridge doesn't forward the packets to the other segments on the network preserves the bandwidth on those segments (their lines aren't cluttered up by data that isn't intended for the computers on that particular segment).

Internetworking with an Ethernet bent

You will find that as the various internetworking devices and internetworking itself are discussed in this chapter, much of the information relates more directly to Ethernet networks than other architectures such as Token Ring and FDDI. The reason for this is simple: Ethernet is the most commonly employed network architecture, and many internetworking devices were devised because of connectivity issues with Ethernet networks. For a wealth of information on Token Ring and other LAN technologies (related to IBM hardware such as Token Ring and FDDI NICs), check out the white papers offered by IBM on its support Web site at http://www.networking.ibm.com/nethard.html. These white papers come in HTML and PDF formats (for Adobe Acrobat Reader) and are a great free resource for network administrators.

A good tutorial on the basics of FDDI can be found at http://www.data.com/tutorials/boring_facts_about_fddi.html. Another good source of networking articles can be found at www.cmpnet.com/, which has links to a large number of sites that provide information on LAN and WAN technologies.

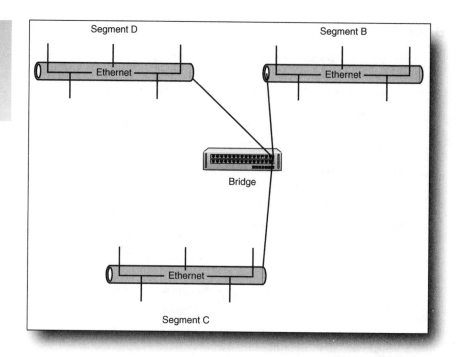

FIGURE 4.3
Bridges segment larger networks to keep segment data traffic localized.

Repeaters, concentrators, and active hubs

Repeaters are also referred to as concentrators. Hubs that have the same signal boosting capabilities as repeaters are referred to as active hubs or multiport repeaters. All these devices (no matter what you call them) operate at the Physical layer of the OSI model.

In another scenario, a computer on segment A transmits data that is intended for a computer on segment C. Again, the bridge will examine the MAC addresses of these packets and in this situation it will forward the packets from segment A to segment C. The bridge is very specific about where it forwards the packets. No packets will be forwarded to segment B.

Although bridging might sound like the ultimate answer to maximizing network throughput, it actually does have some downsides. Bridges forward broadcast packets from the various nodes on the network to all the segments (such as NETBIOS and other broadcasts). Also, in cases in which the bridge is unable to resolve a MAC address to a particular segment on the network, it forwards the packets to all the connected segments.

[handwritten: doesn't forward all to all nodes on network.]

Switches

[handwritten: - preserve bandwith — store - Forward as soon as MAC is read]

Switches are another Layer 2 internetworking device that can be used to preserve the bandwidth on your network using segmentation. Switches are used to forward packets to a particular segment using MAC hardware addressing (the same as bridges). Because switches are hardware-based, they can actually switch packets faster than a bridge.

Switches can also be categorized by how they forward the packets to the appropriate segment. There are store-and-forward switches and cut-through switches.

Switches that employ store-and-forward switching completely process the packet including the CRC check and the determination of the packet addressing. This requires the packet to be stored temporarily before it is forwarded to the appropriate segment. This type of switching cuts down on the number of damaged data packets that are forwarded to the network.

Cut-through switches are faster than store-and-forward switches because they forward the packet as soon as the destination MAC address is read.

Routers

[handwritten: - Hardware/software - prevent broadcast storms]

Routers are internetworking devices that operate at the Network layer (Layer 3) of the OSI model. Using a combination of hardware and software (Cisco Routers use the Cisco IOS—Internetwork Operating System), routers are used to connect networks. These networks can be Ethernet, Token Ring, or FDDI—all that is needed to connect these different network architectures is the appropriate interface on the router.

Because routers are Layer 3 devices, they take advantage of logical addressing to move packets between the various networks on the Internetwork. Routers divide the enterprisewide network into logical subnets, which keep local traffic on each specific subnet. And because routers don't forward broadcast packets from a particular subnet to all the subnets on the network, they can prevent broadcast storms from crippling the entire network.

Transparent bridges build a bridging table

Transparent bridges are employed on Ethernet networks; they forward packets (or drop packets that are part of local segment traffic) on the network based on a bridging table. The bridge builds the table by sampling the packets received on its various ports until it has a complete list of the MAC addresses on the network and the particular network segment that they are present on.

Source-routing bridges

Source-routing bridges on Token Ring networks don't work as hard as transparent bridges on Ethernet networks. Source-routing bridges are provided the path for a particular set of packets it receives within the packets themselves. The bridge only needs to follow the directions contained in the packets to forward them to the appropriate segment.

Because this book is about routers and routing (specifically Cisco Routers and the Cisco IOS), the ins and outs of how routers work and the routing protocols that they use to move packets between subnets are discussed in more detail in Chapter 5, "How a Router Works."

Gateways Lay 4,5,6,7

Gateways are used to connect networks that don't embrace the same network protocol and so protocol translation is necessary between the two disparate networks. For example, a gateway can be used as the connection between an IBM AS400 miniframe and a PC-based LAN.

Gateways function at the upper layers of the OSI model—the Transport, Session, Presentation, and Application (4, 5, 6, and 7) layers. Gateways typically consist of an actual computer that runs software which provides the appropriate gating software that converts the data between the two unlike computing environments. In our example of the gateway between the IBM AS400 and the PC LAN, the gateway computer might be running Windows NT Server with a special translation software package installed.

Gateways typically are situated on high-speed backbones such as FDDI networks, where they connect a mainframe or miniframe to LANs that are connected to the FDDI backbone via routers (see Figure 4.4). Although gateways are certainly necessary to connect networks where data conversion is necessary, they can slow traffic on the network (especially the data traffic moved between the two connected networks). And because gateways typically connect very different systems, their configuration can be relatively more complex than other internetworking devices (*relatively* is the key word; don't ever try to tell someone who configures routers that setting up a gateway is a more difficult task).

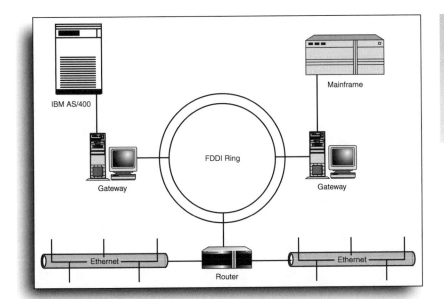

FIGURE 4.4
Gateways provide the connecting point between high-speed backbones and mainframe and miniframe computers.

Building a Campus Network

Before leaving the subject of internetworking, a few words should be said about network scale. A Campus network is defined as a portion of the enterprise network that serves an entire corporation or institution. Network campuses usually are limited to a building or group of buildings and primarily use LAN technologies, such as Ethernet, Token Ring, and FDDI.

Building and maintaining a campus-sized network is really a study in connecting different LAN architectures (using routers) and taking advantage of internetworking devices that help relieve congestion on the network (such as switches and bridges).

Networking the enterprise—connecting the various campus networks—requires the use of WAN technologies, which also employ internetworking devices, particularly routers with the appropriate WAN interfaces.

The next chapter discusses how a router works. This should help you take the puzzle pieces that were provided to you in Chapters 1, 3, and 4 and allow you to better understand how LANs can become WANs and how networking the enterprise isn't an insurmountable task (at least in theory).

I thought routers were gateways

When you configure a particular computer on a network (particularly on a TCP/IP network), you must configure the default gateway for the node. The default gateway is typically the logical address of the router port that the node (and the rest of its subnet) connects to. Don't confuse router interfaces (when they are referred to as gateways) with actual gateways that translate data between two different computer systems.

chapter

5

How a Router Works

Routing Basics

In cases where information needs to be moved between two networks, an internetworking device, called a *router* (you learned a little bit about routers in Chapter 4, "Internetworking Basics"), is responsible for the movement of this data. Routing data on an internetwork requires that a couple of different events take place: an appropriate path for the packets must be determined, and then the packets must be moved toward their final destination.

Both path determination and routing of packets (or *switching* as it is also referred to—packets are switched from an incoming interface to an outgoing interface on the router) take place at layer 3 (Network layer) of the OSI model. Another important layer 3 event is the resolution of logical addresses (such as IP numbers when TCP/IP is the routed protocol) to actual hardware addresses. Additional discussion related to these three layer 3 events will give you a better idea of the overall routing process.

SEE ALSO

➤ *To review the OSI model before continuing with this chapter, see page 35.*

Path Determination

Understanding subnets

Creating subnets is an extremely important part of implementing routing on a network. For now, understand that subnets are logical divisions of a larger corporate network. Creating subnets in a TCP/IP environment will be discussed in great detail in Chapter 10, "TCP/IP Primer."

As discussed in Chapter 4, routers enable you to divide a large network into logical subnets; doing so keeps network traffic local on each subnet, enabling you to take better advantage of the bandwidth available. It's then the job of the router to move data packets between these subnets when necessary. Routers can also serve as the connective device between your network (all your subnets are viewed by other enterprise networks as a single network even though you've divided them into logical parts). Routers also can serve as the connective device to other networks to which your network may be attached. The best example of many different networks connected for communication purposes is the Internet.

For the purpose of discussion, let's create a network that contains subnets that are connected by a router. You will also create a logical addressing system.

Figure 5.1 shows a network that has been divided into two subnets using a router. The type of connections between the subnets (Ethernet, Token Ring, and so on) and the router aren't important at this point in our discussion, so just suppose that the appropriate protocols and interface connections would be used to connect these subnets to the router.

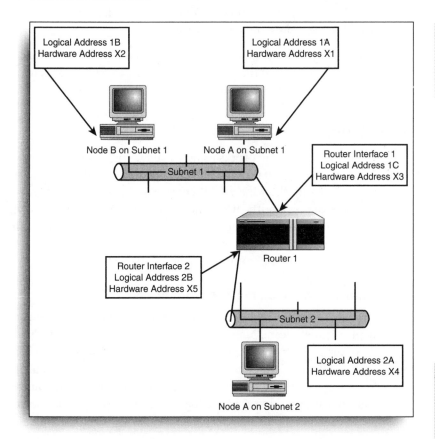

FIGURE 5.1
A network divided into two logical subnets.

Don't try this at home
Be advised that the logical addresses that you assign to your nodes and router interfaces are for our discussion of how the router determines when and when not to forward frames to a network. These aren't real logical addresses. Real logical addresses such as IP addresses would be used on a real-world network.

In this example, the router has two network interfaces, Interface 1 and Interface 2, which are connected to Subnet 1 and Subnet 2, respectively. The logical addressing system that is used to address the various nodes on the network (logical addresses must be assigned to each interface on the router as well) is the subnet number followed by a letter designation. So, Node A on Subnet 1 is assigned the logical address 1A (subnet designation then node designation).

Real-world addresses

To give you an idea of what the addresses for these various router interfaces and nodes would be in a real IP network, each node and interface is listed below with a Class B IP address:

Subnet 1:130.10.16.0

Node A: 130.10.16.2

Node B: 130.10.16.3

Router Interface 1: 130.10.16.1

Subnet 2: 130.10.32.0

Node A: 130.10.32.2

Router Interface 2: 130.10.32.1

Notice that subnetting has taken place on the network and the Subnet 1 nodes and router interface have the third octet value of 16 and the Subnet 2 nodes and router interface have a third octet value of 32; these different numbers identify the different subnets used. You will learn all about this in Chapter 10, "TCP/IP Primer."

Each node on the network will also have a hardware address (remember that a hardware address is actually assigned to each NIC when they are built at the factory; router interfaces are also assigned a burned-in hardware address when they are manufactured). For ease of discussion, the hardware addresses for each of the nodes is an X followed by a number. For example, the hardware address for Node A on Subnet 2 is X4 (remember all hardware addresses are different, that's how the cards are manufactured).

Now that you have a small internetwork, let's take a look at what happens when one of the computers attempts to send packets to another computer on the network.

Logical and Hardware Addresses

When you connect networks using a router, you end up with two different types of data traffic. You end up with local data traffic, where nodes on the same subnet communicate with each other. You also have network traffic where nodes on different subnets are communicating with each other. This type of traffic must pass through the router. The next two sections explain how communication within a subnet and communication between subnets take place.

Communication on the Same Subnet

First, let's look at a situation in which two computers on the same subnet communicate. Node A on Subnet 1 must send data to Node B on Subnet 1. Node A knows that the packets must go to the logical address 1B and Node A knows that 1B resides on the same subnet (so in this case the router will not actively be involved in the movement of packets). However, the logical address 1B must be resolved to an actual hardware address.

Now, Node A might already know that logical address 1B actually refers to the hardware address X2. Computers actually maintain small memory caches where they keep this type of logical-to-hardware address-resolution information. If Node A has no idea what the hardware address of logical address 1B is, it will send a message out to the network asking for the logical address 1B to be resolved to a hardware address. When it receives the information, it will send the packets to Node B, which accepts the packets because they are tagged with its hardware address—X2.

As you can see, node-to-node communication on the same subnet is pretty straightforward.

Communication Between Different Subnets

Now let's look at a scenario where a computer wants to send data to a computer on another subnet.

Node A on Subnet 1 wants to send data to Node A on Subnet 2. So, Node A on Subnet 1 wants to send the data to logical address 2A. Node A on Subnet 1 knows that address 2A isn't on the local subnet, so it will send the packets to its *default gateway*, which is the router interface that is connected to Subnet 1. In this case the logical address of the Node A (on Subnet 1) gateway is 1C. However, again this logical address must be resolved to a hardware address—the actual hardware address of Router Interface 1.

Again, using broadcast messages, Node 1 on Subnet 1 receives the hardware address information related to logical address 1C (the hardware address is X3) and sends the packets on to Router 1 via Router Interface 1. Now that the router has the packets, it must determine how to forward the packets so that they end up at the destination node. It will take a look at its routing table and then switch the packets to the interface that is connected to the destination subnet.

Nodes collect addressing information

Computers use broadcast messages and tables of information (that they build from broadcast information placed out on the network by other computers) to determine which addresses are local and which addresses are remote on an internetwork.

Packet Switching

After the router has the packets, packet switching comes into play. This means that the router will move the packets from the router interface that they came in on and switch them over to the router interface connected to the subnet they must go out on. However, in some cases the packets might have to pass through more than one router to reach the final destination. In our example, only one router is involved. Router 1 knows that the logical address 2A is on Subnet 2. So the packets will be switched from Router Interface 1 to Router Interface 2.

Again, broadcast messages are used to resolve logical address 2A to the actual hardware address X4. The packets are addressed appropriately and then forwarded by the router to Subnet 2. When Node A on Subnet 2 sees the packets with the Hardware Address X4, it grabs the packets.

So, you can see that routing involves both the use of logical addressing and hardware addressing to get packets from a sending computer to a destination computer. Each routable protocol (TCP/IP versus IPX/SPX) uses a slightly different scheme to resolve logical addresses to hardware addresses, but the overall theory is pretty much the same as outlined here (TCP/IP addressing was used as the model for our discussion).

Routing Tables

Before I finish this basic discussion of routing, we should discuss how the router determines which router port it switches the packets to (this information will be reviewed when IP routing is discussed in Chapter 11, "Configuring IP Routing"). Routers use software to create routing tables. These routing tables contain information on which the hardware interface on the router is the beginning route (for the router) that will eventually get the packets to the destination address.

Routers, however, aren't concerned with individual node addresses when they build their routing tables; they are only concerned with getting a particular set of packets to the appropriate network. For example, using your logical addressing system from Figure 5.1, a router's routing table would appear as shown in Table 5.1. Notice that each router interface is mapped to a particular subnet. That way the router knows that when it examines the logical address of a packet, it can determine which subnet to forward the packets to.

Where do routing tables come from?

Routing tables actually have two sources. In *static routing*, the network administrator actually types in the different routes that are available between segments on the internetwork. These network administrator–created routing tables use a series of router commands to build a table that looks somewhat like Figure 5.1. Routing tables can also be built dynamically by routing protocols such as RIP and IGRP (which are discussed later in this chapter). Dynamic routing tables also end up looking like a table (again somewhat like Figure 5.1).

Table 5.1   A Basic Routing Table for Router 1

Subnet Logical Designation	Router Interface
1	1
2	2

Basically, this routing table means that packets that are destined for any node on Subnet 1 would be routed to the Router 1 Interface on the router. Any packets destined for Subnet 2 would be switched to the Router Interface 2 (just as I discussed earlier). Obviously, the logical designation for a subnet on a real-world network would consist of something like a network IP address, such as 129.10.1.0, which designates a class B IP subnetwork. And the router interface would be designated by the type of network architecture it supports, such as E0 for the primary Ethernet interface, or S0 for the primary serial interface on the router.

When multiple routers are involved—on larger networks—the routing tables become populated with more information. For example, let's expand your one router, two-subnet network into five subnets that employ two routers. Figure 5.2 shows this network.

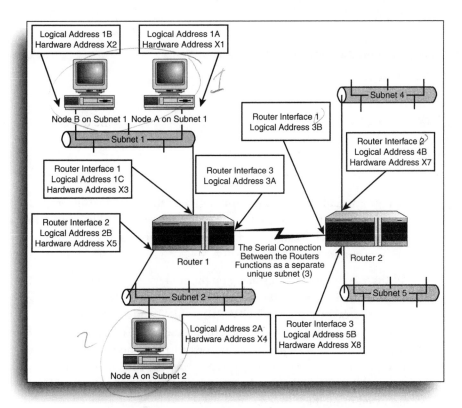

FIGURE 5.2

A network divided into five logical subnets that use two routers.

Now, you might be thinking that you see only four subnets. Actually, any serial connection between two routers is, in effect, a separate subnet and must be provided with unique logical addresses.

With the size of the network expanded and the number of subnets increased, Router 1 will have a decidedly different routing table. It now must potentially pass on packets that go to nodes on Subnets 4 and 5. However, as I stated earlier, a router doesn't worry about getting the packets to the actual recipient nodes; it only forwards the packets so that they get to the correct subnet.

Table 5.2 shows a routing table for Router 1 using your (fictional) logical addressing system for your subnets. Notice that Router 1 forwards packets for Subnets 4 and 5 through the same interface—its Interface 3. So, Router 1 is content with forwarding packets for Subnets 4 and 5 (sent from Subnets 1 or 2) to Router 2. Router 2 is then responsible for switching the packets to the correct interface that is connected to the appropriate subnet.

Table 5.2 An Expanded Routing Table for Router 1

Subnet Logical Designation	Router Interface
1	1
2	2
4	3
5	3

Router 2 would have a similar routing table that would designate that all packets for Subnets 1 and 2 be routed out of its Interface 1 to Router 1. Router 1 would then handle the routing of the packets to the appropriate subnet.

All these routing decisions made by the routers will involve software. Software that is responsible for network transport (network, or *routable*, protocols such as TCP/IP, IPX/SPX, and AppleTalk) and software that helps the router determine the best path for a set of packets to the next step in their journey to a final node destination. This type of software is called a *routing protocol*. Routable protocols (network protocols that can be routed) and routing protocols will be discussed in the next two sections.

SEE ALSO

➤ *For more information on IP routing and routing tables, see page 195.*

Routable Protocols

Before you take a look at the protocols that determine the path for packets routed through the router (and also maintain the routing table used by the router to forward the packets), a few words should be said about routable or *routed protocols*. Chapter 2, "The OSI Model and Network Protocols," discussed commonly used network protocols: TCP/IP, IPX/SPX, AppleTalk, and NetBEUI. Of these four protocols only TCP/IP, IPX/SPX, and AppleTalk are routable. This is because these three protocols all provide enough information in the Network layer header of their packets for the data to be sent from sending node to destination node even when the packets must be forwarded across different networks (by a device such as a router).

SEE ALSO

➤ *To review network protocols such as TCP/IP, see page 44.*

Routing Protocols

Whereas routable protocols provide the logical addressing system that makes routing possible, *routing protocols* provide the mechanisms for maintaining router routing tables. Routing protocols allow routers to communicate, which allows them to share route information that is used to build and maintain routing tables.

Several different routing protocols exist, such as Routing Information Protocol (RIP), Open Shortest Path First (OSPF), and Enhanced Interior Gateway Protocol (EIGRP). And while these different routing protocols use different methods for determining the best path for packets routed from one network to another, each basically serves the same purpose. They help accumulate routing information related to a specific routed protocol such as TCP/IP (IP is the routed portion of the TCP/IP stack).

It's not uncommon in LANs and WANs to find host and server machines running more than one network protocol to communicate. For example, an NT server in a *NT Domain* (an NT Domain is a network managed by an NT server called the Primary Domain Controller) may use TCP/IP to communicate with its member

---

Why isn't NetBEUI routable?

NetBEUI does provide a logical naming system to deliver packets to computers; it uses NetBIOS names, (the name you give your computer when you set it up), which are then resolved to MAC addresses on computers using a series of NetBIOS broadcasts. Unfortunately, the NetBIOS naming system doesn't have a Network layer logical addressing system that can be used to direct packets across a router on an internetwork. NetBIOS names just don't provide enough information (no network information at all) for the packets to be moved between the various networks connected by a router. Plus the NetBEUI/NetBIOS network stack doesn't contain a routing protocol. So, in NetBEUI's case it has two strikes and no route.

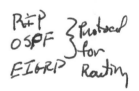

clients. But it may also serve as a gateway to various printers and file servers that use the Novell NetWare operating system; meaning that the NT server will also embrace IPX/SPX as a network protocol. These protocols basically operate in their own tracks simultaneously and do not interfere with each other (see Figure 5.3).

This same concept of simultaneously but independently running protocols is also embraced by routing protocols. Multiple independent routing protocols can run on the same router, building and updating routing tables for several different routed protocols. This means that the same network media can actually support different types of networking.

FIGURE 5.3
Networks can embrace multiple network protocols, and routers can simultaneously route multiple network protocols using multiple routing protocols.

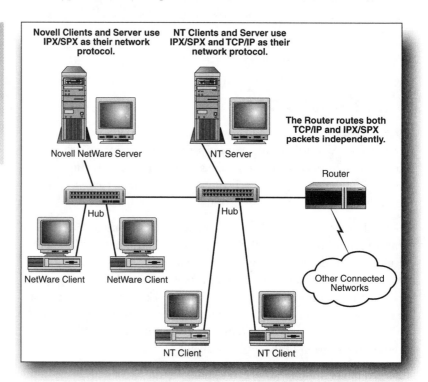

SEE ALSO

➤ *For a quick look at two theoretical routing tables, see page 82.*

➤ *For more information on the types of routing protocols and specific routing protocols, see page 91.*

Routing Protocol Basics

Routing protocols must not only provide information for router routing tables (and be able to adequately update routers when routing paths change), they are also responsible for determining the best route through an internetwork for data packets as they move from the sending computer to the destination computer. Routing protocols are designed to optimize routes on an internetwork and also to be stable and flexible. *optimize route on diff Network*

Routing protocols are also designed to use little processing overhead as they determine and provide route information. This means that the router itself doesn't have to be a mega computer with several processors to handle the routing of packets. The next section discusses the mechanism that routing protocols use to determine paths.

Routing Algorithms

An algorithm is a mathematical process that is used to arrive at a particular solution. In terms of routing protocols, you can think of the algorithm as the set of rules or process that the routing protocol uses to determine the desirability of paths on the internetwork for the movement of packets. The routing algorithm is used to build the routing table used by the router as it forwards packets.

Algor - Build routing tables

Routing algorithms come in two basic flavors: *static* and *dynamic* algorithms. Static algorithms aren't really a process at all, but consist of internetwork mapping information that a network administrator enters into the router's routing table. This table would dictate how packets are moved from one point to another on the network. All routes on the network would be static—meaning unchanging.

static - input Into table
dynamic

The problem with static algorithms (other than it's a real pain to have to manually enter this information on several routers) is that the router cannot adapt to changes in the network topology. If a particular route becomes disabled or a portion of the internetwork goes down, there is no way for the routers on the network to adapt to these changes and update their routing tables so that data packets continue to move toward their final destinations.

Routed protocols and routing protocols are configured on the router

Although this chapter delves into the theoretical aspects of how a router works and discusses the relationship between routed and routing protocols, keep in mind that these are all issues that you deal with on the router when you actually configure it. The Cisco IOS provides the commands and functions that enable you to set the routed and routing protocols used by a specific router. More on the Cisco IOS is discussed in Chapter 9, "Working with the Cisco IOS."

Convergence is the key for dynamic routing protocols

When an internetwork experiences a downed link or some other network problem, it's very important for all the routers on the network to update their routing tables accordingly. *Convergence* is the time it takes for all the routers on the network to be up-to-date in terms of the changes that have taken place in the network topology (such as the unavailability of a certain route because of a downed line). The longer it takes for all the routers on the internetwork to converge, the greater the possibility that packets will be routed to routes that are no longer available on the network. This type of problem is certainly not unheard of on the Internet either, and this is why email can end up traveling a road to nowhere and never get to its destination.

Dynamic algorithms are built and maintained by routing update messages. Messages that provide information on changes in the network prompt the routing software to recalculate its algorithm and update the router's routing table appropriately.

Routing algorithms (and the routing protocols that employ a certain algorithm) can also be further classified based on how they provide update information to the various routers on the internetwork. *Distance-vector routing algorithms* send out update messages at a prescribed time (such as every 30 seconds—an example is the Routing Information Protocol—RIP). Routers using distance-vector algorithms pass their entire routing table to their nearest router neighbors (routers that they are directly connected to). This basically sets up an update system that reacts to a change in the network like a line of dominos falling. Each router in turn informs its nearest router neighbors that a change has occurred in the network.

For example, in Figure 5.4, Router 1 realizes that the connection to Network A has gone down. In its update message (sent at 30-second intervals), it sends a revised routing table to Router 2 letting its neighbor know that the path to Network A is no longer available. At its next update message, Router 2 sends a revised routing table to Router 3, letting Router 3 know that Router 2 no longer serves as a path to Network A. This updating strategy continues until all the routers on the network know that the Network A line is no longer a valid path to the computers on that particular part of the entire internetwork.

The downside of distance-vector routing is that routers are basically using hearsay information to build their routing tables; they aren't privy to an actual view of a particular router's interface connections. They must rely on information from a particular router as to the status of its connections.

Another strategy for updating routing tables on an internetwork is the link-state routing algorithm. Link-state routing protocols not only identify their nearest neighbor routers, but they also exchange link-state packets that inform all the routers on the internetwork about the status of their various interfaces. This means that only information on a router's direct connections is sent, not the entire routing table as in distance-vector routing.

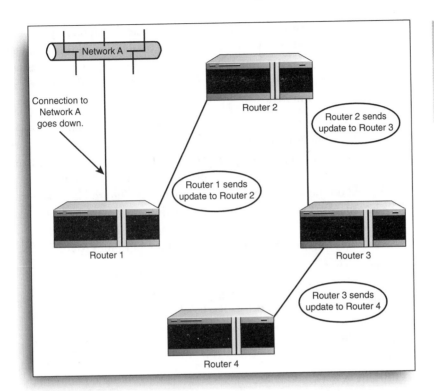

FIGURE 5.4
In distance-vector routing, nearest neighbors provide updated routing tables.

This also means that link-state routers are able to build a more comprehensive picture of the entire internetwork and make more intelligent decisions when choosing paths for the routing of packets. Convergence also takes place more rapidly on a link-state routing system then it does when distance-vector routing is used.

Routing Metrics

Now that you have learned the different types of routing algorithms (static versus dynamic) and the two ways that they update their router tables (distance vector versus link state), you should take a look at how routing protocols actually determine the best route between a sending computer and a destination computer when more than one route is available.

Static versus dynamic routing

Although you might get the impression that dynamic routing is a much better way to manage the demands of internetworking (when compared to static routing), dynamic routing does require more overhead (in terms of bandwidth and processing power) from internetworking devices such as routers because of all the broadcast messages and editing of the routing tables. Dynamic routing is, obviously, a much more "fun" process to monitor. However, in some cases, setting up static routing tables can provide an overall faster throughput on the network as packets are routed.

Routing algorithms use a *metric* to determine the suitability of one path over another. The metric can be several different things such as the path length, the actual cost of sending the packets over a certain route, or the reliability of a particular route between the sending and receiving computers.

For example, RIP, a distance vector routing protocol, uses *hop count* as its metric. A hop is the movement of the packets from one router to another router. If two paths are available to get the packets from one location to another, RIP will choose the most desirable path based on the smallest number of hop counts. Figure 5.5 shows an internetwork where two paths are possible for the routing of packets between the sending and receiving computers. Because Route A requires only one hop, it is considered the optimum route for the packets.

Routing updates are sent to all nearest neighbors

Although Figure 5.4 is concerned with updates related to the problem with the connection to Network A, remember that the routers send updates to all their nearest neighbors. So, while Router 1 is updating Router 2, Router 2 also sends an update to Router 1 as well as Router 3 when it sends its updated routing table.

FIGURE 5.5
Routing algorithms use a metric, such as hop count, to determine the optimum path for data packets.

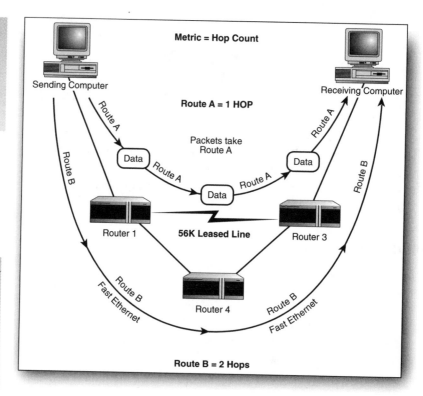

Hybrid routing protocols

Some routing protocols, such as OSPF, are considered hybrids because they use distance-vector and link-state information to update routing tables.

The problem with routing protocols that use only one metric (such as hop count) is that they become very single minded in their pursuit of the best route for a particular set of packets. RIP, for example, doesn't take the speed or reliability of the lines into account when it chooses the best path, just the number of hops. So, as shown in Figure 5.5, even though Route A is the best path according to the number of hops (and RIP), you are forced to route your packets over a slower line (the 56-kilobit leased line). This line is not only slow, it also costs you money. Route B is actually over wire that the company owns (part of the network infrastructure) and is actually a faster medium (fast Ethernet at 100Mbps). However, when you use a routing protocol that uses hop count as the metric it will choose Route A.

To overcome the lack of flexibility provided by hop count as a metric, several other routing protocols that use more sophisticated metrics are available. For example, the Interior Gateway Routing Protocol (IGRP) is another distance-vector routing protocol that can actually use 1 to 255 metrics depending on the number set by the network administrator. These metrics can include bandwidth (the capacity of the lines involved), load (the amount of traffic already being handled by a particular router in the path), and communication cost (packets are sent along the least expensive route). When several routing metrics are used together to choose the path for packets, a much more sophisticated determination is made. For example, in the case of Figure 5.5 a routing protocol that uses metrics other than hop counts (such as communication cost) would choose the route with more hops but less cost to move the packets to their destination.

Types of Routing Protocols

Real-world internetworks (particularly those for an entire enterprise) will consist of several routers that provide the mechanism for moving packets between the various subnets found on the network. To move packets efficiently it's not uncommon to divide several connected routers into subsets of the internetwork. A subset containing several member routers is referred to as an *area*. When several areas are grouped into a higher-level subset, this organizational level is called a *routing domain*.

91

Figure 5.6 shows an internetwork divided into areas. Each area is terminated by a high-end router called a border router (or core router as mentioned in the sidebar). The two border routers are connected to each other, which, in effect, connects the two routing domains (or autonomous systems on an IP internetwork).

FIGURE 5.6
Internetworks can be divided into areas that are connected by area border routers.

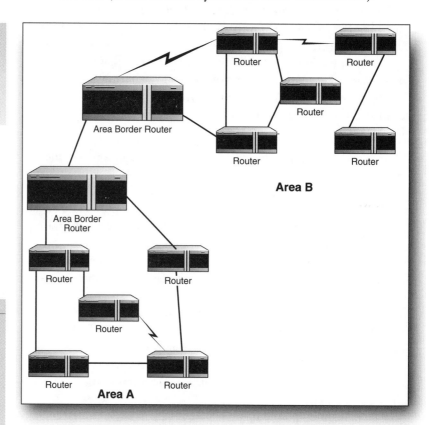

IP internetworks can be divided into routing domains

In cases where link-state routing protocols are used that require greater memory and processing capabilities from the routers on the network, it's not uncommon to divide the internetwork into routing domains. In IP networks, a routing domain is referred to as an *autonomous system*. Routing domains (or if you prefer, autonomous systems) are typically connected by a higher-end router called *a border router* or *core router*.

The fact that internetworks can be divided into logical groupings such as routing domains (or autonomous systems) gives rise to two different kinds of routing protocols: routing protocols that provide the routing of packets between routers in a routing domain and routing protocols that provide the routing of packets between routing domains.

Interior Gateway Protocols (IGPs) provide the routing of packets within the routing domain. IGPs such as RIP or IGRP would be configured on each of the routers in the router domain.

Protocols that move data between the routing domains are called *Exterior Gateway Protocols* (EGPs). Examples of EGPs are Border Gateway Protocol (BGP) and Exterior Gateway Protocol (EGP).

Interior Gateway Protocols

The Interior Gateway Protocols consist of distance-vector and link-state routing protocols. Several different IGPs are available and vary on the number of metrics used to determine optimum routing paths. The oldest IGP is the Routing Information Protocol and is discussed in the following section, along with some of the other commonly used IGPs.

Routing Information Protocol

Routing Information Protocol (RIP) is a distance-vector, IP-routing protocol that uses hop count as its metric. And although it is the oldest IGP, RIP is still in use.

RIP sends out a routing update message every 30 seconds (by Cisco default), which consists of the router's entire routing table. RIP uses the User Datagram Protocol—UDP—(part of the TCP/IP stack) as the encapsulation method for the sending of routing advertisements.

RIP is limited, however, in that the maximum number of hops that it will allow for the routing of specific packets is 15. This means that RIP is fine for smaller, homogenous internetworks, but doesn't provide the metric flexibility needed on larger networks.

SEE ALSO

➤ *For information on configuring RIP on a Cisco router, see page 202.*

Interior Gateway Routing Protocol

The Interior Gateway Routing Protocol (IGRP) was developed by Cisco in the 1980s. IGRP is a distance-vector routing protocol.

IGRP uses a composite metric that takes into account several variables; it also overcomes certain limitations of RIP, such as the hop count metric and the inability of RIP to route packets on networks that require more than 15 hops.

A real-world example

If you have a small or medium-sized company that has an internetwork, your entire network could be considered a routing domain. It would use Interior Gateway Protocols such as RIP or IGRP to move packets between the subnets or areas in the domain. Your connection to the Internet (the global internetwork) would be managed by an Exterior Gateway Protocol such as Border Gateway Protocol. More about these individual routing protocols is provided in the remainder of the chapter.

Implementing RIP

RIP is an IP network routing protocol. The logical division of IP networks is the subnet. Proper subnetting and a consistent use of IP subnet masks is crucial when using RIP on your routers. Subnetting and IP subnet masks will be discussed in Chapter 11.

IGRP is all Cisco

Because IGRP was developed by Cisco and remains a Cisco proprietary protocol, IGRP will only be available on Cisco routers. In comparison, RIP is a universal routing protocol that you will find on IP networks whether they are routed using Cisco boxes or products from another vendor such as 3Com.

Enhanced IGRP builds on IGRP's capabilities

Cisco now provides an enhanced version of IGRP called Enhanced IGRP (EIGRP). Although it uses the same metrics as IGRP, EIGRP provides updates at irregular intervals to reflect that a particular metric such as load or the network topology has changed. And because router updates only include routing information that has changed, EIGRP is less of a bandwidth hog when compared to IGRP.

IGRP (when compared to RIP) also employs a longer time period between routing updates and uses a more efficient format for the update packets that are passed between routers. IGRP also supports the use of *autonomous systems* (similar to the areas discussed earlier in the chapter), so routers running IGRP can be sequestered into domains where the router traffic in a particular domain remains local. This cuts down on the amount of router broadcast communications using up valuable bandwidth throughout the entire internetwork.

IGRP's metric consists of a composite that takes into consideration bandwidth, delay, load, and reliability when determining the best route for data moving from a sending node to a particular destination node. The following list describes how each of these network parameters is viewed by IGRP when the routing algorithm is used to build or update a router's routing table:

- *Bandwidth* is the capacity of a particular interface in kilobits. A serial interface may have a bandwidth of 100,000 kilobits (this would be a serial interface connected to an ATM switch, which typically supplies this amount of bandwidth). Unfortunately, the bandwidth of a particular interface isn't measured dynamically (measuring the actual bandwidth available at a particular time) but set statically by the network administrator using the `band-width` command. More about setting serial interfaces will be discussed in Chapter 15, "Configuring WAN Protocols."

- *Delay* is the amount of time it takes to move a packet from the interface to the intended destination. Delay is measured in microseconds and is a static figure set by the network administrator using the `delay` command. Several delays have been computed for common interfaces such as Fast Ethernet and IBM Token Ring. For example, the delay for a Fast Ethernet interface is 100 microseconds.

- *Reliability* is the ratio of expected-to-received keepalives on a particular router interface. (*Keepalives* are messages sent by network devices to tell other network devices, such as routers, that the link between them still exists.) Reliability is measured dynamically and is shown as a fraction when the `show interface` command is used on the router. For example, the fraction 255/255 represents a 100% reliable link.

- *Load* is the current amount of data traffic on a particular interface. Load is measured dynamically and is represented as a fraction of 255. For example, 1/255 would be an interface with a minimal amount of traffic, whereas 250/255 would be a fairly congested interface. Load can be viewed on the router using the show interface command.

As you can see, IGRP takes a lot of information into consideration when it uses its algorithm to update a router's routing table. It is often implemented in larger internetworks where RIP would be ineffectual.

SEE ALSO

➤ *For information on configuring IGRP on a Cisco router, see page 204.*

Open Shortest Path First Routing Protocol

Open Shortest Path First (OSPF) is a link-state protocol developed by the Internet Engineering Task Force (IETF) as a replacement for RIP. Basically, OSPF uses a shortest path first algorithm that enables it to compute the shortest path from source to destination when it determines the route for a specific group of packets.

OSPF employs the Hello Protocol as the mechanism by which routers identify their neighbors. Hello packet intervals can be configured for each interface on the router that is using OSPF (the default is every 10 seconds). The command for adjusting the Hello Interval is ip ospf hello-interval.

OSPF routing networks can also take full advantage of the autonomous systems feature on large IP networks (also discussed in this chapter as areas and domains), which keeps link-state advertisement of member routers local to a particular autonomous system. Area border routers are used to connect the various autonomous system areas into one internetwork.

Exterior Gateway Protocols

As mentioned earlier, Exterior Gateway Protocols (EGPs) are used to route traffic between autonomous systems (routing domains). *Border Gateway Protocol (BGP)* is a commonly used routing protocol for inter-domain routing. It is the standard EGP for the Internet.

Why does 255 keep popping up?

You probably noticed that both reliability and load use the number 255 as the measure of a completely reliable or completely congested (in terms of load) router interface. This is because, even though hop count isn't one of IGRP's metrics, IGRP can only move packets on internetworks that consist of 255 hops or fewer. This means that theoretically packets could be moved between 255 devices as the packets move from source to destination. This is why the number 255 is used in the measurement of reliability and load.

BGP handles the routing between two or more routers that serve as the border routers for particular autonomous systems. These border routers are also referred to as *core routers*. Basically, these core routers serve as neighbors and share routing table information with each other. This enables the core routers to build a list of all the paths to a particular network.

BGP uses a single metric to determine the best route to a particular network. Each link is assigned an arbitrary number that specifies the degree of preference for that link. The preference degree number for a particular link is assigned by the network administrator.

part

II

ROUTER DESIGN AND BASIC CONFIGURATION

Understanding Router
Interfaces

Router Interfaces

A router interface supplies the physical connection between the router and a particular network medium type. Cisco interfaces are often referred to as *ports*, and each port will be physically designed to appropriately connect the type of network technology it is supposed to serve. For example, a *LAN interface*, such as an Ethernet port on the router, will consist of a female RJ-45 connector (which is connected to an Ethernet hub using a twisted-pair cable with male RJ-45 connectors on either end).

Built-in ports are designated by their connection type followed by a number. For example, the first Ethernet port on a router would be designated as E0. The second Ethernet port would be E1, and so on (in some cases, the Ethernet port will be set up as a hub, such as on the 2505 router). Serial ports are designated likewise with the first serial port being S0. Figure 6.1 shows two serial ports and their numeric designation on a Cisco 2505 router and the Ethernet 0 hub ports (1 through 8).

FIGURE 6.1
Ports such as serial ports are designated by a number, starting with 0. Ethernet interfaces can be set up as Hub ports.

(1) Serial ports

(2) Ethernet hub ports

Cisco routers such as those in the 2500 Series family basically are off-the-shelf routers that come with a predetermined number of LAN, WAN, and serial ports. Higher-end routers like the Cisco 4500 are modular and actually contain empty slots that can be filled with several different interface cards.

Not only are different interface cards available (such as LAN versus WAN), but the number of ports on the card can also be selected. For example, one of the three empty slots on the 4500 router can be filled with an Ethernet card that contains six Ethernet ports. Figure 6.2 shows the Cisco ConfigMaker hardware configuration screen for the Cisco 4500 router (you will work with ConfigMaker in Chapter 16). Three slots are available (shown on the right of the screen) and can be filled with several different cards (listed on the left of the screen).

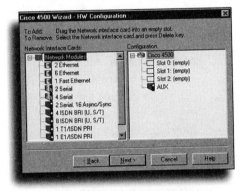

FIGURE 6.2
Modular routers such as the 4500 allow you to fill empty slots with different interface cards.

Modular routers (like the 4500) designate their ports by connection type, followed by slot number, followed by port number. For example, the first Ethernet port on an Ethernet card placed in the router's first slot would be designated as Ethernet 1/0 (the slot is designated first, followed by the port number).

Viewing the interfaces (and their status) on a particular router is handled by the show interfaces command. Figure 6.3 shows the results of the show interfaces command on a 2505 router that has one Ethernet port (E0) and two serial ports (S0 and S1). The status of the various ports is related to whether the ports have been connected (physically to the internetwork) and whether they have been configured.

```
Tera Term - COM2 VT
File  Edit  Setup  Control  Window  Help

router2>show interfaces
Ethernet0 is up, line protocol is up , using hub 0
  Hardware is Lance, address is 0010.7b3a.50b3 (bia 0010.7b3a.50b3)
  Internet address is 10.48.1.0 255.240.0.0
  MTU 1500 bytes, BW 10000 Kbit, DLY 1000 usec, rely 255/255, load 1/255
  Encapsulation ARPA, loopback not set, keepalive set (10 sec)
  ARP type: ARPA, ARP Timeout 4:00:00
  Last input never, output 0:00:08, output hang never
  Last clearing of "show interface" counters never
  Output queue 0/40, 0 drops; input queue 0/75, 0 drops
  5 minute input rate 0 bits/sec, 0 packets/sec
  5 minute output rate 0 bits/sec, 0 packets/sec
     0 packets input, 0 bytes, 0 no buffer
     Received 0 broadcasts, 0 runts, 0 giants
     0 input errors, 0 CRC, 0 frame, 0 overrun, 0 ignored, 0 abort
     0 input packets with dribble condition detected
     1089 packets output, 102933 bytes, 0 underruns
     0 output errors, 0 collisions, 1 interface resets, 0 restarts
     0 output buffer failures, 0 output buffers swapped out
Serial0 is down, line protocol is down
  Hardware is HD64570
  Internet address is 10.32.3.0 255.240.0.0
  MTU 1500 bytes, BW 38 Kbit, DLY 20000 usec, rely 255/255, load 1/255
  Encapsulation HDLC, loopback not set, keepalive set (10 sec)
  Last input never, output never, output hang never
  Last clearing of "show interface" counters never
  Output queue 0/40, 0 drops; input queue 0/75, 0 drops
  5 minute input rate 0 bits/sec, 0 packets/sec
  5 minute output rate 0 bits/sec, 0 packets/sec
     0 packets input, 0 bytes, 0 no buffer
     Received 0 broadcasts, 0 runts, 0 giants
     0 input errors, 0 CRC, 0 frame, 0 overrun, 0 ignored, 0 abort
     0 packets output, 0 bytes, 0 underruns
     0 output errors, 0 collisions, 310 interface resets, 0 restarts
     0 output buffer failures, 0 output buffers swapped out
     0 carrier transitions
     DCD=down  DSR=down  DTR=down  RTS=down  CTS=down
Serial1 is down, line protocol is down
  Hardware is HD64570
 --More--
```

Configuring a particular interface depends on the type of network protocol used by the network to which the interface port is connected. For example, an Ethernet port connected to an IP network will be configured for the routing of IP. An Ethernet port connected to an AppleTalk network will be configured for AppleTalk routing. Interface configuration is covered in Chapters 11, "Configuring IP Routing," 12, "Routing Novell IPX," and 13, "Routing AppleTalk."

SEE ALSO
➤ *Connecting LAN and serial ports to network media is discussed on page 119.*

LAN Interfaces

Cisco routers support several commonly used LAN networks. The most common LAN router interfaces are Ethernet, Fast Ethernet, IBM Token Ring, and Fiber Distributed Data Interface (FDDI).

All these LAN protocols mentioned embrace the same Data Link layer physical addressing system (the MAC hardware address on a NIC or the MAC hardware address found on the controller of the router interface). These addresses are unique for each device.

Each LAN technology is discussed briefly in the list that follows:

- Ethernet provides a network throughput of up to 10Mbps. It is a passive network architecture that uses carrier sense multiple access with collision detection (CSMA/CD) as its network access strategy. A Cisco router can be used to segment an Ethernet network into logical subnets (such as IP subnets). Typically, a router is connected to an Ethernet network using UTP cable with an RJ-45 connector. Some routers, such as the Cisco 2505, provide direct hub connections that can be used to directly connect workstations to hub ports built into the router (see Figure 6.4).

FIGURE 6.4
The 2505 router provides hub ports as the connection to the Ethernet interface built into the router.

① Hub ports

- Fast Ethernet operates at speeds of up to 100Mbps. It uses the same access strategy as regular Ethernet (CSMA/CD) and runs on UTP cable (as does regular Ethernet). Fast Ethernet does require special interfaces on routers (Fast Ethernet Interfaces) and Fast Ethernet NICs on nodes. Any hubs used as part of the network topology must also be Fast Ethernet hubs.

- Token Ring is a proprietary network architecture developed by IBM. Token Ring networks run on a logical ring (the ring is provided internally by the multi access units (MAUs) that are used to connect the various nodes on the network. Token Ring

Routers can handle more than one network protocol

Remember that routers can route more than one network protocol (such as IP and IPX/SPX) at the same time. They also can run more than one routing protocol at a time (which may be dictated by the network protocols that must be routed). Routed and routing protocols are discussed in Chapter 5, "How a Router Works."

103

Checking the MAC address of a router interface

Router LAN interfaces have unique MAC addresses just like network interface cards. To view the MAC address for your router interfaces, use the `show interface` command (refer to Figure 6.3).

networks use token passing as the network access strategy. Routers used on Token Ring networks must contain a special Token Ring interface for connection to the network. Parameters such as the speed of the ring (either 4Mbps or 16Mbps) must be set on the router's Token Ring interface so the throughput speed matches that of the Token Ring network.

- FDDI is a token passing network that uses two redundant rings (passing tokens in opposite directions) as a fault tolerance method (*fault tolerance* is keeping the network up and running when one of the rings breaks down). FDDI, which is often employed as a fiber-optic backbone for larger networks or municipal area networks (MANs), can provide network throughput of up to 100Mbps. Routers used on FDDI networks must have an FDDI interface.

All the LAN protocols require a matching interface on the router that serves them. For example, a Token Ring network can only be attached to a router with the appropriate Token Ring interface. Specifications for some of the routers built by Cisco are discussed in Appendix C, "Selected Cisco Router Specifications." You can also view the various specifications of Cisco routers on Cisco's Web site at www.cisco.com. It is obviously important that when you plan your internetwork, you purchase a router that will provide you with all the necessary interfaces that your various LAN connections will require. Figure 6.5 shows the diagram of a network where several different LAN architectures have been connected using routers (the diagram is actually based on the network map of a real company's internetwork).

SEE ALSO

➤ *MAC addresses are discussed on page 41.*

➤ *For more information on LAN architectures such as Ethernet or FDDI, see page 25.*

Serial Interfaces

Serial router interfaces provide a way to connect LANs using WAN technologies. WAN protocols move data across asynchronous and synchronous serial interfaces (on routers), which are connected via leased lines and other third-party connectivity technologies.

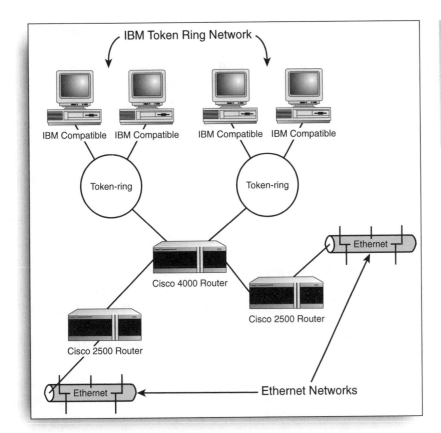

FIGURE 6.5
Routers can provide the connection between different LAN architectures such as the Token Ring and Ethernet networks shown here.

Some of the commonly used WAN Data Link layer technologies are High Level Data Link Control (*HDLC*), X.25, Frame Relay, Integrated Services Digital Network (ISDN), and Point to Point Protocol (PPP). All the WAN protocols discussed are configured on particular router interfaces (such as a serial interface or an ISDN interface) when the router is in the configuration mode. The actual command sets and the ins and outs of configuring WAN protocols on a Cisco router are discussed in Chapter 15, "Configuring WAN Protocols."

- HDLC is a Data Link layer protocol that provides the encapsulation of data transferred across synchronous data links. This means that a device such as a *DCE* (Data Communication Equipment) provides a connection to the network and provides a clocking signal that synchronizes the transfer of data between

HDLC - Default for Cisco

usually for PPP

PPP - Data Link Layer
good for Interconnecting

the two ends of the serial link. Serial ports on a router are connected to a modem or other CSU/DSU device via special cables such as a V.35 cable. HDLC is the default WAN protocol for Cisco routers. Cisco's HDLC implementation is proprietary, however, and will not communicate with other vendor's HDLC (this is why trying to mix routers from different vendors such as Cisco and 3Com can be a real nightmare). HDLC is considered a point-to-point protocol and provides a direct connection between sending and receiving devices (such as two routers).

- Point to Point Protocol (PPP) is another Data Link layer point-to-point protocol supported by Cisco routers. It isn't proprietary, so it can be used to connect Cisco routers to internetworking devices from other vendors. PPP actually operates in both synchronous and asynchronous modes (meaning it can provide either encapsulation type). A flag (which is actually several bits inserted into the data stream) is used to signify the beginning or end of a frame or datagram of information flowing across the PPP connection. PPP can be used for connecting IP, AppleTalk, and IPX networks over WAN connections.

PPP is configured on the serial port of the router that provides the connection to a leased line or some other WAN connection. You may already be familiar with PPP because it is the protocol used to connect workstations to Internet service providers over analog phone lines via a modem.

Synchronous versus asynchronous communications

Synchronous serial connections use a clocking device that provides the precise timing of the data as it moves from sending to receiving end across a serial connection. *Asynchronous* connections rely on start and stop bits to make sure that the data is completely received by the destination interface.

X.25
- switched network

slow Due
to error
checking

- X.25 is a packet-switching protocol for use over public switched telephone networks. Data is passed along the switched network using virtual circuits (such as permanent virtual circuits). X.25 is a slow protocol when compared to newer WAN technologies like Frame Relay because it provides a great deal of error checking (which was a must when X.25 was first implemented several years ago over fairly low-grade telephone lines). X.25 is typically implemented between a DTE device and a DCE device. The DTE is typically a Cisco router, and the DCE is the X.25 switch owned by the public switched network. Figure 6.6 shows how two routers would be connected across an X.25 serial connection.

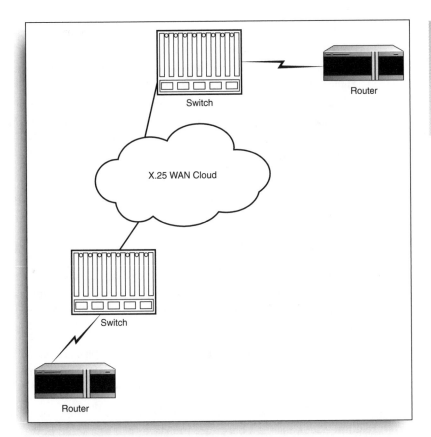

packet switch

- Frame Relay is a packet switching Data Link layer protocol that was originally developed for use over ISDN connections. It has now replaced X.25 as the protocol of choice over switched networks, and it uses virtual circuits to define a route between two devices (such as two routers) communicating over the WAN. In a Frame Relay connection, a DTE such as a router is attached to a DCE such as a CSU/DSU (most CSU/DSUs can be connected to the router using a V.35 serial cable). Or the router can be connected directly to the phone company's switching equipment. Frame Relay[nd]based WANs looked similar to the X.25 packet switching network depicted in Figure 6.6.

- Integrated Services Digital Network (ISDN) uses digital technology to move data, voice, and video over existing phone lines. It is an asynchronous WAN protocol. ISDN requires that the

X.25 and Frame Relay use serial port connections

Both of the packet switching WAN protocols, X.25 and Frame Relay, have their hardware components (DCEs such as CSU/DSUs or phone network switches) connected to the router via one of the router's serial ports. Even a low-end router such as the 2505 (as simple as it is) can have its serial interfaces configured for these WAN technologies, whereas in the case of ISDN, it is typically connected to an ISDN port that is provided by a specific model of router.

network be connected to the phone line using terminal equipment that is commonly referred to as an ISDN modem. However, Cisco routers can be purchased that have a BRI interface (BRI stands for Basic Rate Interface) included on the router. The BRI interface is then connected directly to the phone lines. In cases where your router doesn't have the BRI port, you will have to connect one of the existing serial ports to an ISDN modem (or buy a new router).

SEE ALSO

➤ *WAN protocols and how they work are discussed in greater detail on page 53.*

Logical Interfaces

Before we conclude our discussion of router interfaces, we must take at look at logical interfaces. A *logical interface* is a software-only interface and is created using the router's IOS. Cisco's IOS is explored in Chapter 9, "Working with the Cisco IOS."

Logical interfaces don't exist as actual hardware interfaces on the router. You can think of logical interfaces as *virtual interfaces* that have been created with a series of router software commands.

These virtual interfaces can be viewed by devices on the network as real interfaces, just as a hardware interface such as a serial port is a real interface. You can configure different types of logical interfaces on a router including Loopback interfaces, Null interfaces, and Tunnel interfaces.

Logical interfaces on high-end routers

Logical interfaces are a little bit beyond the scope of this book but you should be familiar with their existence. They are sometimes configured on higher-end routers, such as the Cisco 4000 and 7500 series routers, which serve as central site access routers and core routers on very large internetworks. Logical interfaces can be used on higher-end routers as clever ways to either access or restrict traffic to a particular portion of the internetwork.

Loopback Interfaces

A *Loopback interface* is a software-only interface that emulates an actual physical interface on the router. Loopbacks are typically configured on a high-end router that serves as the core router between two corporate internetworks or between a corporate network and the Internet. Routers serving as core routers will be configured with an exterior gateway protocol such as Border Gateway Protocol that routes the packets between the two separate internetworks.

Because the router serves as such an important link between inter-networks, you don't want it dumping data packets if a particular physical interface goes down on the router. So the Loopback virtual interface is created and configured as the termination address for the Border Gateway Protocol (BGP) sessions. In this way the traffic is processed locally on the router, which assures you that the packets get to their final destination.

BGP

Null Interfaces

Another logical interface is the *Null interface*. It is set up on a router using the appropriate router commands and serves as a brick wall that can be used to keep out certain traffic. For example, if you don't want traffic from a particular network to move through a particular router (but move through the internetwork by other routes) you can configure the Null interface so that it receives and dumps any pack-ets that the network sends to the router. Normally Access lists (dis-cussed in Chapter 14, "Filtering Router Traffic with Access Lists") are used to filter traffic on an internetwork and define valid routes for certain networks. The Null interface is pretty much a sledgeham-mer approach to a process that is normally handled with jeweler's tools.

only allows packed to certain traffic

Tunnel Interfaces

A *Tunnel interface* is another logical interface that can be used to move packets of a particular type over a connection that doesn't typi-cally support these types of packets. For example, a Tunnel interface can be set up on each of two routers that are responsible for routing AppleTalk packets from their LANs. These two routers are con-nected by a serial connection (see Figure 6.7). The Tunnel interface can be configured to route IP. And although AppleTalk would not be typically routed over an IP interface, the AppleTalk packets are encapsulated (stuffed in a generic envelope) and then moved across the Tunnel as if they were IP packets. Cisco routers provide the Generic Route Encapsulation Protocol (GRE), which handles the encapsulation of packets moved over a Tunnel interface.

GRE - Bundles the packets & encapsulate them

FIGURE 6.7
AppleTalk packets are routed over a virtual IP Tunnel.

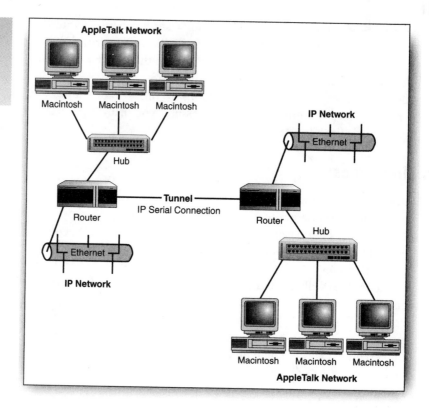

chapter 7

Setting Up a New Router

Becoming Familiar with Your Router

Routers provide the hardware and software necessary for routing. They are important internetworking devices for connecting LAN subnets and for making wide area connections between subnets. Chapter 5, "How a Router Works," provided the theory behind how a router works, and now we will take a look at the nuts and bolts of actually getting a router out of the box and ready for deployment on the network. Figure 7.1 shows the front and back of the Cisco 2505 router. The 2505 router provides only three interfaces, one LAN and two serial interfaces, and is typically used to connect subnets over serial connections such as ISDN, T1 leased lines, and other WAN alternatives.

FIGURE 7.1
The Cisco 2505 router is typically used to connect LANs over serial connections.

① Ethernet port/hub

② Serial ports

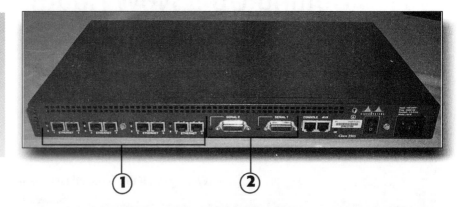

Several different Cisco Router models are available; each designed to satisfy a particular networking or set of networking needs. The number of ports and the type of ports on the different router models will vary, and rightly so because you will want to acquire a router (or routers) with the appropriate connections to fill your internet-working requirements. (Many of the higher-end routers allow you to customize the type and number of interfaces found on the router.)

Cisco Router Design

Cisco routers must be able to build routing tables, execute commands, and route packets across network interfaces using routing protocols. This means that the router must have processing power, some sort of storage capacity, and available random access memory. Appropriate software such as an operating system that can be used to configure routed and routing protocols is also necessary (and is discussed in Chapter 9, "Working with the Cisco IOS").

Router CPUs

Routers aren't unlike PCs in that they contain a microprocessor. And just like PCs, different Cisco router models come with different processors. For example, the Cisco 2505 Router (which is the router that you will see in the various figures throughout this book) contains a 20MHz Motorola 68EC030 processor. A higher-end router like the Cisco 7010 Router contains a 25MHz Motorola MC68040 CPU. (Many of the lower-end routers use some of the same Motorola processors that are used in a variety of Apple Macintosh computers. Some of the very high-end routers use Risc processors that you would typically find on miniframe computers or very high-end servers.)

SEE ALSO
➤ *For more information on specific Cisco routers, see page 337.*

Router Memory Components

As already mentioned, routers not only need processing power, they also need a place to store configuration information, a place to boot the router operating system (IOS), and memory that can be used to hold dynamic information as the router does its job of moving packets on the internetwork. Cisco routers actually contain different types of memory components that provide the storage and dynamic

Getting the right router

Obviously, you will want to purchase the appropriate router or routers to fill your particular networking needs. The Cisco Web site at www.cisco.com provides a great deal of information on the various internetworking products that they sell. Also check out Appendix C, "Cisco Router Specifications List," which provides some descriptions and specifications for some of the Cisco routers available.

caching required. The following list provides information on the different memory components found in a Cisco router:

hold IOS

- **ROM**—Contains the Power-on Self-Test (POST) and the boot-strap program for the router. The ROM chips also contain either a subset or the complete router IOS (for example, the ROM on the 2505 router only contains a subset of the IOS, whereas the 7000 series contains the full IOS). Because the IOS is available on the ROM, you can recover from major disasters such as the wiping out of your Flash RAM. The ROM chips on Cisco routers are removable and can be upgraded or replaced.

startup config
& config

- **NVRAM (nonvolatile RAM)**—Stores the startup configuration file for the router. NVRAM can be erased, and you can copy the running configuration on the router to NVRAM. The great thing about NVRAM is that it retains the information that it holds even if the router is powered down (which is extremely useful considering you won't want to have to reconfigure the router every time after the power goes down).

erase & reprogram

- **Flash RAM**—Flash is a special kind of ROM that you can actually erase and reprogram. Flash is used to store the Cisco IOS that runs on your router. You can also store alternative versions of the Cisco IOS on the Flash (such as an upgrade of your current IOS), which makes it very easy for you to upgrade the router. Flash RAM actually comes in the form of SIMMS (Single-Inline Memory Modules) and depending on the router you have, additional Flash RAM may be installed.

hold config until saved in NVRAM

- **RAM**—Similar to the dynamic memory you use on your PC, RAM provides the temporary storage of information (packets are held in RAM when their addressing information is examined by the router) and holds information such as the current routing table. RAM also holds the currently running router configuration (changes that you make to the configuration are kept in RAM until you save them to NVRAM).

These various memory components all play an important role in what happens when you boot the router. The various possibilities revolving around the router system startup and where the router finds its IOS and start-up configuration files are discussed in the next chapter.

SEE ALSO

➤ *The role that the different memory types play in the router boot up sequence are discussed in the next chapter, beginning on page 126.*

SEE ALSO

➤ *The Cisco Router interfaces are another important hardware component of the router. They are discussed in Chapter 6, starting on page 99.*

Connecting the Console

With an overview of the internal components of the router and the router interfaces (in the previous chapter) taken care of, it's now time to walk through the steps of getting a new router out of its box and connecting it to the LANs that it will service (either by direct connection using a LAN port such as an Ethernet port or by connecting LANs using WAN connections). Configuring the router is discussed in Chapter 8, "Basic Router Configuration," with additional IOS configuration commands discussed in Chapters 9, 11, 12, 13, and 15.

Before you attempt to connect the router, it makes sense to take a look at the contents of the box that were shipped to you by Cisco or your Cisco reseller. Make sure you got what you paid for. Check the cable specifications (they are printed on the cable near the connectors), check the IOS that was shipped (the router won't work with the wrong IOS version), and make sure that the router contains the interfaces you ordered. If anything is missing or the router doesn't contain the correct interfaces (or interface cards used on the higher-end routers), get on the phone to Cisco (1-800-462-4726) or your local Cisco reseller.

After you have inventoried the router, cables, and software that you were shipped, you can start to put the router together. Connect the router's power cord to the router and a power source (make sure that the router is turned off); the next step is to connect a PC to the router to act as the router's console. The console can be pretty much any PC that has a serial port and can run some type of terminal emulation software. The PC, in effect, becomes a dumb terminal and provides you with the interface that you use to configure and monitor the router.

Getting the right IOS

After you determine which router will work for a specific internetworking task, you also must decide which version of the Cisco IOS you will use. The Cisco site (www.cisco.com) also provides information on all the versions of the IOS available and provides a planner that helps you choose the appropriate IOS for your router (such as a 2505 router versus a 4500 router). The IOS that you select must also support the type of routing that you want to do. If you only want to route IP, you can choose a version of the IOS that only routes IP. If you must route IP, IPX, and AppleTalk, you must choose the correct version of the IOS. And be advised: The IOS is a separate purchase, so don't forget to order the appropriate IOS when you buy your router.

The console computer and the router are connected by the *roll-over cable* that ships with the router. The cable is terminated on both ends with an RJ-45 connector (see Figure 7.2).

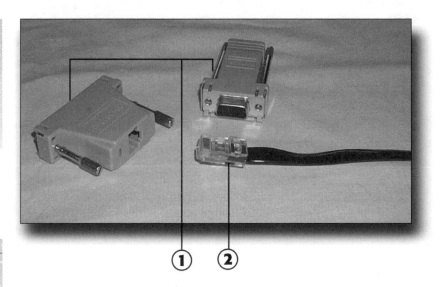

FIGURE 7.2
The roll-over cable is used to connect the router to the PC console.

① Serial adapters

② Roll-over cable

Installing the router

You will want to position the router where it can be connected to the various LANs between which it will route information. This might mean that the router will be in a server closet or positioned where it can be connected to a leased line from your local telephone provider. Most Cisco routers come with mounting brackets that make it easy for you to install the router into hub racks and other server closet equipment racks. If the router will be placed in a very inaccessible spot, you can configure the router (discussed in Chapter 8) before you connect it to the various lines and LAN connections.

The router also comes with several different *serial adapters* that contain an RJ-45 port so that they can be connected to the roll-over cable and then to the serial port on the PC that you will use as the router's *console* (see Figure 7.2). After you've selected the appropriate serial adapter you are ready to connect the router and the console.

Connecting the router and the console

1. Place the RJ-45 male adapter on the roll-over cable in the port on the back of the router marked CONSOLE (see Figure 7.3).

2. Attach the serial adapter to the appropriate serial port on the PC that will serve as the console.

With the physical connection of the router to the PC taken care of, you now must set up some type of *terminal emulation software* on the PC. Terminal emulation software and the communication settings necessary to talk to the router are covered in the next section.

FIGURE 7.3
The roll-over cable is attached to the CON-SOLE port on the router using the male RJ-45 connector.

Configuring the Router Console

The PC serving as the console communicates with the router using terminal emulation software. A number of these software packages exist, such as HyperTerminal (which ships as part of the Windows 95, 98, and Windows 2000 Professional operating systems) and ProComm Plus (a commercial communication program that offers faxing, terminal emulation, and other communication possibilities). A number of other possibilities are available on the Internet and can be downloaded as freeware or shareware (such as Tera Term Pro, an extremely easy-to-use and configure terminal emulator shown in Figure 7.4 and used throughout this book).

```
Tera Term - COM2 VT
File  Edit  Setup  Control  Window  Help
          170 West Tasman Drive
          San Jose, California 95134-1706

Cisco Internetwork Operating System Software
IOS (tm) 3000 Software (IGS-I-L), Version 11.0(16), RELEASE SOFTWARE (fc1)
Copyright (c) 1986-1997 by cisco Systems, Inc.
Compiled Tue 24-Jun-97 12:20 by jaturner
Image text-base: 0x0301E644, data-base: 0x00001000

cisco 2505 (68030) processor (revision K) with 2048K/2048K bytes of memory.
Processor board ID 08867035, with hardware revision 00000000
Bridging software.
X.25 software, Version 2.0, NET2, BFE and GOSIP compliant.
1 Ethernet/IEEE 802.3 interface.
8 Ethernet/IEEE 802.3 repeater ports.
2 Serial network interfaces.
32K bytes of non-volatile configuration memory.
8192K bytes of processor board System flash (Read ONLY)


Press RETURN to get started!

%LINK-3-UPDOWN: Interface Ethernet0, changed state to up
%LINK-3-UPDOWN: Interface Serial0, changed state to down
%LINK-3-UPDOWN: Interface Serial1, changed state to down
%LINEPROTO-5-UPDOWN: Line protocol on Interface Ethernet0, changed state to up
%LINEPROTO-5-UPDOWN: Line protocol on Interface Serial0, changed state to down
%LINEPROTO-5-UPDOWN: Line protocol on Interface Serial1, changed state to down
%SYS-5-CONFIG_I: Configured from memory by console
%SYS-5-RESTART: System restarted --
Cisco Internetwork Operating System Software
IOS (tm) 3000 Software (IGS-I-L), Version 11.0(16), RELEASE SOFTWARE (fc1)
Copyright (c) 1986-1997 by cisco Systems, Inc.
Compiled Tue 24-Jun-97 12:20 by jaturner
router2>
```

FIGURE 7.4
Terminal emulation software (such as Tera Term Pro) is used to communicate between the console and the router.

Make sure your terminal emulation software supports serial communication

Many terminal emulation software packages on the Internet are designed to telnet between computers connected to the Internet. This means that they don't support or allow you to configure the terminal software for communications via your serial ports. Before you spend a lot of time downloading and installing a particular package, make sure that it will allow serial connections. Windows HyperTerminal is available as part of your operating system and can be configured for serial communications (with the settings shown in Table 7.1).

After you have installed a particular terminal emulation software package, you must set up the communication parameters for the serial port that you will use to talk to the router. Table 7.1 shows the communication settings to be used by the software.

Table 7.1 Terminal Communication Settings

Parameter	Setting
Terminal Emulation	VT100
Baud rate	9600
Parity	none
Data bits	8
Stop bits	1 (2 stop bits for the 2500 series)

Working with the Terminal Emulation Software

Each terminal emulation package will operate a little differently, but each will provide some sort of menu/dialog box system that gives you access to the various settings for the software. Figure 7.5 shows the Serial port setup dialog box in Tera Term. Communication settings are configured using drop-down boxes.

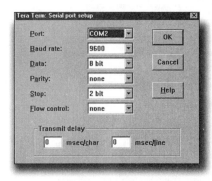

FIGURE 7.5
Communications setting for the serial port will be available in a dialog box in most Windows-based terminal emulators.

After you've correctly configured the console's terminal emulator, it's really quite easy to establish communications with the router.

Establishing communications between the router and the console

1. Start your terminal emulator and make sure that you have selected the appropriate serial port for communications (and set the communication parameters shown in Table 7.1)

2. Power on the router (press the on/off switch on the router—it's on the back, left of the 2500 Series routers).

The banner for the router (as shown in Figure 7.4) should appear. If you seem to have a connection with the router, check your serial and console connections (on the roll-over cable) and make sure that you have specified the correct serial port for the communication session in the terminal emulator.

Routers right out of the box will not be configured. This means that none of the interfaces has been prepared for communications nor have the appropriate routed and routing protocols been set up on the new router. To configure a new router you'll need to follow the steps for router configuration found in Chapter 8.

SEE ALSO

➤ *Configuring a new router is discussed in the next chapter, starting on page 123.*

Connecting the Router to the Network

After the router is connected to the console you have a means to configure the various router parameters (other methods of configuring the router also are available, as outlined in the next chapter). The next step is connecting the router to the networks that it will service.

As discussed in Chapter 6, "Understanding Router Interfaces," several different interfaces can be available on your router (depending on the router model and the configuration that you chose for the router). For a basic walk through of some of the connection options, we will take a look at a 2505 Cisco Hub/Router.

LAN Connections

Depending on the type of router you have, LAN connections are typically made to an Ethernet or Token Ring interface port on the router and then to a hub or MAU (Multistation Access Unit, see

Chapter 1 for more information) that supplies the connections for the various computers on the network. Let's assume that we are connecting an Ethernet LAN to our router. Typically a hub will be connected to the Ethernet port using CAT 5 twisted pair (the Ethernet interface provides an RJ-45 female port). The various computers on the network will then be connected to the hub.

To use a straight-through CAT 5 twisted pair cable (the cable used for connecting PCs to hubs), you must switch the MDI/MDI-X switch on the router to the MDI-X position. For routers such as the Cisco 2505 and 2507 routers (which don't have the MDI/MDI-X switch), the router must be connected to a hub using a crossover cable (a cross-over cable is a modified straight-through twisted pair cable, where the pairs have been "reorganized" to reverse the transmit and receive electrical signals).

Some routers, such as the Cisco 2505 Router, actually provide the Ethernet interface in the form of a hub (see Figure 7.6). This negates the need for a separate hub, and PCs can be plugged directly into the hub ports available on the router. If more hub ports are required, a crossover cable can be used to connect one of the hub ports on the router to a port on an additional hub.

FIGURE 7.6
The Cisco 2505 provides one Ethernet interface in the form of an 8-port hub.

① Hub ports

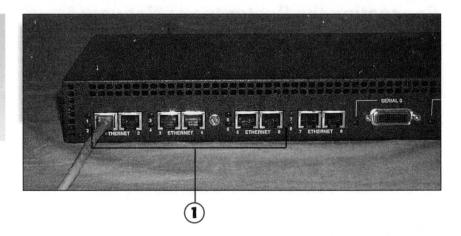

SEE ALSO
➤ *For more information on twisted pair cabling, see page 17.*

Serial Connections

Serial connections on the router can be configured for several different WAN protocols. The actual physical serial connection on Cisco routers is a 60-pin female port (see Figure 7.7).

The Cisco 2505 Router (shown in Figure 7.6) supplies two serial ports. The serial port supports several different signaling standards including V.35, X.21bis, and EIA-530. Figure 7.8 shows a V.35 cable that supplies the male 60-pin connector for connection to the router's serial port. The other end of the V.35 cable would typically be placed in a CSU/DSU or other device in WAN connections. Table 7.2 lists some of the signaling standards supported by Cisco serial interfaces.

Daisy-chained hubs

If you plan on daisy-chaining (connecting hub-to-hub) several hubs to an Ethernet port on a router, remember that you are limited to four hub devices in the data path between Ethernet devices.

Check your connections

If you've physically connected a particular interface correctly, you will typically find that the router acknowledges the connection. For example, connecting a serial connection from your router to the appropriate device will usually register on the router as the fact that the particular interface is up, meaning it is active (even if an appropriate protocol has not yet been configured for the interface).

Table 7.2 Serial Signaling Standards

Standard	Specification
V.35	Synchronous communications between networks and packet-switching WANS
X.21bis	Defines communications between DTEs and DCEs in an X.25 WAN
EIA-530	RS232 standard for unbalanced serial communications

A Final Word on Physical Router Connections

Whether you should configure the router before connecting it to the serial and LAN interfaces that it will service, or connect the router and then configure it, is pretty much a chicken-or-egg dilemma. Configuring the router with a very basic configuration so that it can be seen on the network can allow you to then connect the router to all its various physical connections and then complete the configuration of the router using a virtual terminal over the network (virtual terminals are discussed in the next chapter).

If the router can be connected to the various LAN and WAN devices before you configure the router, this allows you to fully configure and test the connections immediately. However, if the router is placed in an area that is somewhat difficult to access (such as a small closet on a hub rack), it might be difficult to directly connect a PC to the router for configuration purposes.

Whatever the case, the next chapter discusses how to configure a new router right out of the box.

chapter 8

Basic Router Configuration

Configuring a Router

Setting up a basic configuration for a router is a matter of enabling the various interfaces on the router and setting the software settings for the routed and routing protocols. For example, if you are routing IP, the interfaces must be assigned appropriate IP addresses. Routing protocols must also be configured (if you are going to use RIP or IGRP, you must configure these protocols). And any serial interfaces that you use must also be configured with an appropriate WAN layer 2 protocol (such as HDLC or Frame Relay). Basic configuration information may also include bandwidth information and timing information for WAN connections.

HDLC or Frame

Bottom line—the configuration file for your router uses software settings that tell the router what to route and how to route it. All the commands that you use to configure the router are part of the Cisco IOS command set. You will also find that there are several different ways that you can configure the router, either directly by using the router console, or by loading a configuration file that has been placed on a Trivial File Transport Protocol (TFTP) server on your network. The following list shows some of the possibilities for loading configuration information onto a router:

- Router Console—You can configure the router directly from a PC—the *router console*—that is connected to the router console port using the rollover cable that comes with the router. The PC must be running terminal emulation software that allows you to connect to the router through the PC's serial port. You also can connect directly to the router using the router's auxiliary port, which is typically housed next to the console port on the back of the router.

- Virtual Terminal—If the router has already been provided a basic configuration that gets at least some of the interfaces up and running on the network (such as an Ethernet port), you can Telnet to the router via a *virtual terminal*. This simply means that a computer on the network that is running a Telnet program can connect to the router and configure the router (if the appropriate passwords are known—which will be discussed in more detail later in this chapter).

- Network Management Workstation—Routers can also be configured from a workstation on the network that runs special network management software, such as Cisco's CiscoWorks or a similar product from Hewlett Packard known as HP OpenView.

- Cisco ConfigMaker—This graphics-based program (see Figure 8.1) allows you to build a configuration for a router or routers on a network and then load the configuration to a router that is directly connected to a router console (the PC that is running ConfigMaker) or other routers that are connected to the network. Delivering router configurations from ConfigMaker to routers on the network requires that the network interfaces on these routers already be configured. ConfigMaker will be discussed in greater detail in Chapter 16, "Configuring the Router with Cisco ConfigMaker."

- TFTP Server—A configuration for a router can be loaded from a TFTP server on the network. Saving configurations to a TFTP server and then downloading them to a particular router is very straightforward. TFTP servers will be discussed in Chapter 17, "Using a TFTP Server for Router Configuration Storage."

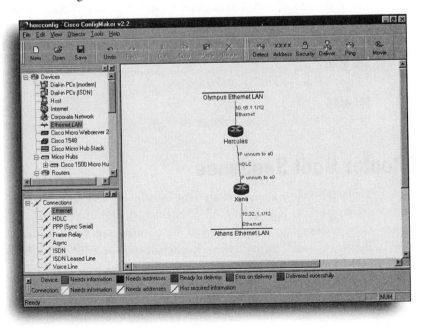

FIGURE 8.1
Software such as Cisco's ConfigMaker allows you to diagram your internetwork and then load your configurations to a router or routers.

Of all the configuration methods available, probably the easiest and the most directly hands-on is configuring the router by directly connecting a PC to the router console port (see Figure 8.2). This not only allows you to quickly set up a basic configuration on the router using the router System Configuration dialog, but it also allows you to fine-tune your configuration in the router Configuration mode. Both of these configuration methods will be discussed in the chapter.

FIGURE 8.2
A PC can be directly connected to a router using the console or auxiliary ports.

① Console port

② Auxiliary port

Before you take a look at how to set up a basic configuration using the System Configuration dialog on a new router, let's take a look at the router boot sequence. This will also give us some insight into where the router looks for a configuration file when it comes online.

SEE ALSO
➤ *For more information about TFTP servers, see page 289.*

SEE ALSO
➤ *For more information about basic router commands and configuring a router, see page 141.*

As good as gold

Configuring a router correctly and appropriately for the internetwork it serves is really the most important aspect of working with routers (of course, I'm downplaying internetwork design and troubleshooting for the moment). This is why Cisco Certified Internetworking Engineers are highly paid and respected internetworking professionals. A proper configuration really becomes as important as gold. You will look at different ways of saving (and protecting) your configuration files as you work through this chapter.

Router Boot Sequence

You've already learned the different memory types found in the router (such as RAM, NVRAM, Flash RAM, and ROM). And all these memory types play a part in the boot sequence of a router. Before you walk through the sequence of steps to configure a brand new router right out of the box, some discussion is required to explain the router boot sequence and the various places that the router will look for a configuration file.

When you power the router on, the ROM chip runs a *Power On Self Test (POST)* that checks the router's hardware such as the processor, interfaces, and memory. This test isn't unlike the power-on test that a PC runs when you power it on (RAM, CPU, and other hardware is checked).

The next step in the router boot-up sequence is the execution of a bootstrap program that is stored in the router's ROM. This bootstrap program searches for the CISCO IOS. The IOS can be loaded from the ROM itself (routers either have a partial or complete copy of the CISCO IOS in ROM), the router's FLASH RAM, or from a TFTP server on the network (commands for loading the IOS from various locations will be discussed in the next chapter). The IOS is typically stored in the router's Flash RAM.

After the router's IOS is loaded, the router searches for the configuration file. The configuration file is normally held in NVRAM (a copy command is used to copy a running configuration to NVRAM). As with the IOS, however, the configuration file can be loaded from a TFTP server (again, the location of the configuration file would be dictated by information held in the router's NVRAM).

After the router loads the configuration file, the information in the file enables the interfaces and provides parameters related to routed and routing protocols in force on the router. Figure 8.3 provides a summary of the router start-up process. Keep in mind that loading the IOS from a source other than Flash RAM requires a notation in the ROM's configuration Registry and that to load the configuration file from a source other than NVRAM, information pointing to the location of the file has to be contained in NVRAM.

If a configuration isn't found in NVRAM or in another place specified (such as a TFTP server), the Setup mode is entered and the System Configuration dialog appears on the router console screen. The next section discusses how to set up a basic router configuration using the dialog.

SEE ALSO

➤ *To review the different memory components on a router, see page 113.*

SEE ALSO

➤ *For more about the Cisco IOS command set, see page 142.*

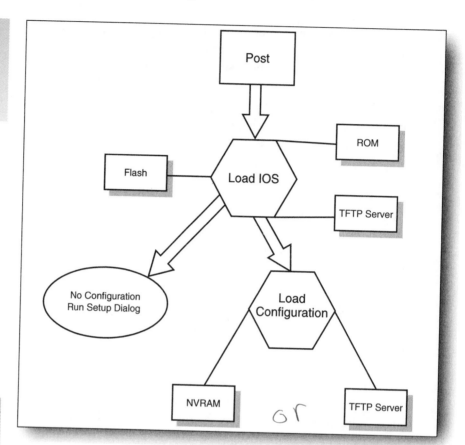

FIGURE 8.3
The router boot sequence loads the router IOS and the router configuration file.

Configuring a router from scratch

You can erase the configuration file for a router and then start over, building a new basic configuration using the configuration dialog. At the enable prompt type `erase startup-config`, and then press **Enter**. This erases the configuration file from NVRAM. To restart the router type `reload`. Then press **Enter** to confirm the reload. The router will reboot and the System Configuration dialog will appear on the Router Console screen.

Working with the System Configuration Dialog Box

When you boot up a new router (or a router where the configuration file has been deleted), the System Configuration dialog is loaded (see Figure 8.4). This Setup mode asks you a series of questions; the answers to those questions provide a basic configuration for the router.

Working through the Setup dialog is very straightforward. You do need to know certain parameters related to the configuration of the router, however, such as which network protocols you will route (IP, IPX, AppleTalk) and the parameters related to the various interfaces. For example, if you route IP you will need to know the IP addresses of the router interfaces that you want to configure (the following steps provide sample addresses). If you have a router that you want to configure, follow the steps provided.

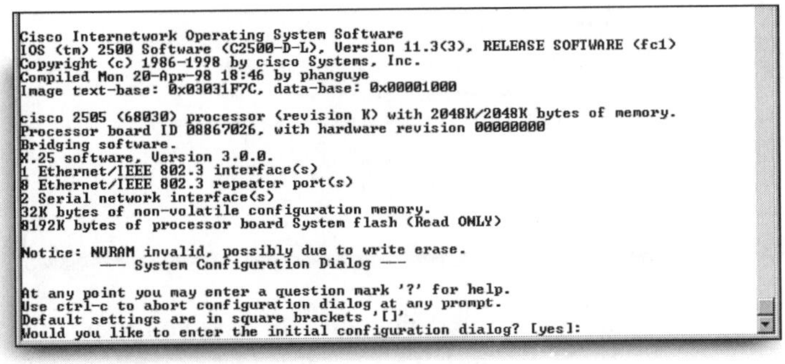

```
Cisco Internetwork Operating System Software
IOS (tm) 2500 Software (C2500-D-L), Version 11.3(3), RELEASE SOFTWARE (fc1)
Copyright (c) 1986-1998 by cisco Systems, Inc.
Compiled Mon 20-Apr-98 18:46 by phanguye
Image text-base: 0x03031F7C, data-base: 0x00001000

cisco 2505 (68030) processor (revision K) with 2048K/2048K bytes of memory.
Processor board ID 08867026, with hardware revision 00000000
Bridging software.
X.25 software, Version 3.0.0.
1 Ethernet/IEEE 802.3 interface(s)
8 Ethernet/IEEE 802.3 repeater port(s)
2 Serial network interface(s)
32K bytes of non-volatile configuration memory.
8192K bytes of processor board System flash (Read ONLY)

Notice: NVRAM invalid, possibly due to write erase.
        ---- System Configuration Dialog ----

At any point you may enter a question mark '?' for help.
Use ctrl-c to abort configuration dialog at any prompt.
Default settings are in square brackets '[]'.
Would you like to enter the initial configuration dialog? [yes]:
```

FIGURE 8.4
The Setup dialog helps you build a basic configuration for a new router by asking a series of questions.

SEE ALSO
➤ *For more about IP addressing, see page 195.*

Starting the Setup Dialog Box

The Setup dialog can ask you quite a few questions related to setting various passwords for the routers and configuring the interfaces on the router. The first part of the setup configuration relates to setting up enable and virtual terminal passwords for the router.

Starting the configuration process with the Setup dialog

1. You will be asked Would you like to enter the initial configuration dialog? (see Figure 8.4). Press **Enter** to answer yes (the default option) and continue.

2. You will then be asked if you want to see the current interface summary. This allows you to view the interfaces on the router. Press **Enter** to continue. A summary of the interfaces on the router will be provided as shown in Figure 8.5. Note that the Ethernet 0 interface is up, but that both the serial interfaces on this router are down. Also, no IP numbers have been assigned to the interfaces.

3. Next, you are asked to provide a name for the router. Type a name (such as ciscokid) and then press **Enter**.

> **IOS version and supported network protocols**
>
> The 2505 router configured in the figures in the following sections is running Cisco IOS 11.3. This version of the IOS supports IP, IPX, AppleTalk, and DECnet routing. This book will discuss the routing of IP, IPX, and AppleTalk, the most commonly routed network protocols.

```
At any point you may enter a question mark '?' for help.
Use ctrl-c to abort configuration dialog at any prompt.
Default settings are in square brackets '[]'.
Would you like to enter the initial configuration dialog? [yes]:

First, would you like to see the current interface summary? [yes]:

Any interface listed with OK? value "NO" does not have a valid configuration
Interface          IP-Address      OK? Method Status                Protocol
Ethernet0          unassigned      NO  unset  up                    up
Serial0            unassigned      NO  unset  down                  down
Serial1            unassigned      NO  unset  down                  down

Configuring global parameters:

  Enter host name [Router]:
```

4. The next Setup dialog question asks you to provide an enable secret password. This password is encrypted and will provide you with access to the router's Enable mode (the mode that allows you to make changes to the router's configuration). Type an appropriate password, and then press **Enter**.

5. You are then asked to provide an "enable" password, which seems redundant because you have already provided a secret password for the Enable mode. This second password is related to earlier versions of the Cisco IOS that didn't provide the capability to create an encrypted password for the Enable mode. Because you aren't allowed to leave this password blank (even though you won't use it), type a value (something you can remember but isn't apparent to someone trying to access the router who shouldn't). In this case I will use password. Press **Enter** to continue.

6. You will then be asked to provide a virtual terminal password for the router. This password is used by virtual terminals that Telnet to the router over the network. This enables you to monitor (and even configure a router) from a remote workstation on the network. Provide a virtual terminal password, and press **Enter** to continue.

7. The next Setup dialog question asks you if you want to enable *SNMP (Simple Network Management Protocol)*. This protocol provides baselines for network operations and provides a way to monitor changes in the network using a management station (which requires software such as CiscoWorks). If you won't use management software to manage the routers, there is no reason to enable SNMP). In this case you won't enable it. Type no at the prompt and press **Enter** to continue.

Configuring Routed Protocols

The next portion of the Setup dialog is related to the configuration of routed and routing protocols that will be used on the router. You will be asked if you want to enable each of the routed protocols supported by your version of the IOS and to choose which routing protocols you want to enable.

Configuring protocols with the Setup dialog

1. In the case of the 2505 router that you are configuring, the next prompt asks if DECnet should be enabled (*DECnet* is a protocol stack supported by the Digital Equipment Corporation). The default response is **No**. Press **Enter** to continue.

2. In the case of our 2505 router, the next dialog prompt asks if AppleTalk should be configured. For now, you will respond with no (the default). Chapter 13, "Routing AppleTalk," covers the ins and outs of AppleTalk routing and I'll defer AppleTalk until then. Press **Enter** to continue.

3. The next dialog prompt asks if IPX should be configured (IPX is covered in detail in Chapter 12, "Routing Novell IPX,"). To answer no, press **Enter**.

4. The next prompt asks if IP should be configured and the default answer is Yes (see Figure 8.6). Although IP will be covered in great detail in Chapters 10, "TCP/IP Primer," and 11, "Configuring IP Routing," it makes sense to enable IP at this point. This enables you to get the router up and running on the network, and then you can further configure the router using a virtual terminal or by loading a ready-made configuration file from Cisco ConfigMaker or a TFTP server. Press **Enter** (to say yes) and continue.

5. You will then be asked if you want to configure IGRP on the router. IGRP is one of the IP routing protocols. Configuring IGRP and RIP will be covered in Chapter 11, so for the moment you can say no. Type no and press **Enter** to continue.

6. You will then be asked to configure RIP. No is the default, so press **Enter** to continue.

7. The next dialog asks if bridging should be enabled on the router. Press **Enter** to continue (No is the default).

```
Configuring global parameters:

  Enter host name [Router]: ciscokid

The enable secret is a one-way cryptographic secret used
instead of the enable password when it exists.

  Enter enable secret: password

The enable password is used when there is no enable secret
and when using older software and some boot images.

  Enter enable password:
% No defaulting allowed
  Enter enable password: cisco
  Enter virtual terminal password: password
Configure SNMP Network Management? [yes]: no
Configure DECnet? [no]:
Configure AppleTalk? [no]:
Configure IPX? [no]:
Configure IP? [yes]:
```

Configuring Router Interfaces

The next part of the Setup dialog is related to the configuration of the router's interfaces. You will be asked which router interfaces will be in use on the router (such as Ethernet and serial interfaces). Also, because IP was enabled for routing, you will have to supply IP addresses for the various interfaces on the router. How these IP addresses were arrived at will be discussed in Chapter 10.

Configuring interfaces with the Setup dialog

1. The next prompt relates to the first interface on the router, which in the case of the 2505 router is the Ethernet 0 interface. You will be asked if this interface is in use. Yes is the default value, so to enable the interface, press **Enter**.

2. The next prompt asks if IP should be configured on the interface (E0). The default value is Yes; press **Enter** to continue.

3. The next prompt asks for the IP address of the interface (interfaces on the router use IP addresses just like any other node on the network). Type 10.16.1.1 as the address for the E0 interface (see Figure 8.7). Then press **Enter** to continue.

4. The next prompt asks how many bits are in the subnet field. This number relates to how many IP subnets have been created for your internetwork. This will be discussed in Chapter 10. For now, trust that I've divided the available network addresses (which are class A addresses) into 14 subnets, which requires 4 bits in the subnet field (this will make sense after you read Chapter 10). Type 4 and then press **Enter**.

```
Configuring interface parameters:

Configuring interface Ethernet0:
  Is this interface in use? [yes]:
  Configure IP on this interface? [yes]:
    IP address for this interface: 10.16.1.1
```

FIGURE 8.7
An IP address is assigned to the Ethernet 0 port on the router.

5. Because the 2505 router's E0 interface is actually an eight-port hub, you are asked if you want to enable all ports on the hub. The default is Yes (and you want to say yes), so press **Enter** to continue.

6. You are then asked if you want to configure the next interface on the router, which in this case is serial 0. Yes is the default. Press **Enter** to continue.

7. You are then asked if you want to configure IP on the S0 inter- *Serial* face. Press **Enter** and continue.

8. You are given the option of configuring the S0 interface as IP unnumbered (this means that the interface will route IP but doesn't require its own IP number). This is done to actually save your IP addresses (from the pool of IP addresses that you have available). Configuring serial interfaces with IP addresses will be handled in more detail in Chapter 11. For now, press **Enter** to say no.

9. You are then asked to provide an IP address for the S0 interface. Type 10.32.1.1. Then press **Enter**.

10. You will then be asked to provide the subnet field bits. This is defaulted to 4, which was entered in step 4. Press **Enter** to use the same bit count.

11. You are now asked to configure the Serial 1 interface. Press **Enter** to say yes.

12. Press **Enter** to say no to IP unnumbered.

13. Type the IP address 10.48.1.1 at the prompt (see Figure 8.8). Then press **Enter**.

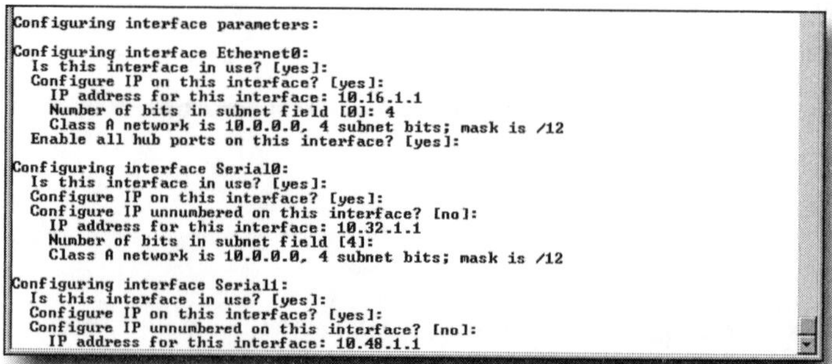

FIGURE 8.8

IP addresses given to each of the serial interfaces on the router.

```
Configuring interface parameters:

Configuring interface Ethernet0:
  Is this interface in use? [yes]:
  Configure IP on this interface? [yes]:
    IP address for this interface: 10.16.1.1
    Number of bits in subnet field [0]: 4
    Class A network is 10.0.0.0, 4 subnet bits; mask is /12
  Enable all hub ports on this interface? [yes]:

Configuring interface Serial0:
  Is this interface in use? [yes]:
  Configure IP on this interface? [yes]:
  Configure IP unnumbered on this interface? [no]:
    IP address for this interface: 10.32.1.1
    Number of bits in subnet field [4]:
    Class A network is 10.0.0.0, 4 subnet bits; mask is /12

Configuring interface Serial1:
  Is this interface in use? [yes]:
  Configure IP on this interface? [yes]:
  Configure IP unnumbered on this interface? [no]:
    IP address for this interface: 10.48.1.1
```

Save to NV Ram for New config

The next prompt is where you enter the subnet bits (4 is supplied as the default number of subnet bits). Then press **Enter**.

After you press **Enter**, the screen will scroll rapidly, showing link tests for the interfaces that you have configured. You will be asked if you want to use the current configuration. Type yes and then press **Enter** to save the configuration file that you created using the System dialog. The router will build the configuration and save it to NVRAM.

The next time you press **Enter**, the router will take you to the router's User mode prompt. You are now ready to view the configuration parameters on the router or edit the configuration of the router.

Using the Different Router Modes

After the router contains a basic configuration, you can begin to examine the different router modes available. The router supplies you with three basic levels of access: *User mode*, *Privileged mode*, and *Configuration mode*.

Each of the basic router modes provides a higher degree of access to the router's configuration and also gives you greater capabilities to edit the configuration of the router. The list that follows briefly describes the three router modes:

- User mode—This mode provides limited access to the router. You are provided with a set of nondestructive commands that allow examination of certain router configuration parameters. You cannot, however, make any changes to the router configuration.

Other router modes

Other router modes exist that enable you to configure a router that cannot find a valid IOS image in Flash RAM or in cases where you want the router to load the IOS from a source other than Flash RAM. The ROM Monitor mode is entered when the router doesn't find a valid IOS image. You can configure the router from the ROM Monitor prompt. The RXBoot mode is used to actually help the router book when it doesn't find a valid IOS image. An important use of the ROM Monitor is changing forgotten passwords. See "Getting Around Lost Passwords," later in this chapter, for information about getting around lost passwords.

- Privileged mode—Also known as the Enabled mode, this mode allows greater examination of the router and provides a more robust command set than the User mode. After you enter the Privileged mode using the secret or enable password (if a secret encrypted password was not set), you have access to the configuration commands supplied in the Configuration mode, meaning you can edit the configuration for the router.

- Configuration mode—Also called the Global Configuration mode, this mode is entered from the Privileged mode and supplies the complete command set for configuring the router. Subsets of the Configuration mode exist for protocols, interfaces, and other aspects of the router operation.

User (Unprivileged) Mode

As I've already noted, the User mode enables you to do a limited survey of the router's configuration. The User mode is the default mode when you reboot a router. Even access to the User mode can be protected by a console password (see the "Configuration Mode" section that follows for information on the various password commands).

Figure 8.9 shows the user prompt on the router you configured using the System dialog. The prompt is the router's name followed by > (the greater than sign). This figure also shows a portion of the results from the show interfaces command.

```
ciscokid>show interfaces
Ethernet0 is up, line protocol is up , using hub 0
  Hardware is Lance, address is 0010.7b3a.50c3 (bia 0010.7b3a.50c3)
  Internet address is 10.16.1.1/12
  MTU 1500 bytes, BW 10000 Kbit, DLY 1000 usec, rely 255/255, load 1/255
  Encapsulation ARPA, loopback not set, keepalive set (10 sec)
  ARP type: ARPA, ARP Timeout 04:00:00
  Last input never, output 00:00:02, output hang never
  Last clearing of "show interface" counters never
  Queueing strategy: fifo
  Output queue 0/40, 0 drops; input queue 0/75, 0 drops
  5 minute input rate 0 bits/sec, 0 packets/sec
  5 minute output rate 0 bits/sec, 0 packets/sec
     0 packets input, 0 bytes, 0 no buffer
     Received 0 broadcasts, 0 runts, 0 giants, 0 throttles
     0 input errors, 0 CRC, 0 frame, 0 overrun, 0 ignored, 0 abort
     0 input packets with dribble condition detected
     445 packets output, 47601 bytes, 0 underruns
     0 output errors, 0 collisions, 2 interface resets
     0 babbles, 0 late collision, 0 deferred
     0 lost carrier, 0 no carrier
     0 output buffer failures, 0 output buffers swapped out
--More--
```

FIGURE 8.9
The User mode allows you to view router configuration information using a limited command set.

The User mode is pretty much a "you can look but don't touch" environment. It can, however, provide a wealth of information about the router and its current status. More about the commands available in the User mode are discussed in Chapter 9, "Working with the Cisco IOS."

SEE ALSO

➤ *For more information about router examination commands available in the User mode, see page 141.*

Privileged Mode

The Privileged mode provides all the commands found in the User mode, but also includes an extended set of commands for examination of the router status (such as the show running-config command for examining the current running configuration on the router). The Privileged mode also supplies the config command, which enables you to enter the Configuration mode for the router.

The Privileged mode really controls the router. So, it's important that the enable password be considered a thing of great value. You don't want just anyone messing with the router's configuration (if you just want to let someone take a look at some of the router parameters, they can use the User mode).

To enter the Privileged mode on a router, type enable at the User mode prompt and then press **Enter**. Provide the enable password (which will be the secret encrypted password that you set for the router) and press **Enter**. Figure 8.10 shows the router in the Privileged mode after the show running-config command has been invoked. The Privileged prompt is the router's name followed by the # (number) symbol.

When you have finished working in the Privileged mode, it makes sense to return to the User mode. Otherwise, you leave the router wide open to be configured by anyone who happens by the terminal. To return to the User mode, type disable and press **Enter**. If you want to totally log off the router, type logout and press **Enter**. This means that the next person to use the console will have to enter the router password (if one exists) to enter the User mode.

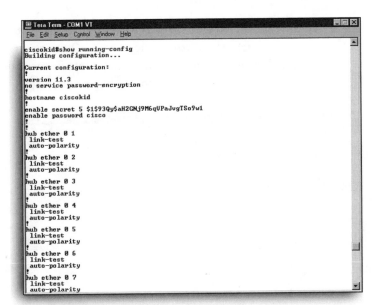

```
Tera Term - COM1 VT
File Edit Setup Control Window Help
ciscokid#show running-config
Building configuration...

Current configuration:
!
version 11.3
no service password-encryption
!
hostname ciscokid
!
enable secret 5 $1$93Qy$aH2GNj9M6qUPaJvgTSo9w1
enable password cisco
!
hub ether 0 1
 link-test
 auto-polarity
!
hub ether 0 2
 link-test
 auto-polarity
!
hub ether 0 3
 link-test
 auto-polarity
!
hub ether 0 4
 link-test
 auto-polarity
!
hub ether 0 5
 link-test
 auto-polarity
!
hub ether 0 6
 link-test
 auto-polarity
!
hub ether 0 7
 link-test
 auto-polarity
```

FIGURE 8.10
The Privileged mode allows you to examine the router configuration with a large command set and to enter the Configuration mode.

Configuration Mode

The Configuration mode allows you to set all the parameters related to the hardware and software running on the router. You can configure interfaces, routed protocols, and routing protocols. You can also set router passwords and configure the WAN protocols used by the router's serial interfaces. Some of the configurable options related to the router can be set on a new router using the System Configuration dialog. The Configuration mode gives you access to absolutely all the commands that you would use to configure or fine-tune the configuration for the router.

The Configuration mode is reached from the Privileged mode. Type config at the Privileged prompt and then press **Enter**. Let's take a look at the global configuration commands that allow you to change the router's name and the various passwords that you can set on the router.

Using the Configuration mode

1. At the Privileged prompt type config, and then press **Enter**.

2. You will be asked if you want to configure from the terminal, memory, or the network. The default is the console terminal, so press **Enter** to continue.

3. To change the name that has been given to the router, type host-name [name], where name is the name you want to give to the router. After entering the command, press **Enter.** The new router name will appear at the Config prompt (see Figure 8.11).

FIGURE 8.11
In the Configuration mode you can change the router name and set the enable and login passwords.

4. To set the enable password, type enable secret [password] at the Config prompt, where [password] is the word that you will use as your secret password to get into the Privileged mode. Then press **Enter.** I've set my password as hamburger (see Figure 8.11).

5. Now you can set a password for the router. This means that anyone logging in to the router will have to provide this password to even access the User mode. To set the password you must get into the Line Console mode. Type line console 0, and then press **Enter.**

6. You are now in the line console Configuration mode; type login, and then press **Enter.**

7. To specify the login password, type password [password], where the [password] is the word you want to use to log in to the router. For example, I've made my login password cisco (see Figure 8.11).

8. When you have completed your configuration changes, press **Ctrl+Z.** This will save your changes to the router's running configuration and return you to the Privileged prompt.

After you have made changes to the running-config, you may want to save them to your startup-configuration in NVRAM. This is the file that is loaded when the router is rebooted or restarted. At the Privileged prompt, type copy running-config startup-config, and then press **Enter**. The new startup-configuration will be displayed on the console screen.

Getting Around Lost Passwords

Sometimes you just forget those passwords, which can be bad news if you need to enter the Privileged mode and change a router's configuration.

Replacing a lost password

1. Turn the router off and after waiting five seconds turn it back on. As the router reboots, press **Ctrl+Break**.

2. You will enter the ROM Monitor mode. Type e/s2000002, and then press **Enter**. Write down the virtual configuration number that appears.

3. Now at the prompt type o/r0x2142 and press **Enter** (this makes the router ignore the configuration file in NVRAM). Type i at the prompt, and press **Enter**. The router will reboot and enter the configuration dialog. Click **No** at the dialog prompt, and then press **Enter**.

4. At the router prompt type enable to enter the Privileged mode. Type copy startup-config running-config, and then press **Enter** to get your original configuration into the router's RAM.

5. At the enabled prompt type config. You are now in the Configuration mode. Type enable secret *new password*, where *new password* is your new secret password. Now you must set the register contents back to the original contents.

6. At the config prompt, type the config-register 0x virtual configuration number (which is the virtual configuration number that you wrote down). Press **Enter**.

7. Now Type end and press **Enter** to get out of the Configuration mode. Reboot the router. Now you should have a new secret password, and the router should be back to its normal configuration.

> **Virtual terminal password**
>
> One password that you didn't work with is the virtual terminal password. This is the password that is used by anyone who wants to Telnet into your router. Telnet is discussed in Chapter 11 in the "Using Telnet" section. To change your virtual terminal password, at the Config prompt type line vty 0 4, and then press **Enter**. This puts you in the virtual terminal Configuration mode. Type login and press **Enter**. Then type password [*password*], where [*password*] is the password you want to use as the Telnet password. Press **Ctrl+Z** to end the configuration session.

Becoming familiar with the various modes of the router and the commands that they offer is an extremely important aspect of overall router management. In the next chapter you will become more familiar with the Cisco IOS and the commands and command structure that it offers. Each of the modes discussed in this chapter will be covered in the context of the IOS commands available in a particular mode.

chapter

9

Working with the Cisco IOS

Introducing the Internetworking Operating System

The Cisco *Internetworking Operating System (IOS)* is the software that provides the router hardware with the capability to route packets on an internetwork. The IOS, like any operating system, provides the command sets and software functionality that you use to monitor and configure the router, and it also provides the functionality for the various protocols—both routed and routing—that make internetworking a reality.

Configuring the router means that you enable the various interfaces and protocols on the router. You must use commands that bring your various hardware interfaces such as Ethernet or serial interfaces to life. You must also provide configuration information for the protocols that are routed, such as IP or IPX/SPX. And you must also configure routing protocols such as RIP and IGRP. After the router is configured, you must manage your configuration files. The list that follows details some of the things you would do with the IOS command set:

- Configure the router LAN interfaces—Configuring the router LAN interfaces should be done after you have made the physical connections, assembling the router hardware and connecting the various cables to LAN or WAN networks. The router interfaces must be configured for use on these networks. For example, on a network that routes IP, each Ethernet interface involved must be configured with an appropriate IP address and subnet mask.

- Configure Serial Connections and WAN protocols—In cases where your router is connected to a WAN by a leased line or some other WAN technology, you must configure the WAN protocol used on the serial interfaces of the router.

- Manage router configuration files—After the router is configured, you will want to maintain copies of the configuration file. You will save the running configuration to NV RAM where it is stored as the startup configuration. You may also want to save a configuration file or load a configuration file from a TFTP server (this is covered in Chapter 17, "Using a TFTP Server for Router Configuration Storage").

- Monitor and maintain the router—You will also use the IOS command set to monitor and troubleshoot problems with the router. A time may also come when you need to update the router IOS in Flash RAM. The command set provides all the tools necessary to keep an eye on the router and update its IOS and feature set if required.

Although this list may seem exhausting in terms of what you must do to maintain routing on your network, it is by no means exhaustive. The Cisco IOS command set is huge and the subject of a number of books. Cisco publishes a software command summary for each of the IOS versions, and these books are as thick as the New York City telephone directory. The command reference for IOS 11.3 is in excess of 1,000 pages. You will find, however, that you will use only a fairly small percentage of all the IOS commands available, even if you become a routing maniac and have an opportunity to work with some of the higher end routers on a large internetwork.

Cisco provides a *Command-Line Interface (CLI)* that you can use to configure and maintain your router. You can access the CLI using a router console or by Telnetting to a router using a virtual terminal.

This chapter will provide an overview of the IOS and the CLI and let you get your feet wet with a very complex and robust operating system. Commands related to configuring IP, IPX, AppleTalk, and router serial interfaces (and WAN protocols) are discussed in subsequent chapters.

If you are a DOS or UNIX aficionado, you will find the CLI familiar. It is a very typical command-line interface. If you aren't familiar with command-line interfaces, figures are provided to keep you on track with the commands discussed. You will find that the command structure is fairly straightforward.

SEE ALSO

➤ *For more information about the routing protocols such as RIP and IGRP, see page 131.*

➤ *For a summary of the IOS commands discussed in this book, see page 324.*

Command Structure

You already worked with the IOS command set briefly in Chapter 8, "Basic Router Configuration," when you explored the different router modes: User, Privileged, and Configuration. Each of these modes provides a different set of commands:

- The User mode provides only basic commands that enable you to view system information and perform basic tests.

- The Privileged mode provides a larger set of commands for viewing router information and also provides access to the Configuration mode.

- The Configuration mode provides the command set that enables you to configure the interfaces and protocols used on the router.

SEE ALSO

➤ *For more information about the different router modes, see page 134.*

Exec Commands

Configuration mode has its own command structure

Although the Configuration mode is kind of an extension of the Privileged mode (you have to be in Privileged mode to get to the Configuration mode), you will find that the configuration commands have a slightly different structure than the Exec commands used in User and Privileged modes. Router configuration commands will be discussed in a number of different chapters in the context of particular configurations such as different LAN protocols in Chapters 11, 12, and 13 and WAN protocols in Chapter 15.

The Cisco IOS uses a command interpreter to execute your commands (it interprets the command and then executes it) called the *Exec*, and the User mode and the Privileged mode are considered different levels of the Exec. So, when you are in the User mode or the Privileged mode, the commands available take on a particular basic structure: the command followed by the router parameter. The command will be one of the IOS commands, such as show, and the router parameter is the item on which you want the command to act.

So, for example, the command show Ethernet 0 will display the parameters related to the first Ethernet interface on the router. Figure 9.1 shows this command and its results on a 2505 router running IOS 11.2.

To actually execute the commands that you use in the various router modes, always press **Enter** after typing the command. The results of the command are then displayed on the router console or virtual terminal screen.

Configuration Mode

The Configuration mode handles its commands in a slightly different way. Whereas the Exec commands are two-part requests where you specify the command and what you want it to act on, the *configuration commands* require that you execute several commands that, layered together, actually change the parameters related to a particular interface or a particular protocol. For example, let's say that you want to select the WAN protocol that you will use on a particular serial interface on the router (in this example, serial 1). Remember that you have to be in the Privileged mode to enter the Configuration mode.

Configuring a WAN protocol for a serial interface

1. At the Privileged prompt type config, and then press **Enter**.

2. You will be asked if you want to configure from the terminal, memory, or the network. The default is the console terminal, so press **Enter** to continue.

3. After you are in the Configuration mode (at the Config prompt), you then have to specify the IOS device that you want to configure. So to configure the serial 1 interface, type interface serial 1 (see Figure 9.2).

```
popeye#config
Configuring from terminal, memory, or network [terminal]?
Enter configuration commands, one per line.  End with CNTL/Z.
popeye(config)#interface serial 1
popeye(config-if)#encapsulation ppp
popeye(config-if)#end
popeye#
04:39:56: %SYS-5-CONFIG_I: Configured from console by console
popeye#
```

4. When you press **Enter**, the prompt changes to config-if, meaning that you have specified a particular interface (in this case, serial 1).

5. Now you can type in the command that will actually change the configuration of the specified interface. To enable point-to-point protocol for example, type encapsulation ppp, and then press **Enter**.

6. You can now type additional commands that will configure parameters related to the serial 1 interface. When you have completed the configuration, type end (or press **Ctrl+Z**), and then press **Enter**. This ends the configuration session for the serial 1 interface.

As you can see, configuration commands move from the general to the specific. First, you let the IOS know that you want to configure something, then you let it know what you what to configure, and then you provide it with the specific configuration parameters. Much of your router configuration takes this format. There are, however, some configuration commands that can be fired off as one-liners such as the hostname command, which enables you to change the name of your router. In fact, router configuration commands can be broken down into three categories:

- Global commands—*Global commands* are self contained, one-line commands that affect the overall global configuration of the router. Examples are hostname and enable secret (which sets the secret password for the Privileged mode). These types of commands are global because they affect a parameter that affects the overall functionality of the router, such as the router's name or the password you type to get in the Privileged mode.

Encapsulation isn't just a fancy word

When you are configuring serial interfaces with particular WAN protocols, you use the encapsulation command followed by the name of the protocol. *Encapsulation* is the packaging of data in a particular protocol header. For example, Ethernet data is encapsulated in an Ethernet header before being placed on the network. In cases where Ethernet frames are moved across a WAN connection, the entire frame is placed in (or encapsulated in) a frame type dictated by the WAN protocol used, such as HDLC or PPP. Encapsulation will be discussed in Chapter 10, "TCP/IP Primer," and Chapter 15, "Configuring WAN Protocols," as it relates to specific protocols.

- Port Commands—*Port Commands* are a set of commands that enable you to specify a particular interface or controller for configuration; these commands must be followed by subcommands that provide additional configuration information related to a particular interface or controller. For example, a port command to specify that serial 0 should be configured would be `interface serial 0`.

- Subcommands—*Subcommands* provide specific configuration information for the interface or controller that you specify with a particular port command. For example, to provide an IP address for a serial interface, you would type `IP Address` followed by a specific IP address and subnet mask.

You will have an opportunity to work in the Configuration mode later in this chapter and subsequent chapters where configuration information is given for specific network protocols such as IP, IPX, and AppleTalk.

The IOS Help System

No matter what mode you are in, the Cisco IOS can provide help. Now, I'm not talking about the handholding type of help you are used to getting with the various Windows-based programs that you probably use, but a more subtle type of help that is pretty decent for a command-line interface.

Suppose you are in the User mode and would like to see a complete list of the commands available. Type `?` and then press **Enter**. The commands are listed on the console screen as shown in Figure 9.3.

Okay, so now after checking out the commands available in the User mode, you find that you would like to use a particular command, but would like additional help on how that command should be entered at the prompt. For example, let's say you would like to see how to use the `show` command. Type `show` (or the command that you want to get help with) at the prompt followed by `?` (place a space between `show` and the question mark or you will get a "bad command" notification), and then press **Enter**. You will be provided with help specific to the chosen command, as shown in Figure 9.4.

FIGURE 9.3
You can get help in any of the router modes; type **?** and then press **Enter**.

FIGURE 9.4
You can get help on specific commands.

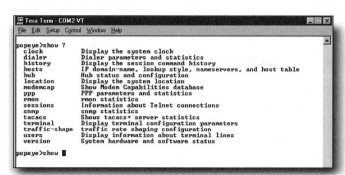

After providing help on the specific command, the command itself is automatically retyped for you at the command prompt (see Figure 9.4). You can then add specific parameters to the command and press **Enter** to execute it. For example, in the case of the show command, you can add version to the command and then press **Enter**. Parameters related to IOS currently installed on the router will be displayed on the screen (see Figure 9.5).

As stated before, the help system is also available in the Privileged
and Configuration modes. The Privileged mode help is similar to
that found in the User mode. You can receive general help by typing
? or more specific help by typing a command followed by ?.

Figure 9.6 shows the Help screen for the Privileged mode. Notice
that it provides a larger number of commands than the User mode
(which makes sense because the Privileged mode is a password-
protected mode that provides greater access to the router).

You can also get help in the Configuration mode. For example, you
may be in the middle of configuring a particular router interface and
would like to see a list of subcommands available. Type ? at the configure interface prompt and you will receive a list of available commands, as shown in Figure 9.7.

How to get more

When the information
provided by a particular
command (such as **?**)
doesn't fit on one console
screen, More will appear
at the bottom of the dis-
played information. To
move down through the
additional information,
press **Enter** to advance one
line and press the
Spacebar to advance one
screen. In cases where you
don't want to view more
information, and want to
return to the console
prompt, press **Escape**
(Esc).

Router Examination Commands

When you work in the Exec modes (User and Privileged) a number
of the commands you use center around examining the various configuration settings and hardware parameters of the router. One of the
most useful commands is the show command. You can use this command to view the status of all the interfaces on the router and view
the statistics for such items as Flash RAM and the network protocols

currently being routed. You will find the show command invaluable in both the User and Privileged modes.

FIGURE 9.6
The Privileged mode provides a larger set of commands than the User mode does.

FIGURE 9.7
Help is available even in the Configuration mode.

You've already seen in the preceding section that the User mode provides you with a set of commands that you can use to examine the router status, and it is actually a subset of commands that are available to you in the Privileged mode. And even though you are working with a subset of types of items you can view with the show command, you can actually learn quite a lot about how the router has been configured in the User mode.

So, suppose you are stuck in the User mode on a router (you don't have the Privileged mode password) and want to examine the router. The first thing you would like to view is the interfaces available on the router.

Using the *show interfaces* command

1. At the User prompt, type show interface.

2. Press **Enter** to execute the command.

The results of the command will appear on the router console screen. Figure 9.8 shows the results of the show interfaces command on a 2505 router that has one Ethernet and two serial interfaces. It shows one screen-full of information; to see the rest of the output, you would have to press the **Spacebar**.

Quite a lot of information is provided by this one command. The hardware address (MAC) and the IP address are shown for Ethernet 0. The status of the interface (such as up or down) and the status of the protocol (or protocols) configured on that interface also appear. Additional information relates to the number of packets that have been input and output by the interface. Because this is an Ethernet interface (which uses CSMA/CD as the network access strategy), the number of collisions and illegal frames (giants and runts) are also provided.

Information on the other interfaces on the router will also be provided by this command. Note the Serial 0 interface information shown in Figure 9.8. The IP address for the interface is shown and the encapsulation type, PPP (which is the WAN protocol being used on this interface).

Command-line savvy

When you are working with the CLI there are some keystrokes that will help you if you make a mistake in a command and want to edit it before you execute it. Press **Backspace** to delete characters to the left of the cursor and then retype them. If you need to move to the beginning of the command line, press **Ctrl+A**. To move to the end of the line press **Ctrl+E**. Remember that you must press the **Enter** key to execute your commands.

FIGURE 9.8

The show interfaces command gives you information related to the interfaces installed on the router.

1. Ethernet interface hardware address (0010.7b3a.50b3)

2. Ethernet interface IP address (130.10.64.1/19)

3. Ethernet encapsulation type (Encapsulation ARPA)

4. Serial 0 IP address (130.10.32.1/19)

5. Serial 0 encapsulation type (Encapsulation PPP)

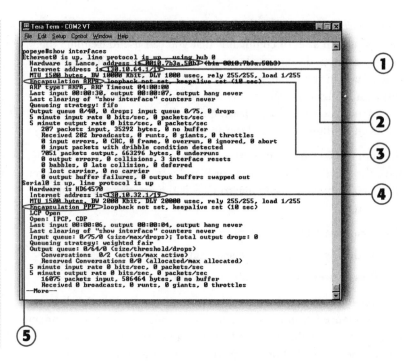

The show interfaces command will give you information on all the interfaces on a particular router. In the case of the 2505 router, I would have to press the **Spacebar** to show the next screen so that I can see the parameters related to the Serial 1 interface on the router. If you are using a higher-end router with several interfaces, you will have to continue to press **Enter** or the **Spacebar** to view the information. When you have come to the end of the information provided by the command, you will be returned to the user prompt.

If you find that show interfaces provides you with more information than you need and you just want to hone in on a particular interface on the router, you can use the show command to view the parameters related to just one interface.

Narrowing the focus of the *show* command

1. At the user prompt, type show interface Ethernet 0.

2. Press **Enter** to execute the command.

You will see results similar to those shown in Figure 9.8, but only the information for the Ethernet 0 interface will be provided.

The show command can also be used to gather other information related to the router. Table 9.1 lists some of the additional show-related commands that you can use in the User mode (all these show derivations will also work in the Privileged mode).

Table 9.1 The *show* Command in the User Mode

Command	Provides
Show clock	The time and date settings for the router
Show version	The version of the IOS currently running on the router
Show protocols	Lists the network protocols configured on the router
Show processes	CPU utilization information
Show history	A list of your last 10 commands
Show hub	Information on the status of the hub ports of a 2505 router

A number of other show-related commands exist. I will discuss several more show commands in the context of the particular network or routing protocol that they are used to monitor.

SEE ALSO

➤ *For more information on using* show *to view IP-related parameters, see page 195.*

➤ *For more information on using* show *to view IPX-related parameters, see page 211.*

➤ *For more information on using* show *to view AppleTalk-related parameters, see page 227.*

Using the Privileged Mode

The Privileged mode also allows you take advantage of all the show commands discussed in the previous section and several others that aren't available in the User mode. You will learn some of these "privileged" show commands, such as show running-config, in the "Checking Router Memory" section of this chapter.

More importantly, the Privileged mode provides you with the capability to access more complete information on the router's configuration and set operating system parameters (and you already know that you must be in the Privileged mode to enter the router's

Abbreviate your commands

You will find that the Cisco IOS commands can be abbreviated in many cases. For example, rather than typing the show command, you can get away with the abbreviation sh. The abbreviated form of interface Ethernet 0 would be int E0. So the entire command to show interface Ethernet 0 would be sh int E0. Try your own abbreviated forms of commands as you work with your router. The worst thing that will happen is that the command interpreter won't recognize the command and let you know that there was invalid input or an incomplete command.

Configuration mode). Let's say that you would like to set the system clock for the router; you must do it in the Privileged mode.

Setting the time and date

1. At the User prompt, type enable, and then press **Enter**.

2. Type the Privileged mode password and press **Enter**. You are now in the Privileged mode.

3. Type clock set followed by the time, day, month, and year; a correct entry for the time would be clock set 21:43:05 (hour, minutes, seconds); a correct entry for the date would be 13 June 1999. Using the example data shown, the complete command would read clock set 21:43:05 13 June 1999, as shown in Figure 9.9.

4. Press **Enter** to execute the command.

5. To check the new settings type show clock, and then press **Enter** (see Figure 9.9).

FIGURE 9.9
You can set the time and date on the router using the clock set command.

① The clock set command

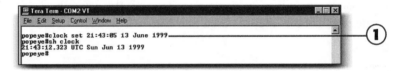

Several other Privileged commands exist that you will use on a regular basis. For example, show cdp neighbors is an internetwork exploratory tool that I will discuss in the "Checking Out the Internetwork Neighborhood" section found later in this chapter. Other Privileged commands are discussed in the next section.

Checking Router Memory

When you configure the various interface and protocol parameters for a router, this information is stored in the router's RAM. It's important that you store this information somewhere, in case the router loses power. In the Privileged mode you can save your running configuration to NVRAM where it becomes the router's startup configuration (and is loaded if the router is rebooted).

The Privileged mode also allows you to examine the contents of RAM and NVRAM using the `show` command. These commands aren't available in the User mode.

Viewing the running configuration

1. At the User prompt, type `enable`, and then press **Enter** (if you aren't in the Privileged mode).

2. Type the Privileged mode password and press **Enter**. You are now in the Privileged mode.

3. Type `show running-config`, and then press **Enter** to execute the command. The command results will appear on the router (see Figure 9.10).

4. To advance through the information on the screen, press **Spacebar** for an entire screen or **Enter** to advance line by line.

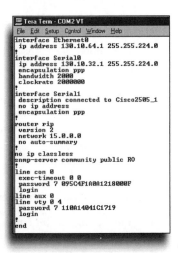

FIGURE 9.10
Show running-config displays the entire running configuration for the router.

The *running configuration* provides information on how the different interfaces are currently configured and which routing protocols have been enabled. It also shows the passwords that have been set on the router (however, remember that the Privileged mode secret password is encrypted, so you can't tell what it is). The `running-config` command provides a complete picture of the parameters running on the router, and this is why it is a Privileged mode command; it's information important to the router's administrator, so it should be protected.

Scroll through a list of recent commands

You can use the Up Arrow key on the keyboard to cycle through the commands that you recently used. Press the Up Arrow and you will see the last command used (it is placed at the router prompt); continue to press the Up Arrow and your commands (the last 10 from most to least recent) will appear one by one. To fire off a recycled command, just use the Up Arrow key to place the appropriate command at the prompt, and then press *Enter*.

Remember to exit the Privileged mode

When you finish working in the Privileged mode type `disable`, and then press *Enter* to return to the User mode. This will protect your router from being reconfigured by an overly zealous coworker or corporate terrorist who is trying to bring down your Silly Putty manufacturing empire.

As you fine-tune your running configuration, a time will come when you would want to save it to NVRAM as the startup configuration. The great thing about the `copy` command is that you can copy information from RAM to NVRAM (running to startup). Or if you mess up your running configuration, you can copy information from NVRAM to RAM (startup to running). The command you use to copy information from one type of memory to another is `copy`.

Copying the running configuration

1. In Privileged mode, type `copy running-config startup-config`.

2. Press **Enter** to execute the command.

The router will pause for a moment. `Building configuration` will be displayed on the screen. Then **"[OK]"** will appear. The running configuration has been copied to the startup configuration. You can quickly check your new startup configuration with the `show startup-config` command (the output will be similar to the `running-config` shown in Figure 9.10). The results of this command also show you how much NVRAM is being used on the system to store the configuration file.

Another memory type on the router is *Flash RAM*. This is where the router's IOS is stored. You can view the contents of Flash in both the User and Privileged mode.

Viewing Flash contents

1. In the Privileged or User mode, type `show flash`.

2. Press **Enter** to execute the command.

The results of the command will appear on the console screen (see Figure 9.11). The IOS filename is given and the amount of free and used Flash RAM is displayed.

FIGURE 9.11
show flash displays the IOS file in flash and the amount of flash available.

① OS filename

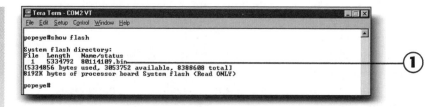

Checking Out the Internetwork Neighborhood

When you work with internetworks, it's important to be able to gather information related to routers that are directly connected to your router. These routers are typically referred to as *neighbors*. Cisco routers have a proprietary protocol, *Cisco Discovery Protocol (CDP)*, that provides you with the capability to access information related to neighboring routers. CDP uses Data Link broadcasts to discover neighboring Cisco routers that are also running CDP (CDP is turned on automatically on routers running IOS 10.3 or newer).

Working with CDP

Before you use CDP to view information about other routers, you may want to check your router interfaces to make sure that CDP is enabled. This is done using the show cdp interface command.

Viewing CDP interfaces

1. At the User or Privileged prompt type show cdp interface.

2. Press **Enter** to execute the command.

The results of the command will appear on the router console screen (see Figure 9.12). The CDP information for all the interfaces on the router will appear.

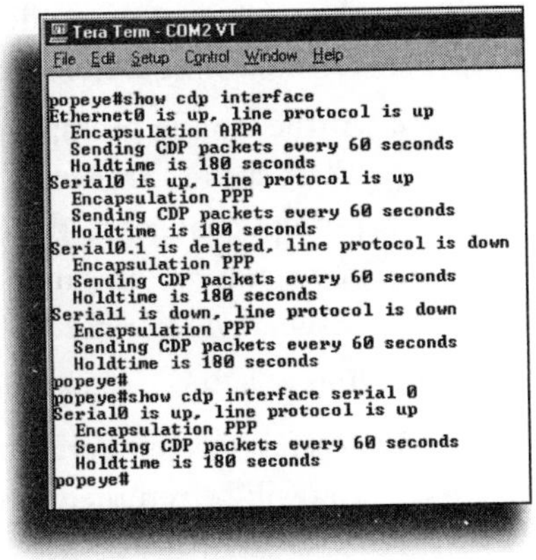

> **Make sure your running configuration works**
>
> You will want to put a new running configuration through its paces (let it run for a while and monitor router parameters using the show command and a command I haven't discussed yet called debug) before you save it as the router's startup configuration. You may also want to back up the original startup configuration to a TFTP server before you save a new running configuration as the startup configuration (covered in Chapter 17).

FIGURE 9.12
The show cdp interface command shows which interfaces are enabled for CDP.

Working with flash

You erase the contents of Flash in the Privileged mode (not generally a good idea) using the erase command; you can also load a new version of the IOS into Flash using a TFTP server and the copy command, which is discussed in Chapter 17.

CDP doesn't care about network protocols

CDP is platform-independent, so it will accumulate information about neighbor routers no matter which network protocol stack they might be running (such as TCP/IP, IPX/SPX, and so on).

Changing CDP holdtime

You can manually set the holdtime for CDP in the configuration mode. At the configuration prompt type cdp holdtime *seconds*, where *seconds* is the time interval for the holdtime.

You can also view the CDP information for a particular interface. For example, in Figure 9.12, the command that follows the initial show cdp interface command is show cdp interface s0. This provides the CDP information for just interface serial 0.

In Figure 9.12, you will see two pieces of information that warrant further discussion: the CDP packet send interval and the CDP hold-time. Notice that CDP packets are sent by CDP-enabled interfaces every 60 seconds. This means that they are broadcasting information to their CDP neighbors every minute.

The *holdtime* refers to the amount of time a router should hold the CDP information that it has received from a neighboring router. If a router doesn't receive an update message from a neighbor within three minutes (180 seconds), it must discard the old CDP information that it holds.

Remember that the purpose of CDP is to stay up to date on the status of your neighboring routers. So, if a line is down or some other problem causes you to lose contact with a neighbor, you don't want your router relying on old information when it makes routing decisions.

If a particular interface isn't enabled for CDP, you can enable it in the configuration mode.

Enabling CDP on an interface

1. At Privileged prompt type config terminal. You are placed in the configuration mode with the console (terminal is the source for the configuration information).

2. At the Config prompt type the interface you want to enable for CDP, such as interface serial 0. Then press **Enter**. The prompt changes to the Config-If prompt, letting you know that you can now enter information for the configuration of the designated interface.

3. Type cdp enable, and then press **Enter**.

4. To end the configuration of the serial interface, press **Ctrl+Z**. You will be returned to the Privileged prompt (see Figure 9.13).

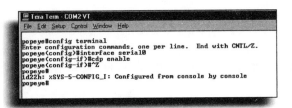

Viewing CDP Neighbors

After you have viewed the status of CDP on your various interfaces, you can use CDP to take a look at platform and protocol information on a neighboring router or routers.

Viewing CDP neighbors

1. At the User or Privileged prompt type show cdp neighbors.

2. Press **Enter** to execute the command.

Figure 9.14 shows the result of this command for a 2505 router that only has one neighbor, which is connected via a serial interface. Table 9.2 describes the information shown in Figure 9.14.

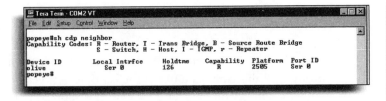

FIGURE 9.14
The show cdp neighbor command lets you check your network neighborhood and view directly connected routers.

Table 9.2 The *show* Command in the User Mode

Parameter	Meaning	Example from Figure 9.14
Device ID	The neighbor's or neighbors' hostname(s)	Olive
Local Interface	The interface on the local router that provides the connection to the neighbor	Serial 0
Capability	Whether the router is configured to serve multiple functions such as routing (R), Bridging (B), and switching (S).	R (this router is only configured to route)

continues...

Table 9.2 Continued

Parameter	Meaning	Example from Figure 9.14
Platform	The type of Cisco router.	2505 (the neighbor is a 2505 router)
Port ID	The interface used on the neighbor to connect to your local router	Serial 0

Obviously, if you are using a higher-end router that is connected to many different neighbors via its various interface ports, the number of neighbors shown using the `show cdp neighbors` command would be greater than that shown in Figure 9.14.

If you want to see more details concerning your CDP neighbors, you can use the `show cdp neighbor details` command. You can enter this command at the User or Privileged prompt. Figure 9.15 shows the results of this command. Notice that this command provides the IP address of the neighbor's interface and the version of the IOS that the neighbor is running.

Using Ping

A command that can be very useful when you are working with routers is ping. And if you use the Internet a great deal you may have already used this command to test the lag time between you and another computer on the Net. *Ping* (which is short for *Packet InterNet Groper*) is used to test the connection between two or more nodes on a network. These nodes can be host computers, servers, or routers.

Ping can be used with a number of Layer 3 protocols such as IP, IPX, and AppleTalk, and uses the logical address assigned to the node on the network. On routers, you can Ping different interfaces because in most cases they will each be assigned a logical address. For example, if you are routing IP, each interface on your router will probably be assigned an IP address.

For example, let's say you want to see whether your connection to another router is up and running. All you have to do is ping the interface on the other router that your router is connected to.

Pinging a neighbor

1. At the User or Privileged prompt type `ping ip address`. In this case you are trying to ping the Olive router that is connected to your router via a serial interface. So, the command reads `ping 130.10.32.2`.

2. Press **Enter** to execute the command.

The results of the Ping command appear in Figure 9.15. Notice that the success rate is 100%. In cases where you can't reach the node that you've pinged, the success rate will be 0%.

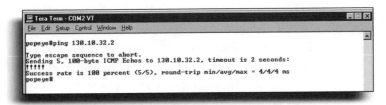

FIGURE 9.15
ping can be used to check your connection to a particular router on the internetwork.

Ping will be discussed in more detail later in this book (as will the Trace and Extended Ping commands in Chapter 18, "Basic Troubleshooting").

SEE ALSO

➤ *For more about ping and extended ping, see page 314.*

➤ *Another TCP/IP protocol stack member, Telnet, can also be used to connect to other routers on the internetwork. For more information, see page 209.*

Creating a Router Banner

You have explored the Cisco IOS in the User and Privileged mode (and worked with a number of different and useful IOS commands) in this chapter, and you should also spend some time working in the Configuration mode. Because several chapters are devoted to configuring specific LAN, WAN, and routing protocols on the router, let's work on something fun in the Configuration mode—the creation of a banner. This banner will appear on your console screen when the router is booted (or rebooted) and will also appear on the screen of virtual terminals that are used to log in to your router (using Telnet, which is discussed in Chapter 11, "Configuring IP Routing").

The router banner is created in the Configuration mode. The command is `banner motd end character`; where the end character is a keyboard character of your choice that tells the configuration mode when you have completed your banner text (`motd` actually stands for message of the day). For example, you will want to choose a character such as the number sign (#), dollar sign ($), or other character that will not appear in the body of your banner (such as most letters of the alphabet).

Creating a router banner

1. At the Privileged prompt type `config terminal`. You are placed in Configuration mode with the console (`terminal` is the source for the configuration information).

2. I will use the dollar sign ($) as our end character. Type `banner motd $`. Then press **Enter**. You will be told to type your banner text and end the banner with the $ character.

3. Type the text for your banner. Use the **Enter** key to place blank lines in the banner text. Use the **Spacebar** to position items from left to right in the banner. Figure 9.16 shows a sample router banner.

4. Type your selected end character ($ in this case) and press **Enter**. You will be returned to Configuration mode.

5. Press **Ctrl+Z** to save your banner and exit Configuration mode.

FIGURE 9.16
You can create a banner for your router in the configuration mode.

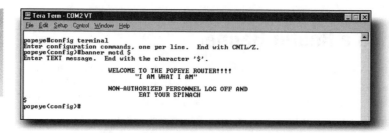

```
popeye#config terminal
Enter configuration commands, one per line.  End with CNTL/Z.
popeye(config)#banner motd $
Enter TEXT message.  End with the character '$'.

                WELCOME TO THE POPEYE ROUTER!!!!
                     "I AM WHAT I AM"

                NON-AUTHORIZED PERSONNEL LOG OFF AND
                     EAT YOUR SPINACH
$
popeye(config)#
```

After exiting the Configuration mode, you may have to press **Enter** once to return to the Privileged prompt. To view your router banner, type `quit` and press **Enter**.

This exits you from the router. When you press **Enter** on the initial router screen, your router banner will appear (see Figure 9.17). If you have set up the router with a login password, you will be asked to provide the password to enter the router.

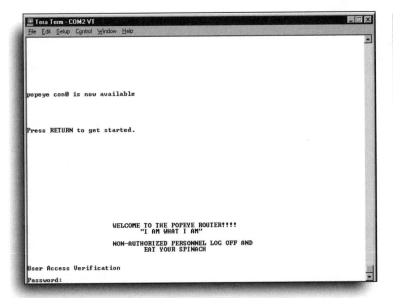

As you can see from this chapter, the Cisco IOS provides a large and robust command set. You will remember the commands that you use often and probably have to look up the commands that you don't. A summary of the basic commands covered in this book is available in Appendix A, "Basic Router Command Summary," as a resource.

SEE ALSO

➤ *For more information on setting passwords on the router (in the Configuration mode), see page 137.*

➤ *The password commands also appear in the command reference in Appendix B; see page 323.*

part

III

ROUTING LAN PROTOCOLS

chapter

10

TCP/IP Primer

The TCP/IP Protocol Stack

TCP/IP (Transmission Control Protocol/Internet Protocol) has become the common language for the networking world and is a commonly deployed protocol suite on enterprise networks. It is also the foundation for the worldwide Internet—the mega network of networks. Many network operating systems (*NOS*), such as Windows NT 4.0 Server, Windows 2000 Server, and Novell Netware 5.0, embrace TCP/IP as their default networking protocol.

I discussed TCP/IP briefly in the Chapter 2, "The OSI Model and Network Protocols." And as you already know, TCP/IP was developed originally as a set of WAN protocols that could be used to maintain communication links between sites even if certain sites became inoperable during a worldwide nuclear war. In light of the kind of fun people have on the Internet today using the TCP/IP stack, it is somewhat ironic (and somewhat depressing) that the suite was originally developed as a sort of wartime network failsafe system by the Department of Defense.

Another point that must be made about TCP/IP is that it has become an integral part of operating and supporting routers on an internetwork. Cisco router administrators use Telnet (a member of the TCP/IP stack) to communicate with remote routers and use TFTP (another TCP/IP protocol) as a mechanism for copying and saving configuration files and loading new IOS software on the router. Most big networks use TCP/IP as their network protocol, so a lack of understanding of the TCP/IP stack will make it pretty hard for you to work with routers and internetworks. TFTP is discussed in more detail in Chapter 17, "Using a TFTP Server for Router Configuration Storage."

SEE ALSO

➤ *To check out some of the other overview information on TCP/IP, see page 45.*

TCP/IP and the OSI Model

TCP/IP was developed in the 1970s and so preceded the completion of the OSI model (in the 1980s). This means that the different protocols in the TCP/IP stack don't map directly to a single layer in the OSI model (although the lower-layer Network and Data Link protocols, such as IP and ARP, do map somewhat closely to their conceptual equivalent in the OSI model).

When TCP/IP was developed, the Department of Defense (DOD) developed its own conceptual model—the *DOD model*—(also known as the DARPA model) for how the various protocols in the TCP/IP stack operate. This reference model divides the movement of data from a sending node to a receiving node into four layers (compared to the seven layers of the OSI model). Figure 10.1 shows how the DOD model maps to the OSI model.

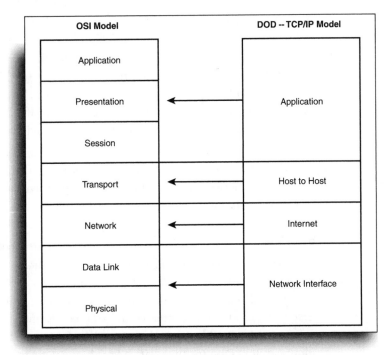

OSI Model	DOD -- TCP/IP Model
Application	Application
Presentation	
Session	
Transport	Host to Host
Network	Internet
Data Link	Network Interface
Physical	

FIGURE 10.1
The DOD four layer model mapped to the seven layers of the OSI model.

Each layer in the DOD-TCP/IP conceptual stack defines the job that TCP/IP protocols do that operate at that particular level (just as the OSI model does). In the next four sections you will take a look at what happens at each layer of the DOD-TCP/IP conceptual stack and the actual TCP/IP stack protocols that operate at these levels. Figure 10.2 shows the TCP/IP stack mapped to the DOD model.

SEE ALSO
➤ *To review the OSI model, see page 34.*

Application Layer

The Application layer protocols provide the user interface for the various protocols and applications that access the network. Application layer protocols in the TCP/IP stack handle file transfer, remote login to other nodes, email functionality, and network monitoring. A number of different protocols reside at this level:

- *FTP (File Transfer Protocol)* is a protocol that provides the capability to transfer files between two computers. FTP is actually a full-blown application (FTP clients can be downloaded from the Internet and used to move files between computers) and a protocol that is supported by other applications such as Web browsers.

- *TFTP (Trivial File Transfer Protocol)* is a stripped down version of FTP that provides a way to move files without any type of authentication (meaning no username or password). TFTP is used in the router world as a way to save router configuration files or update the IOS of a router (this protocol is described extensively in Chapter 17).

- *SMTP (Simple Mail Transport Protocol)* is a protocol that provides mail delivery between two computers. It is a protocol supported by email clients and used for sending and receiving email on the Internet.

- *SNMP (Simple Network Management Protocol)* is a protocol that provides the capability to collect network information. SNMP uses *agents* (software watchdogs that keep an eye on network processes) that collect data on network performance. The collected data can then be compared to baseline information. Software packages like CiscoWorks use SNMP to help network administrators monitor the relative health of a network.

- *Telnet* is a terminal emulation protocol that allows you to connect a local computer with a remote computer (or other device such as a router). The local computer becomes a virtual terminal that has access to applications and other resources on the remote computer. Telnet will be used to log on to a remote router from a local router in Chapter 11, "Configuring IP Routing."

Host-to-Host Layer

The Host-to-Host layer protocols provide flow control and connection reliability as data moves from a sending to a receiving computer. This layer takes the data from the Application layer protocols and begins the process of readying the data for movement out over the network. Two TCP/IP suite protocols inhabit the Host-to-Host layer: TCP and UDP.

- *TCP (Transport Control Protocol)* is a connection-oriented protocol that provides a *virtual circuit* (not unlike establishing a phone call between the sending and receiving nodes) between user applications on the sending and receiving machines. TCP takes the data from the Application layer protocols and breaks it into segments and then makes sure that they are reassembled on the receiving end. TCP requires that the sending and receiving computer establish a synchronized connection, which is done by the exchange of packets carrying sequencing numbers and a synch control bit. TCP requires a lot of network overhead.

- *UDP* (User Datagram Protocol) is a connectionless transport protocol that provides a connection between Application layer protocols that don't require the acknowledgements and synchronization provided by TCP. UDP is like sending a postcard through the mail system. The packet is addressed for the receiving node and sent on its way. UDP is much more passive than TCP. Application layer protocols that use UDP include TFTP and SNMP.

Internet Layer

The Internet layer (corresponding to the OSI Network layer) is responsible for the routing of data across logical network paths and provides an addressing system to the upper layers of the conceptual model. This layer also defines the packet format used for the data as it moves onto the internetwork. The Internet layer really revolves around one protocol—IP. Other protocols at this layer basically provide support for the IP addressing system and packet format. An important job of the Internet layer is resolving logical addresses (such as IP addresses) to the actual hardware (MAC) addresses of the nodes on the network.

IP datagrams are surrounded by MAC layer information

IP datagrams consist of an IP header, which contains the source IP address, the destination IP address (and some other IP related items), and the data provided by the upper-layer protocols. This datagram is sandwiched inside MAC layer header (containing information regarding the media access type, such as Ethernet or Token Ring) and MAC layer trailer, which contains the CRC check for the packet. In our DOD diagram the MAC layer protocols operated at the Network Access layer (described in the next section) and at the Data Link layer of the OSI model. This IP datagram is a good example of how the layers work together to get data to its destination.

Everything you ever wanted to know about IP

The entire TCP/IP stack and IP in particular (RFC 791) have been documented in RFC (Request For Comments) documents. These documents are available at a number of sites on the World Wide Web. Two locations that are good bets for finding a particular RFC are Ohio State's RFC repository at `http://www.cis.ohio-state.edu/hypertext/information/rfc.html`, and the Hyper-RFC site at `http://www.csl.sony.co.jp/rfc/`. Or you can just search the Web with RFC as your keyword.

Ping and traceroute use ICMP

Both ping and traceroute, a router command, use ICMP messages. Ping is introduced in Chapter 9, "Working with the Cisco IOS," and traceroute will be looked at in Chapter 18, "Basic Router Troubleshooting."

- *IP (Internet Protocol)*—IP takes the data from the Host-to-Host layer and fragments the information into packets or *datagrams*. It labels each packet with the IP address of the sending device and the IP address of the receiving device. IP also reassembles datagrams on the receiving machine into segments for the upper-layer protocols. IP is a connectionless protocol that has no interest in the contents of the datagrams. Its only desire is to address and move the datagrams toward their destination.

- *ARP (Address Resolution Protocol)*—When IP prepares a datagram, it knows the IP address of the sending and receiving computers (it receives this information from the upper layer protocols such as Telnet or SMTP). IP also needs the MAC hardware address for the receiving computer because it must provide this information to the Network Access layer protocol used on the network (such as Ethernet). ARP provides the mechanism for resolving the IP address to an actual hardware address. ARP sends out broadcasts with the receiving computer's IP address and asks the computer to reply with its hardware address.

- *ICMP (Internet Control Message Protocol)*—This protocol is a message service provider and management protocol that is used by routers to send messages to host computers that are sending data that must be routed. Routers can let the sending host know when a destination is unreachable or when the router's memory buffer is full of data. Again, ICMP is basically used as a support protocol for IP addressing as ARP is.

➤ *The logical addressing system provided by IP is discussed in greater detail later in this chapter on page 180.*

Network Access Layer

The Network Access layer consists of the protocols that take the datagrams from the Internet layer and envelope them in a specific frame type that is then placed on the network's physical medium as a bit stream. You are already familiar with these protocols, which were previously described as the Data Link layer protocols of the OSI model and include such network architectures as Ethernet, Token Ring, and FDDI. The IEEE specifications described in Chapter 2 provide the specifications for the different frame types used by these network architectures.

Because these protocols reside at the MAC layer (a part of the Network Access Layer of the DOD model and the Data link layer of the OSI model), they are integrally involved in the physical addressing of the data packets. The physical address for a computer is actually burned on the network interface card that is placed in the computer. Router Ethernet, Token Ring, and FDDI interfaces also have MAC addresses burned into the ROM chip of the controller for the interface (serial interfaces on routers don't have MAC addresses).

Figure 10.2 provides a summary of how the OSI model maps to the DOD model and provides the TCP/IP stack mapped to the DOD model. The protocols shown in the TCP/IP stack will be discussed further in respect to how they relate to routers and routing.

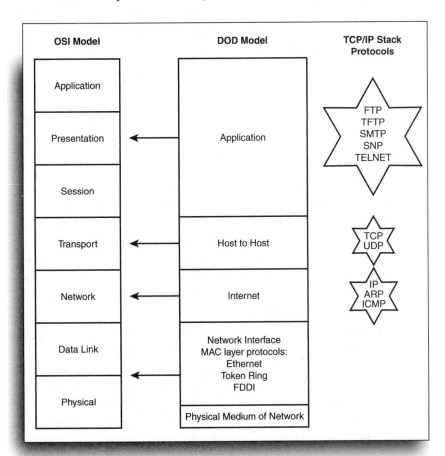

FIGURE 10.2
The DOD model and TCP/IP stack mapped to the OSI model.

An important question arises as to how the logical addressing system provided by IP is resolved to the MAC hardware addresses found on the various network nodes. This subject will be discussed in the next section, which provides a basic overview of IP addressing.

SEE ALSO

➤ *For an overview of network architectures, see page 25.*

➤ *For more information on the IEEE specifications, see page 47.*

Working with IP Addresses

IP addresses are 32 bits long and consist of four 8-bit octets (each octet is one byte). A typical IP address would be 200.1.25.7 (as shown in dotted decimal format). The IP address actually exists as a binary number (1s and 0s), which, as you will see when you get to subnetting, becomes very important in calculating subnets.

An IP address can be written in three different forms:

- Dotted decimal: 200.1.25.7
- Binary: 11001000 00000001 00011001 00000111
- Hexadecimal: C8 1 19 7

IP addresses are hierarchical addresses in that they provide different levels of information; they can tell you the network that the node resides on, the subnet it belongs to, and the actual node address. The IP addressing system isn't unlike the system used to designate your home address by the U.S. Post Office. A letter to you provides your street address, city, and state (and of course zip code). A number of people can live in your city or state, but only you live at the particular postal address.

IP addresses use this same strategy, so part of the IP address tells you the network the node is on, part of it tells you the subnet, and most importantly part of the IP address tells you the node designation. This type of addressing system makes routing practical because data can be forwarded by routers using the network and subnet information (they don't have to actually know the physical MAC address of the receiving node) to the router that serves that particular subnet (meaning it is connected to that subnet).

After the router that serves a particular subnet has the packets for a node that resides on that subnet, it can make sure the packets get to their final destination by resolving the IP address in the packet to the MAC address on the receiving computer. Again, this is like your home address; if you reside in California, mail from the East Coast is forwarded to intermediary post offices in the Midwest using the Zip Code and eventually arrives at your local post office. From your local post office your mail is "resolved" to your home address and delivered by a mail carrier.

Having a network portion to the address means that a router only has to know how to get the packets to that network address (through a maze of routers). And it gets help from the other routers on the internetwork as the packets hop from router to router on the way to their final destination.

Understanding which part of the IP address refers to the network subnet, and which part refers to the node, is a very important aspect of working with IP addresses. The next section explores the different IP classes and the subnet masks they use to make this whole IP addressing thing work.

IP Classes

IP addresses have been broken down into 3 classes based on the size of the network that they serve. There are Class A, Class B, and Class C IP internetworks.

- *Class A* is used for very large networks and supplies over 16 million node addresses for the network. Because of the way IP addresses are structured, a Class A network can serve a huge number of host computers (nodes), but there can only be 127 class A networks. The reason for this will become apparent shortly—read on! ARPAnet (built in the early days of the Internet) is an example of a Class A network.

- *Class B* is used for networks that still need a lot of node addresses, such as a large company or institution. There are 16,384 Class B network addresses, with each Class B supplying over 65,000 host addresses.

The reason MAC addresses aren't used for routing

The alternative to using a hierarchical addressing system like IP is to use flat addressing (there are MAC addresses on all the computers with network cards). However, with flat addressing systems like MAC addresses, routers would have to remember all the unique MAC addresses in the world (a technical impossibility). It would be like using social security numbers to deliver mail. A letter to you would be addressed with your social security number, meaning the routing of it to your home would require a Herculean effort by the postal system.

Getting your own IP numbers

There are a couple of ways that your company can be issued a range of IP numbers. You can get your IP addresses from your Internet Service Provider (which supplies you with a portion of the address pool that they have purchased). Or you can be issued your IP numbers directly by the American Registry for Internet Numbers. IP ranges aren't cheap, and you can check out the details at http://www.arin.net/. You will also need a domain name if you are going to have a company presence on the Web, go to www.internic.net for more information on establishing a domain name (such as Microsoft.com or Habraken.net).

Network 127 is reserved for loopback

In Table 10.1, you will notice that Class A networks end with a first octet decimal value of 126 and Class B networks begin with a first octet value of 128. So what happened to network 127? It is reserved for loopback testing that allows computers to send a packet to themselves without tying up network bandwidth.

- *Class C* is used for small networks and there are over 2 million Class C network addresses available. Class C networks only provide 254 node addresses, however.

Each of these classes used a certain number of *octets* in an IP address to denote the network portion of the address and the node portion of the address. For example, a Class A IP address such as 10.5.25.8 denotes the IP network using the first octet. This means that the network number is 10. The rest of the address, 5.25.8, denotes the host address. So, if only the first octet is used for network addresses, there can only be a limited number of network addresses in a Class A (because you limit the possibilities to one octet), whereas you are using three octets to specify the host address, which gives you a lot of different possible combinations. This is why there are only a limited number of Class A networks available, but each Class A network supplies a huge number of host addresses (over 16 million).

Contrasting this Class A address with a Class C address, 200.44.26.3, will help emphasize the point. The first three octets of a Class C address denote the IP network number (200.44.26). Only the last octet is available to assign host numbers. So, you can see that having three octets available for network numbers gives you a huge number of possibilities; whereas using only one octet as a source of host addresses really limits the possibilities.

Figure 10.3 shows each of the IP Network classes and the octets that they use for network addresses and for host addresses. The greater the number of octets used for host addresses, the more possible hosts. The greater the number of octets used for network addresses, the greater the number of possible networks; it's that straightforward.

Table 10.1 summarizes the decimal range for the first octet of each of the IP network classes and the number of networks and nodes that are available with each class. A sample IP address is also provided for each of the different classes.

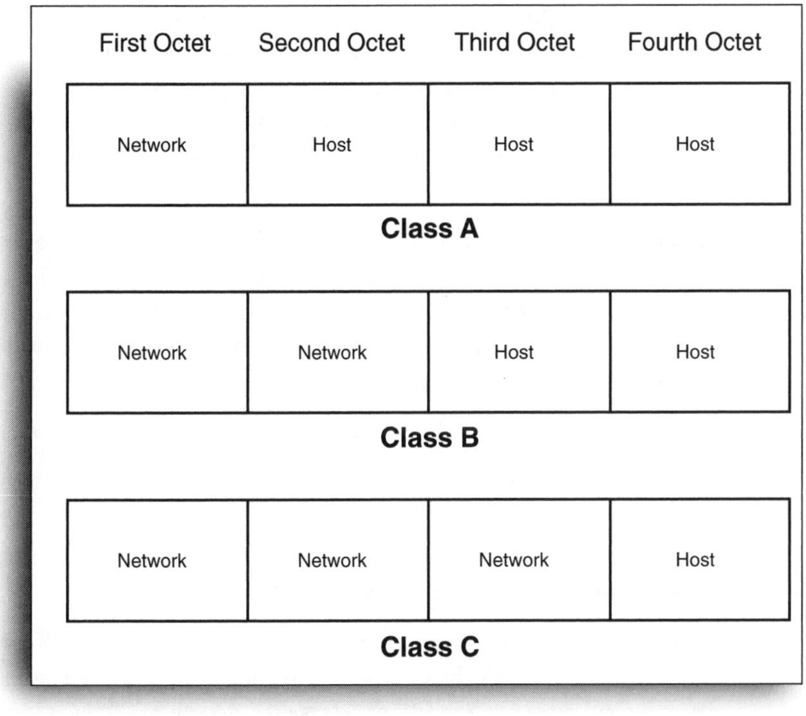

FIGURE 10.3
Each of the IP classes uses a certain number of octets for network addressing and a certain number of octets for node addressing.

Table 10.1 IP Network Classes

Class	First Octet Range	Number of Networks	Number of Hosts	Sample Address
A	1-126	127	16,777,214	10.15.121.5
B	128-191	16,384	65,534	130.13.44.52
C	192-223	2,097,152	254	200.15.23.8

Binary Equivalents and First Octets

Remember that when you see an IP address such as 200.1.25.7 (and the sample addresses shown in Table 10.1), you are actually looking at a convenient dotted decimal representation of a series of 32 bits that are divided into four 8-bit octets. Each octet consists of 8 bits, which is one byte. So in actuality the IP address 200.1.25.7 is really a series of 32 1s and 0s—11001000 00000001 00011001 00000111.

Class D and Class E addresses

Two additional classes of IP network addresses exist: *Class D* and *Class E*. Class D network addresses are used by multicast groups receiving data on an internetwork from a particular application or server service. An example of a multicast use of Class D addresses is Microsoft NetShow, which can broadcast the same content to a group of users at one time. Class E addresses belong to an experimental class, which isn't available for use by folks like you and me.

Converting decimal to binary or vice versa

You can quickly convert decimal to binary or binary to decimal using the Windows calculator. Start the Calculator (from the **Start** menu, choose **Programs**). Click the **View** menu and select **Scientific**. The default numbering system is decimal type in the decimal number from any octet in an IP address such as 126. Then click the **Bin** (binary) radio button on the format bar of the calculator. The number is converted to binary—1111110. Note that the calculator doesn't place the lead zeros in the binary numbers so to show all 8-bit places for an IP address octet, you would have to add the lead 0 to this number—01111110. To convert binary to decimal, click **Bin** and then type in the 8-bit binary number (1 and 0s) for the octet. Then click **Dec** to convert to decimal.

How the decimal number 200 is converted to the binary number 11001000 or vice versa will be discussed in "Subnetting IP Addresses," later in this chapter. So, for now, you only need to understand that IP addresses are written in the dotted decimal format really as a convenience and they actually exist as a series of 1s and 0s.

Rules have been established for the *leading bits* in the first octet of each of the classes you've discussed (A, B, and C). This enables a router to look at the first octet of an IP address and immediately know which class of IP address it is looking at (it's also a convenient way for you to quickly tell a Class A address from a Class B or C address).

- In Class A addresses the first bit of the first octet is set to 0.
- In Class B addresses the first bit of the first octet is set to 1, and the second bit is set to 0.
- In Class C addresses the first two bits of the first octet are set to 1 and the third bit is set to 0.

Figure 10.4 shows the first octet of a Class A, B, and C IP address in binary format respectively. Converting binary to decimal is a subject that you shall cover in a moment. However, you should take a look at IP subnet masks before you get into the math.

Basic Subnet Masks

Another aspect of IP addressing that is extremely important to how IP addressing works is the use of *subnet masks*. An IP address without the appropriate subnet mask is like Laurel without Hardy (or I guess now that's Beavis without Butthead). The subnet mask for a particular IP address is actually used by the router to resolve which part of the IP address is providing the network address and which part of the address is providing host address.

The basic subnet masks for each class are provided in Table 10.2. Subnet masks also consist of four octets of information. A router matches up the information in the subnet mask with the actual IP address and determines the network address and the node address.

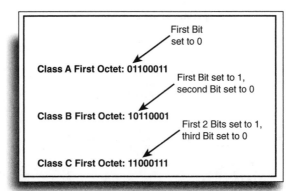

Table 10.2 Basic Subnet Masks

Class	Subnet Mask
A	255.0.0.0
B	255.255.0.0
C	255.255.255.0

In the basic subnet masks (where no subnetting has been done) the octet either has all the bits turned on (represented by 1s) or all the bits turned off (represented by 0s). When all the bits are turned on (all 8 bits are represented by 1s) the decimal equivalent is 255. When all the bits are set to the binary 0, the decimal equivalent is 0. Figure 10.5 shows the binary equivalent of the Class B basic subnet mask.

The big question is how does a router use the subnet mask to determine which part of an IP address refers to the network address. It actually uses a process called *anding* where it "ands" the bits in the subnet mask with the bits in the IP address to determine the network address.

Here's how anding works: the IP address and the subnet mask are both viewed by the router in binary format (which you will learn to do in the next section of this chapter). The bits in the subnet mask are then "anded" with the corresponding bits in the IP address. Table 10.3 shows the results of anding binary bits (1s and Os).

An early bird brain teaser

Even though you haven't talked about converting binary numbers to decimal yet, take my word for it that the first bit in an octet when represented by the binary 1 has the decimal value of 128. Because Class A addresses always have the first bit set to 0, it isn't worth anything (meaning it's 0 in decimal too). So, the first octet value for Class A networks is always less than 128 (take a look at the first octet decimal range for Class A addresses in Table 10.1).

FIGURE 10.5
Subnet masks can also
be represented in deci-
mal or binary.

Class B Subnet Mask
Decimal: 255.255.0.0
Binary: 11111111 11111111 00000000 00000000

Table 10.3 Anding

Bit Combination	Result
1 and 1	1
1 and 0	0
0 and 0	0

Let's take a look at some actual anding. In Figure 10.6 a Class B IP address and its basic subnet mask are converted to binary. The binary equivalents of the IP address and the subnet mask are anded. The result is the IP address for the network (in this case 180.20.000.000).

FIGURE 10.6
The network number is
resolved by anding the
IP address and the
Subnet mask.

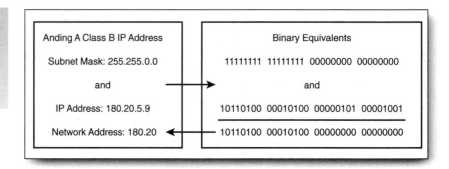

Anding A Class B IP Address

Subnet Mask: 255.255.0.0

and

IP Address: 180.20.5.9

Network Address: 180.20

Binary Equivalents

11111111 11111111 00000000 00000000

and

10110100 00010100 00000101 00001001

10110100 00010100 00000000 00000000

Subnetting IP Addresses

Now that you've been introduced to the format for IP addresses and their subnet masks, you can tackle subnetting. Basically, subnetting enables you to take a number of LANs and connect them together into one internetwork. It also provides you with the capability to break a large network into subnets that are connected with routers. Segmenting a large network using routers allows you to maximize the bandwidth of the network because the routers keep the traffic on each subnet local; the data isn't broadcast to the entire network.

Each of the classes that you discussed in the previous section (Class A, B, and C) can be subnetted. Before you get into the actual math involved in determining subnets and the new network subnet mask, let's look at how dotted decimal IP addresses are converted to decimal and vice versa.

SEE ALSO

➤ *To review how routers work, see page 78.*

Binary and Decimal Conversions

Each octet in the IP address (although represented as a decimal number) consists of 8 bits. Each bit position has a decimal equivalent. That decimal equivalent isn't realized, however, unless the bit is represented as a 1 (0 bits have no decimal value). Figure 10.7 shows the decimal value of each bit position in the octet and the total value for the octet when certain bits have the binary value of 1.

The first bit in any octet of an IP address will have a decimal value of 128 followed by a bit that has a decimal value of 64. The bits on the far left of the octet are referred to as the *high-order bits*. If you move down to the right end of the octet, where the last bit's decimal value is 1 (followed by a bit on the left that has a decimal value of 2), you are working with the *lower-order bits*.

Decimal Value of Bit Positions								
128	64	32	16	8	4	2	1	Decimal Total
1	0	0	0	0	0	0	0	128
1	1	0	0	0	0	0	0	192
1	1	1	0	0	0	0	0	224
1	1	1	1	0	0	0	0	240
1	1	1	1	1	0	0	0	248
1	1	1	1	1	1	0	0	252
1	1	1	1	1	1	1	0	254
1	1	1	1	1	1	1	1	255

Does the router have common sense?

You're probably looking at Figure 10.7 and thinking, "Why doesn't the router just look for 255 in the subnet mask and then use the numbers in the IP address that appear in the same octet as the Network address. Well, in effect it does, although it must crosscheck the numbers in binary because it receives the data in a bit stream (a stream of 1s and 0s). Also, when you throw in subnets and have subnet masks that include subnetting bits, it isn't quite as obvious which part of the address is network information and which part of the address is providing subnet or node information.

FIGURE 10.7
Decimal equivalent for octet bit combinations.

Figure 10.7 gives you the total decimal value for an octet when you turn on bits (bit values of 1) working from the high-order bits to the low-order bits. Note that when all the bit values are set to 1, the total decimal value is 255.

Obviously, you will run across IP address octets where only lower order bits have decimal values. For example, if the first low-order bit and the second low-order bit are both set to the binary 1, you have an octet decimal value of 3 (1+2).

When you do IP subnetting, you work with both the high-order and low-order bits. And although the math involved in the subnetting process has you hopping from one end of the octet to the other (using the low-order bits for some calculations and the high-order bits for others), the process is pretty straightforward.

Just to make a point, let's convert the octet 01110001 to decimal using the information in Figure 10.8. The answer would be 64+32+16+1=113. All you have to do is add the decimal equivalents of the bits in the octet that are set to 1.

Creating Subnets on a Class A Network

The easiest way to learn subnetting is to actually do it. So let's take a look at a Class A network and walk through the steps of subnetting it (remember that they are only very few Class A networks, but the subnetting math is actually easiest when working with Class A and Class B networks).

The first octet of a Class A network can be in the decimal range of 1-126. So let's say that you've been assigned the network address 10.0.0.0.

In Class A networks, the first octet defines the network address. The remaining three octets provide the node address information because you have all the possible bit combinations available in 3 octets. That's 24 bit positions, so the number of node addresses available would be 2^{24}-2 or 16,777,214 (you take 2 to the power of the number of bits that are available to create node addresses—in this case 3 octets or 24 bits).

When to subnet?

Subnetting IP networks is required when you attach remote sites together using routers. Another reason to subnet is when you have a network with a huge number of nodes that is really chewing up your bandwidth. So, while you may never work with a Class A IP network, a network providing that many possible hosts would certainly be subnetted.

The reason that you must subtract 2 from the possible node addresses (2^{24}) is that you lose two possibilities because the bits in the node octets cannot be set to all 1s or 0s. When the node octets are all set to 1, that address is used to broadcast messages to all the nodes on the network—it means all nodes—and so can't be used for an actual node address. When the node octets are all set to 0, that address signifies the network wire address. In our case, if all the node octets are set to 0, you get the address 10.0.0.0, which remember is our network address, which becomes very important when you configure IP networks on a router.

Figure 10.8 summarizes what you've talked about so far. Now you also know that you take the number of bits available for node addresses and can quickly figure out how many possible node addresses that gives you by raising 2 to the power of the node bit total and then subtracting 2.

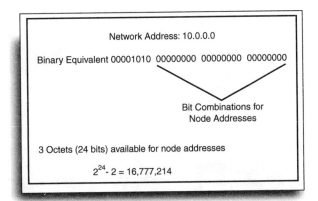

FIGURE 10.8
The number of node addresses available can be determined using the number of bits available for node addressing.

Now, if you're with me so far, you probably feel pretty good, but you've only scratched the surface of this whole subnetting issue. The next step is to determine how many subnets you will need for your network. If you have a Class A network, your operation will probably be spread across a wide geographical area and use both LAN and WAN technology. Let's keep this simple, however. Say you want to divide your large network into 30 subnets (you will also have to have a separate router interface to service each subnet so, even for 30 subnets you are talking about several routers that each have a number of interfaces (such as Ethernet interfaces) to connect to the different subnets).

Figure 10.9 shows a portion of the network that you are dividing into 30 subnets. You are looking at just one location (one building) in the larger network, where six subnets out of the total 30 will be used. Each LAN will be its own subnet (meaning the LAN interface on the router connected to the LAN will be part of the same subnet). The serial connection between the two routers also requires that it be a separate subnet, so one of the subnets you create will be used for that set of interfaces (on both the routers).

FIGURE 10.9
A subnetted network will consist of separate LAN subnets and WAN subnets that connect routers.

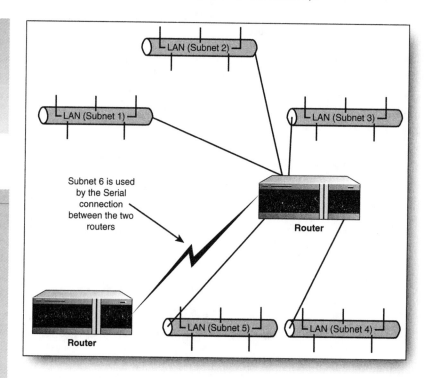

How many subnets should I create?

When you divide your network into logical subnets, you want to create enough subnets to take care of the current locations on your networks (using both LAN and WAN connections). You also want to keep growth in mind as well. You really only want to do this subnetting math once because IP addresses will be assigned to the various routers and computers on the network. Having to do this all over because you only created six subnets and now need 14 is probably not going to set well with your boss. Oh, well, you can always work in sales.

Now that you know how many subnets you need, you can begin to work through the process of stealing bits to create our subnets. The first thing that you will do is create the new subnet mask that will be used for the entire network.

Creating the Network Subnet Mask

You want 30 subnets. Right now our network address 10.0.0.0 only supplies bits for the network address (the first octet) and bits for node addresses (the other three octets). So, how do you create subnets? You steal some bits from the node octets and use them to create our subnets (you can't steal bits from the network octet because this is provided to you by the people who assign IP networks—it is basically cast in stone).

So, you will steal bits from the first node octet to create our subnets (the second octet in the 10.0.0.0 address—from left to right). This means that the possible number of node addresses is going to be decreased because you are going to take some of the bits to create subnets (with bits removed for subnets, you get less node addresses).

Stealing the bits will not only let us compute ranges of IP addresses for each subnet (each of the 30 subnets will have a different range of IP addresses), but it also lets us create a new subnet mask for the entire network. This new subnet mask will let routers and other devices on the network know that you have divided our network into subnets and it will also tell them how many logical subnets have been created.

But first things first, you must figure out how many bits you need to steal to come up with 30 subnets. Remember that each bit in an octet has a decimal value. For example, the first low-order bit on the far right of the octet has a decimal value of 1, the bit to its left has a value of 2 and so on. So, to create 30 subnets you add the lower order bits' decimal values until you come up with a value of 31. Why 31 and not 30? You cannot use subnet 0, which is what you derive when you steal only the first lower-order bit. So the formula is actually: total decimal value of stolen lower-order bits minus 1. Figure 10.10 shows you how five lower order bits were used to come up with 30 subnets.

When you know how many bits it takes to create 30 subnets—5 bits—you can create the new subnet mask for the entire Class A network. Forget for the moment that you used lower order bits (adding from right to left) to come up with the 30 subnets.

Take the first five high-order bits (128, 64, 32, 16, and 8) working from left to right. Add them together: 128+64+32+16+8=248. The 248 is very important. Normally, a Class A subnet mask is 255.0.0.0. But this Class A network has been subnetted (using bits in the second octet). So the new subnet mask is 255.248.0.0.

This new subnet mask tells routers and other devices that this Class A network contains 30 subnets. Now that you have the subnet mask for the entire network (this subnet mask would be used as the subnet mask for router interfaces and computers on the network no matter which of the 30 subnets that node is on) you can figure out the range of IP addresses that would be available in each of the 30 subnets.

You may have to create more subnets than you need

When you figure out the number of subnets that you need, you may find that when you start converting lower order bits to decimal and start adding them, you end up with more subnets than you actually want. For example, if you want 26 subnets, you will have to create 30 subnets because the decimal equivalents of the bits themselves. This doesn't mean you have to use them all, you can still set up 26 subnets on your network; it's just that you can't create that exact number.

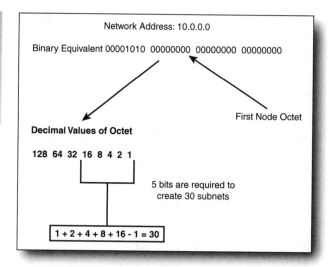

Calculating IP Subnet Ranges

Calculating the subnet ranges is pretty straightforward. You used five high-order bits to determine the binary number used in the second octet of our new subnet mask for the network. These high-order bits also provide the secret for determining the IP address ranges for each subnet. The high-order decimal values that you used for the subnet mask were: 128, 64, 32, 16, and 8.

Take the lowest of the high-order bits that you used to calculate the new subnet mask, in this case 8. This number becomes the increment used to create the IP address ranges for the 30 subnets.

For example, the first subnet (of our 30) will begin with the IP address 10.8.0.1. The 8 is used as the starting increment for the second octet in the IP address. Remember, it was the second octet that you stole the bits from to create our subnets. So, all IP addresses that have a second octet decimal value of less than 8 are invalid values. To calculate the beginning number of our next subnet add 8 to the second octet, you get 16. So, the starting address for the second subnet will be 10.16.0.1. Continue to add 8 to the second octet to determine the start address for all 30 of the subnets.

Now, you probably wonder where I came up with the 0 in the third octet and the 1 in the fourth octet. The possible decimal values of any octet range from 0 (where all bits are set to 0) to 255 (where all bits are set to 1). So the first IP address in the subnet can have all 0s in the third octet. So, why does the fourth position start with 1? Remember, I said earlier that the node address could not be represented by octets containing all 0s or all 1s. If the fourth octet was 0, both the node octets (the third and the fourth) would be all 0s, which is used to denote the subnetwork address, and so it isn't a legal address for a node.

To determine the range of addresses for a particular subnet, you take that subnet's starting address and use all the addresses that are between it and the starting address of the next subnet. For example, the first subnet will contain all the addresses between 10.8.0.1 and 10.16.0.1 (but not including 10.16.0.1).

Table 10.4 gives the start and end address for the first 10 of the 30 subnets that you created. To figure out the other 20 ranges, simply add the increment (8) to the second octet (the subnet octet).

Table 10.4 IP Address Ranges for Subnets (First 10 of 30)

Subnet #	Start Address	End Address
1	10.8.0.1	10.15.255.254
2	10.16.0.1	10.23.255.254
3	10.24.0.1	10.31.255.254
4	10.32.0.1	10.39.255.254
5	10.40.0.1	10.47.255.254
6	10.48.0.1	10.55.255.254
7	10.56.0.1	10.63.255.254
8	10.64.0.1	10.71.255.254
9	10.72.0.1	10.79.255.254
10	10.80.0.1	10.87.255.254

Calculating Available Node Addresses

Why does the end address for each subnet stop at 254?

Remember that the node portion of the IP address (in this case the third and fourth octet) cannot be all 1s (or 255 in decimal format). So, you can have all 1s in the third octet (255), but can only go to 254 in the fourth octet.

I've already stressed the importance of creating the appropriate number of IP subnets for your network (with growth figured in). But you also need to make sure that the number of node addresses available for each subnet will accommodate the number of computers and other devices that you plan to deploy on the subnets. Each subnet is a mini-network unto itself and you can't steal IP addresses from one of the other subnets, if you find that you don't have enough addresses for all your devices.

How many IP addresses do you lose when subnetting?

Be advised that subnetting (stealing bits for subnets) reduces the number of IP addresses available for your network nodes. For example, a Class A network that isn't subnetted provides 16,777,214 node addresses. Now, you computed that if you create 30 subnets on a class A network you get 524,286 IP addresses per subnet. Multiply 524,286 by 30. You get 15,728,580. So, 16,777,214 minus 15,728,580 is 1,048,634. You lose a lot of potential node addresses by subnetting.

Calculating the number of node addresses available in each subnet is very straightforward. In our Class A network, you originally had 24 bits dedicated to node addressing. To create the 30 subnets, you had to steal 5 bits from the second octet. This means that now only 19 bits (24-5) are available to create node IP addresses. To calculate the nodes addresses per subnet, take 2 and raise it to the 19th power and then subtract 2 (2^{19}-2). This results in 524,286 IP addresses per subnet. Obviously, Class A networks provide a huge number of addresses and coming up short is pretty improbable. But when you work with the subnetting of Class B and Class C addresses, you need to make special note of how many addresses you have available in each subnet.

Creating Class B and Class C Subnets

The process of creating Class B and Class C subnets is very similar to creating Class A subnets. The math is all the same, however, you are working with a smaller pool of potential node addresses when you subnet. Let's look at each of these classes briefly.

Class B Subnetting

Class B networks that aren't subnetted provide 2 octets (16 bits) for node addressing. This provides 65,534 node addresses. The basic subnet mask for a Class B network is 255.255.0.0.

Let's say that you've been assigned a Class B network address of 180.10.0.0. To subnet this network, you will have to steal bits from the third octet. You have determined that you want to create six subnets. Figure 10.11 walks you through the process of creating the subnets and creating the new subnet mask.

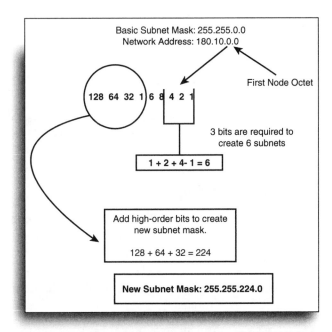

Basic Subnet Mask: 255.255.0.0
Network Address: 180.10.0.0

First Node Octet

128 64 32 1 6 8 4 2 1

3 bits are required to create 6 subnets

1 + 2 + 4 - 1 = 6

Add high-order bits to create new subnet mask.

128 + 64 + 32 = 224

New Subnet Mask: 255.255.224.0

FIGURE 10.11
Determine the lower order bits needed to create the subnets and then add the same number of higher order bits to create the subnet mask.

The new subnet mask for the network would be 255.255.224.0 (see Figure 10.12). To figure out the range of IP addresses in each of the six subnets, you use the lowest of the high-order bits that were added to determine the new subnet mask number for the third octet. This would be 32 (again, taken from Figure 10.12). So, the first address in the first subnet would be 180.10.32.1 (180.10.32.0 is reserved as the subnetwork address and so cannot be used as a node address). To come up with the starting IP address of the second subnet, add 32 to the third octet (64). The second subnet would start with 180.10.64.1. Table 10.5 shows the ranges for the six subnets created from this Class B network address.

Table 10.5 IP Address Ranges for Class B

Subnet #	Start Address	End Address
1	180.10.32.1	180.10.63.254
2	180.10.64.1	180.10.95.254
3	180.10.96.1	180.10.127.254
4	180.10.128.1	180.10.159.254
5	180.10.160.1	180.10.191.254
6	180.10.192.1	180.10.223.254

Because you took 3 bits to create your subnets, you are left with 13 bits for nodes. So, 2^{13}-2= 8190. That's 8190 IP addresses available per subnet.

Class C Subnetting

Class C subnetting is a little more problematic than Class A and B networks because you only have one octet to steal bits from to create your subnets. Class C networks are also small to begin with (only 254 IP addresses are available), so creating more than just a few subnets will leave you with a very small number of node addresses available in each subnet.

Let's walk through an example that allows us to examine the idiosyncrasies of Class C subnetting. The network address is 200.10.44.0. One octet is available for node addresses (the fourth octet). This is also the octet that you must borrow bits from to create your subnets.

You will divide the Class C network into two subnets. To create the two subnets you must borrow the first two lower order bits that have the decimal value of 1 and 2 (1+2-1=2 subnets). You then move to the other end of the decimal bit values and use the first 2 high-order bits (because you borrowed 2 bits for the subnets) to create the new subnet mask for the network. The two high-order bits are 128 and 64. Add them together and you get 192. So the new subnet mask for the network is 255.255.255.192.

Figure 10.12 summarizes the steps that were followed to create the new network subnet mask by borrowing the appropriate number of bits to create 2 subnets.

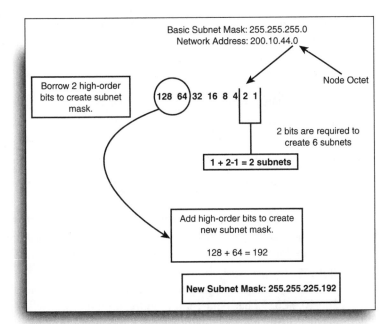

FIGURE 10.12
Use the number of lower order bits used to create the appropriate number of subnets and take the same number of high-order bits to create the subnet mask.

Now you need to figure out the range of IP addresses that will be available in the two subnets. The lowest of the high-order bits used to create the new subnet mask was 64, which becomes the increment for the subnet ranges. So, using what you learned when creating Class A and Class B subnets, you would assume that the start address of the first subnet would be 200.10.44.64. However, remember that an address in the range must be reserved as the subnetwork address. Because you are working with only one octet, the first usable address in the range of IP addresses for the subnet must be reserved as the subnetwork address. So, 200.10.44.64 is reserved for the subnet address.

That means that the beginning of the range of IP addresses in the first subnet that you can use for node addresses begins with 200.10.44.65. And the next subnet, which begins with 200.10.44.128 (you add the increment to itself to get the start of the next subnet range) also reserves the first address (200.10.44.128) as the subnetwork address (it identifies the subnet as a separate entity on the whole network). So the second subnet range of addresses that can be used for nodes begins with 200.10.44.129.

A name is just a name

I've been referring to the address provided by your ISP (such as 200.10.44.0) as the network address. This is also sometimes referred to as the major network address. And I've been identifying the address reserved for the subnet as the subnetwork or subnet address. In cases where the network address is referred to as the major network address, the subnetwork may be referred to as the network address. Just remember that the address you procure from InterNIC or your ISP is the network or major network address and the subnet addresses you create are subnetwork or network addresses.

Calculating available node addresses

To quickly calculate the number of IP addresses that would be available for each of our Class C subnets use the formula $2^{[\text{bits available for node addresses}]}$ minus 2. In our case this would be $2^6 - 2=62$. You have 2 subnets so $62\times2=124$.

Table 10.6 shows the ranges for the two Class C subnets and also shows addresses such as the subnetwork address that cannot be used for node addressing.

Table 10.6   IP Address Ranges for Class C Subnets (2)

Subnet	Subnetwork Address	Start Address	End Address	Broadcast Address
1	200.10.44.64	200.10.44.65	200.10.44.126	200.10.44.127
2	200.10.44.128	200.10.44.129	200.10.44.190	200.10.44.191

The big problem with subnetting a Class C network is that you lost a lot of normally usable IP addresses. You lost 2 addresses in each subnet, one for the subnetwork address, and one for the broadcast address. You also lost all the addresses that come before 200.10.44.64. That means you lose 200.10.44.1 through 200.10.44.63. That's quite a few addresses, especially when you don't get that many addresses with a Class C anyway.

Understanding Subnet 0

There is a way to "cheat" and use these lost addresses for your network nodes (in our case addresses 200.10.44.2 through 200.10.44.62-200.10.44.1 is reserved for the subnetwork address and 200.10.44.63 would be the broadcast address). These "lost" addresses are referred to as subnet 0 and normally cannot be used. However, you can configure your router to take advantage of the subnet 0 IP addresses: type the ip subnet-zero command at the config prompt and then press Enter (this is a global configuration command, so you don't have to enter it for any particular router interface).

Using subnet 0 means that only 1 bit needs to be stolen to create subnet 0 and subnet 1. So, the subnet mask would now be 255.255.255.128 (only 1 high-order bit is used to create the new subnet mask). The range of IP addresses for the two subnets would be 200.10.44.1-200.10.44.126 (200.10.44.127 is the broadcast address) for subnet 0 and 200.10.44.129-200.10.44.254 (200.10.44.128 is the subnetwork number and 200.10.44.255 is the broadcast address) for subnet 1.

Because using subnet 0 makes the calculation of subnets a little more difficult (when compared to Class A or B), Table 10.7 provides a summary of the fourth octet numbers that would be available for each subnet when a Class C network is subnetted with subnet 0 used as a valid subnet. Values are provided for 2, 4, and 8 subnets on the Class C network.

The big thing to remember when using subnet 0 is that you don't subtract 1 from the low-order bits when you determine the number of bits you must steal to create the required number of subnets.

Table 10.7 IP Address Ranges for Class C Subnets Using Subnet 0

# of Subnets	Subnet Mask	Start Address	End Address	Broadcast Address
2	255.255.255.128	x.x.x.1	x.x.x.126	x.x.x.127
		x.x.x.129	x.x.x.254	x.x.x.255
4	255.255.255.192	x.x.x.1	x.x.x.62	x.x.x.63
		x.x.x.65	x.x.x.126	x.x.x.127
		x.x.x.129	x.x.x.190	x.x.x.191
		x.x.x.193	x.x.x.254	x.x.x.255
8	255.255.255.224	x.x.x.1	x.x.x.30	x.x.x.31
		x.x.x.33	x.x.x.62	x.x.x.63
		x.x.x.65	x.x.x.94	x.x.x.95
		x.x.x.97	x.x.x.126	x.x.x.127
		x.x.x.129	x.x.x.158	x.x.x.159
		x.x.x.161	x.x.x.190	x.x.x.191
		x.x.x.193	x.x.x.222	x.x.x.223
		x.x.x.225	x.x.x.254	x.x.x.255

A Final Word on Subnetting

On any network that uses internetworking connectivity strategies, you will most likely face the issue of dividing a particular IP network into a group of subnets. And understanding the simple math presented in this chapter will make it very easy for you to create subnets on any class of network; however, sometimes it can be even simpler to just look up the information on a chart.

Table 10.8 provides a summary of the subnet mask and the number of hosts available when you divide a Class A network into a particular number of subnets (subnet 0 has not been allowed). Table 10.9 provides the same information for Class B networks (subnet 0 has not been allowed).

Table 10.8 Class A Subnetting

# Of Subnets		Bits Used	Subnet Mask	Hosts/Subnet
2		2 255.192.0.0		4,194,302
6		3 255.224.0.0		2,097,150
14		4 255.240.0.0		1,048,574
30		5 255.248.0.0		524,286
62		6 255.252.0.0		262,142
126		7 255.254.0.0		131,070
254	8	255.255.0.0		65,534

Table 10.9 Class B Subnetting

# Of Subnets	Bits Used	Subnet Mask	Hosts/Subnet
2	2	255.255.192.0	16,382
6	3	255.255.224.0	8,190
14	4	255.255.240.0	4,094
30	5	255.255.248.0	2,046
62	6	255.255.252.0	1,022
126	7	255.255.254.0	510
254	8	255.255.255.0	254

Configuring IP Routing

Configuring Router Interfaces

As you've already heard several times in this book, TCP/IP is the de facto network protocol for the networks of the world (due to the Internet explosion—everyone wants to be part of this planetwide network). It is a routable and robust network protocol stack. You learned all about IP addresses and IP subnetting in Chapter 10, "TCP/IP Primer." Now, you can take some of the concepts learned in that chapter and apply them directly to router configurations.

Routing IP on an internetwork requires that you complete two main tasks: configure LAN and WAN interfaces with the correct IP and subnet mask information, and then enable an IP routing protocol on your router or routers. (IP routing is automatically enabled on the router in contrast to IPX and AppleTalk, which aren't.) When routing IP, you have more than one choice for your routing protocol (such as RIP versus IGRP).

Let's walk through the steps of configuring LAN interfaces on a router first and apply some of the information that you picked up on IP subnetting in Chapter 10. For example, assume your example network is a Class B network with the network address 130.10.0.0. You will create 6 subnets on this network. The new subnet mask for the network would be 255.255.224.0.

Table 11.1 provides the range of IP addresses for the 6 subnets.

Table 11.1 IP Address Ranges for 6 Subnets on 130.10.0.0

Subnet #	Start Address	End Address
1	130.10.32.1	130.10.63.254
2	130.10.64.1	130.10.95.254
3	130.10.96.1	130.10.127.254
4	130.10.128.1	130.10.159.254
5	130.10.160.1	130.10.191.254
6	130.10.192.1	130.10.223.254

Figure 11.1 shows a diagram of a portion of a company internetwork. IP addresses (from our range in Table 11.1) have been assigned to the router interfaces on each of the routers. This figure will help provide some context to the IOS commands that you are going to work with in this chapter.

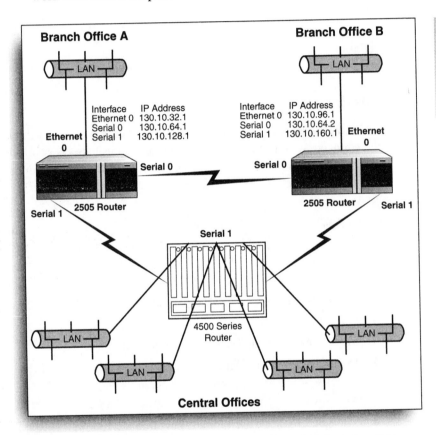

Interface	IP Address
Ethernet 0	130.10.32.1
Serial 0	130.10.64.1
Serial 1	130.10.128.1

Interface	IP Address
Ethernet 0	130.10.96.1
Serial 0	130.10.64.2
Serial 1	130.10.160.1

FIGURE 11.1
Two remote sites connected to a central office. IP addressing provided for remote sites.

You will configure the 2505 router at the Branch A location. This means that the router (which has three interfaces, one Ethernet, and two serial) must have each interface configured with a different IP address that is in a different subnet range. Table 11.2 lists the IP addresses (also shown in Figure 11.1) that you will use to configure this router. You will learn about configuring LAN interfaces (such as Ethernet ports) in the next section, "LAN Interfaces" and WAN interfaces in the section after that, "WAN Interfaces."

Table 11.2 IP Addresses for 2505 Router Interfaces

Interface	IP Address
Ethernet 0	130.10.32.1
Serial 0	130.10.64.1
Serial 1	130.10.128.1

SEE ALSO

➤ *For an overview of IP routing protocols such as RIP and IGRP, see page 93.*

LAN Interfaces

LAN interfaces, such as Ethernet ports or Token Ring ports, will be the connection point between the router and a local area network. The number of subnets at a particular location will dictate the number of LAN interfaces required on the router (if only one router is used).

Each of these LAN interfaces will be on a separate subnet. The simplest way to assign IP addresses to a LAN interface is to use the first IP address available in the address range of the subnet that the interface will connect to.

Configuring IP addressing for a LAN interface

1. At the Privileged prompt type config t, and then press **Enter**. You are placed in the Global Configuration mode.

2. To configure a particular LAN interface, type the name of the interface at the prompt, such as interface ethernet 0. Then press **Enter**. The prompt changes to the config-if mode.

3. Now you can enter the ip address command followed by the IP address for the interface and the subnet mask for the network. In this example, the command would be ip address 130.10.32.1 255.255.224.0 (see Figure 11.2). Press **Enter** to complete the command.

4. To end the configuration of the interface, press **Ctrl+Z**.

5. Press **Enter** again to return to the privileged prompt.

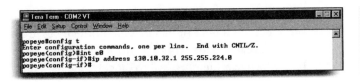

FIGURE 11.2
Individual LAN interfaces must be configured with an IP address and subnet mask.

You can quickly check the configuration parameters for a LAN port using the show ip interface command. For example, to see the IP addressing for Ethernet 0, you would type show ip interface e0 and then press **Enter**. Figure 11.3 shows the results of this command on our 2505 router.

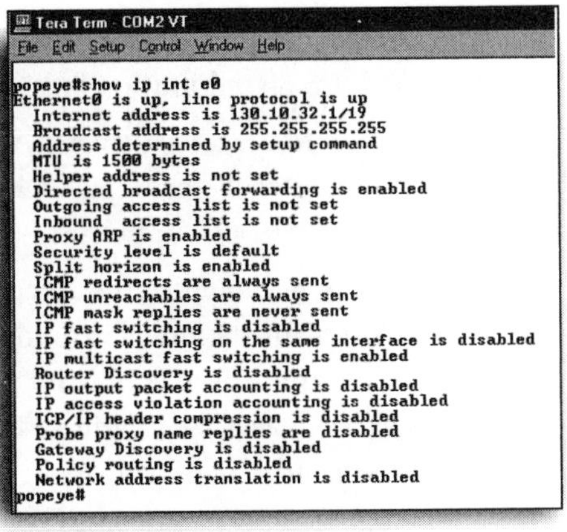

FIGURE 11.3
Check the IP addressing for an interface with the show ip interface command.

If you look at the IP information provided in Figure 11.3, the IP address reads as 130.10.32.1/19, and no subnet mask information is provided. You entered 130.10.32.1 as the IP address for the interface in the previous set of steps. So, what does the /19 mean? Actually, this is the router's way of telling you the subnet mask.

The 19 is the number of bits that are used for network addressing plus the number of bits used to create the subnets on this network. Normally, a Class B network uses two octets (16 bits) to define the network number for the network: in this case 19–16=3. This shows you the number of bits stolen for subnetting. If you take the first three high-order bits and add them (128+64+32), you get 224, which tells you that the subnet mask is 255.255.224.0.

Show all interface IP addressing

If you type the show ip interface command and don't specify a particular router interface, the IP addressing of all the interfaces on the router will be displayed.

Saving your router configuration

When you make changes to your router's configuration, you will want to save the configuration changes from RAM to NVRAM. This makes the currently running configuration file the startup configuration if the router is rebooted or powered back on after a power failure. At the privileged prompt, type `copy running-config startup-config`, and then press **Enter**. The configuration will be built and saved to NVRAM.

Whenever you see notation like the /19, just take that number and subtract the number of bits that are normally used for the class of network that you are working with. This always gives you the subnet bits, which can then be used to quickly calculate the subnet mask.

WAN Interfaces

WAN interfaces can be configured with IP addresses exactly in the same way that you configure LAN interfaces. To configure a serial 0 interface on a router, you would complete the following steps.

Configuring IP addressing for a serial interface

1. At the Privileged prompt, type `config t`, and then press **Enter**. You are placed in the Global Configuration mode.

2. To configure a particular LAN interface, type the name of the interface at the prompt, such as interface serial 0. Then press **Enter**. The prompt changes to the `config-if` mode.

3. Now you can enter the IP address command followed by the IP address for the interface and the subnet mask for the network. In this example, the command would be `ip address 130.10.64.1 255.255.224.0` (see Figure 11.4). Press **Enter** to complete the command.

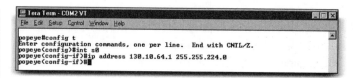

FIGURE 11.4
Individual WAN interfaces must be configured with an IP address and subnet mask.

4. To end the configuration of the interface, press **Ctrl+Z**.

5. Press **Enter** again to return to the privileged prompt.

You can use the `show ip interface s0` command to check the configuration of the serial interface.

One issue relating to the number of IP addresses you have available to configure the routers, hosts, and servers on your network rears its ugly head when you are configuring WAN interfaces. An entire subnet (an entire range of IP addresses) must be wasted to configure the serial interfaces on two routers that are connected by a particular WAN connection.

For example, in the case of our two 2505 routers in Figure 11.1, they are connected by their serial 0 interfaces (using a particular WAN connection and protocol). This connection must be configured as a separate subnet, meaning the serial 0 interface on the Branch Office A router will use one address in the chosen subnet range and the serial 0 interface on the Branch Office B router will use one address from that same subnet range. So, you basically fritter away all the other addresses in that subnet range.

To overcome this obvious waste of IP addresses, you can configure your serial interfaces without IP addresses (they will still route IP packets even though they are designated as *IP unnumbered*). The command used at the configuration prompt for the interface is ip unnumbered [interface or virtual interface]. The interface or virtual interface parameter is the designation of an actual interface, such as Ethernet 0, or a virtual interface such as loopback 0, that has been configured with an IP address (see Figure 11.5).

FIGURE 11.5
Serial interfaces can be configured as ip unnumbered, which saves IP addresses for other routers and nodes on your network.

If you use ip unnumbered on a serial interface, the serial interface that it connects to via a WAN connection must also be configured as IP unnumbered. The drawbacks of configuring a serial interface as IP unnumbered, is that you cannot Telnet to that serial interface or ping that interface (because it doesn't have its own IP address). Also, if the interface to which you "hooked" the serial port, such as Ethernet 0 (shown in Figure 11.5) goes down, you might not be able to reach the connection that the serial interface is attached to.

Configuring a Routing Protocol

After you have the interfaces on the router configured with the appropriate IP addresses and subnet mask, you can configure a routing protocol. Different Interior Routing Protocols (protocols used for routing on your internal internetwork) are available and your choice of a routing protocol will depend on the size of your internetwork. For example, RIP is fine for small internetworks but is limited to 15 hops (from router to router), making its use on large internetworks a problem. For larger internetworks you may want to use IGRP or OSPF. You will look at the configuration of RIP and the configuration of IGRP in the next two sections of this chapter.

SEE ALSO

➤ *For an overview of IP routing protocols such as RIP and IGRP, see page 93.*

Configuring RIP

RIP is a distance-vector routing protocol that uses hop count as its metric. RIP summarizes the information in the routing table by IP network numbers (also referred to as major network numbers).

Configuring RIP is very straightforward. You must first select RIP as your routing protocol and then let RIP know the major network number for each interface you have enabled for IP routing. In the sample network that you have been discussing (see Figure 11.1), you are working with only one major network number, 130.10.0.0. So, you only need to specify this network when configuring RIP on our router.

Configuring RIP

1. At the privileged prompt, type `config t`, and then press **Enter**. You are placed in the Global Configuration mode.

2. At the config prompt, type `router rip`, and then press **Enter**. This selects RIP as the routing protocol.

3. Type `network [major network number]` at the config prompt. The *major network number* is the network address for a class A, B, or C network that is directly connected to the router. In your case, you are connected to one major network 130.10.0.0. Therefore, the command would be `network 130.10.0.0` (see Figure 11.6). Press **Enter** to continue.

4. Repeat the `network [major network number]` for each IP network that the router is directly connected to. For example, if different Class C networks are connected to several Ethernet interfaces, you must repeat the `network` command for each of the network addresses for these Class C networks.

Enabling IP routing

If IP routing has been disabled on the router (it is enabled by default), you will want to enable it before configuring your routing protocol. At the config prompt, type the global command `ip routing`, and then press **Enter**. To exit the Configuration mode press **Ctrl+Z**. If for some reason you want to disable IP routing on a router, you can use the configuration command `no ip routing`.

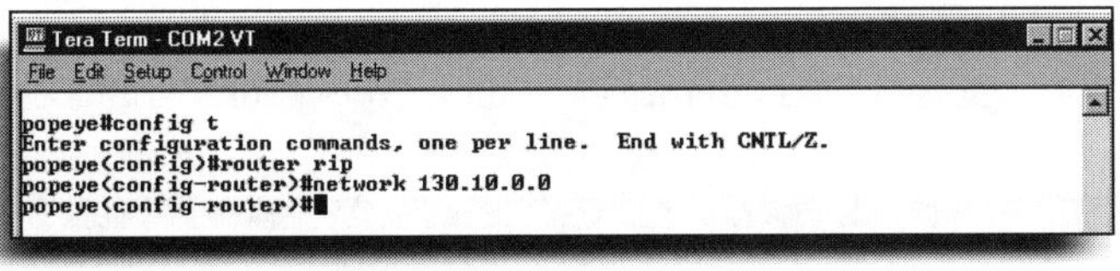

FIGURE 11.6
Router RIP selects RIP as the routing protocol and the network command specifies IP networks connected to the router.

5. When you have finished entering the directly connected networks, press **Ctrl+Z** to end the configuration session.

6. Press **Enter** to return to the Privileged prompt.

After you've configured RIP on your router, you can use the IOS commands that provide a view of RIP routing information such as the routing table and the settings for RIP broadcasts.

To view the RIP routing table, type show ip route at the user or privileged prompt and then press **Enter**. Figure 11.7 shows the results of this command on a 2505 router that is connected to another 2505 router via a serial connection. Subnets that are directly connected to the router are marked with a C (interfaces that were configured on that router). Other subnets that are reached by a particular directly connected subnet are marked with an R (these network locations are learned by RIP).

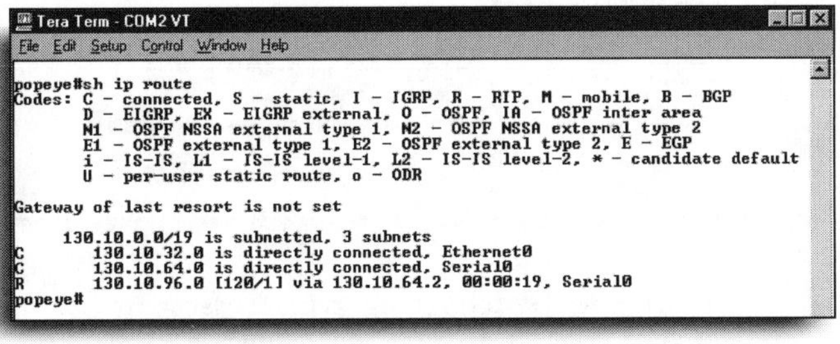

FIGURE 11.7
The show ip route command provides a view of the RIP routing table on the router.

You can use the show ip protocol command to view the timing information related to RIP. For example, RIP updates are sent every 30 seconds. The hold-down time for RIP is 180 seconds. This means that if a router doesn't receive a RIP update from a connected router, it waits 180 seconds from the last received update and then flags the subnet path as suspect. After 240 seconds, the router will actually remove the path information related to the other router from the routing table because it considers the path no longer usable.

Type show ip protocol at the user or privileged prompt and then press **Enter**. Figure 11.8 shows the results of this command.

FIGURE 11.8
The show ip proto-col command provides a view of the RIP timing settings and the net-works that are provided routing by RIP.

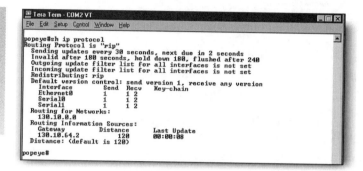

If you want to view RIP update messages as they are sent and received by a router, you can use the debug ip rip command. Type debug ip rip at the privileged prompt and then press **Enter**. Figure 11.9 shows the results of this command.

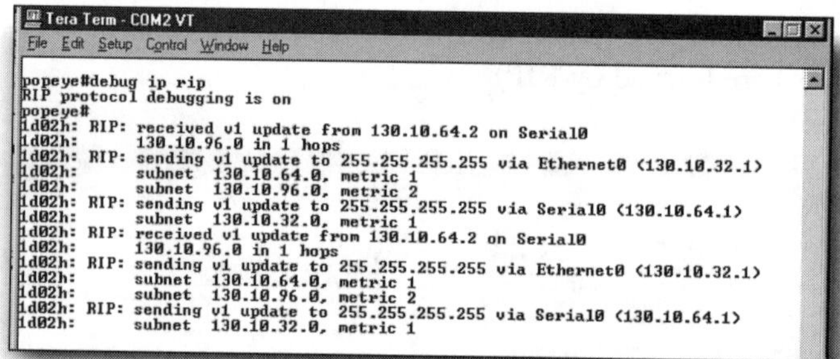

FIGURE 11.9
Use the debug ip rip command to view RIP updates on the router.

To turn off RIP debugging, type no debug ip rip and press **Enter** (otherwise the update messages will drive you crazy if you are trying to work on the router).

SEE ALSO

➤ *For information on how routers work and using routing protocols to build routing tables, see page 82.*

Configuring IGRP

Because RIP is limited to routes of less than 16 hop counts, interme-diate and large internetworks need a routing protocol that can handle the scale of the network. IGRP is a distance vector routing protocol like (RIP) that uses several metrics such as delay, bandwidth, and reliability. IGRP doesn't use hop count as a metric but it can provide routing information for a path of up to 255 hops, which makes it ideal for large internetworks.

Configuring IGRP is similar to configuring RIP. You must enable the IGRP protocol and specify the major IP networks that are directly connected to the router's interfaces. However, because IGRP is used on larger internetworks (such as a complete corporate network), you must specify the autonomous system number for the autonomous system (AS) that the router belongs to. Several different networks (Class A, B, or C) can be part of a particular autonomous system. Autonomous systems are tied together by core routers that run an Exterior Gateway Protocol, such as Border Gateway Protocol (BGP).

Configuring IGRP

1. At the privileged prompt, type `config t`, and then press **Enter**. You are placed in the Global Configuration mode.

2. At the config prompt, type `router igrp [autonomous system number]`, where the autonomous system number is the AS number assigned to the AS to which your router belongs. For example, `router igrp 10` would enable IGRP routing and specify the AS number 10. After entering the command, press **Enter**.

3. Type `network [major network number]` at the config prompt. The *major network number* is the network address for a Class A, B, or C network that is directly connected to the router. In this case, you are connected to one major network, 130.10.0.0, so the command would be `network 130.10.0.0` (see Figure 11.10). Press **Enter** to continue.

4. Repeat the `network [major network number]` for each IP network that the router is directly connected to. For example, if different Class C networks are connected to several Ethernet interfaces, you must repeat the `network` command for each of the network addresses for these Class C networks.

Creating autonomous systems

In cases where a company merges with another company or a company's network grows in leaps and bounds, you may want to employ autonomous systems (you have to if you are using IGRP as your routing protocol). Autonomous system numbers can be between 1 and 65,655. You arbitrarily assign them to your different internetworks (but use some kind of numbering system to keep it all straight). The autonomous systems are then tied together by large core routers that run an Exterior Gateway Protocol. See Appendix C, "Selected Cisco Router Specifications," for information on the 7500 series of Cisco that might be used as Core routers.

FIGURE 11.10
Router igrp [AS number] selects IGRP as the routing protocol and specifies the autonomous system that the router belongs to.

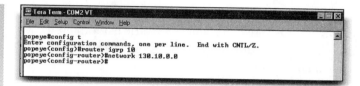

FIGURE 11.10
Router igrp [AS number] selects IGRP as the routing protocol and specifies the autonomous system that the router belongs to.

5. When you have entered the directly connected networks, press **Ctrl+Z** to end the configuration session.

You can also use the show commands (and variations of these commands related to IGRP) that were discussed in the section on RIP routing. For example, the show ip route command now shows the routing table built by IGRP (see Figure 11.11). Network addresses marked with a **C** are directly connected to the router; addresses marked with an **I** are those discovered by IGRP.

FIGURE 11.11
The show ip route command allows you to view the IGRP routing table.

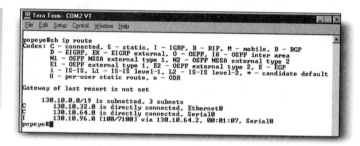

IGRP sends updates every 90 seconds (as opposed to RIP's 30-second interval). Routes not confirmed for 630 seconds are flushed from the router's routing table. You can view this information using the show ip route command.

To view a summary of the IGRP routing update messages as they exit and enter the router, use the debug ip igrp events command at the Privileged prompt. Figure 11.12 shows the results of this command.

If you want to see information related to the update messages such as the metric used (a number representing a value based on all the IGRP metrics), use the debug ip igrp transaction command. Figure 11.13 displays the results of this command.

Turn off all that debugging

To turn off all the debugging you may have enabled on a router, type no debug all at the Privileged prompt and then press **Enter**.

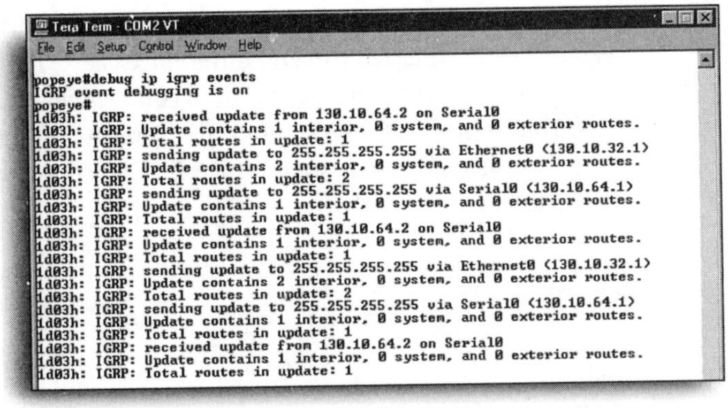

FIGURE 11.12
The debug ip igrp events command enables you to view the outgoing and incoming IGRP updates on the router.

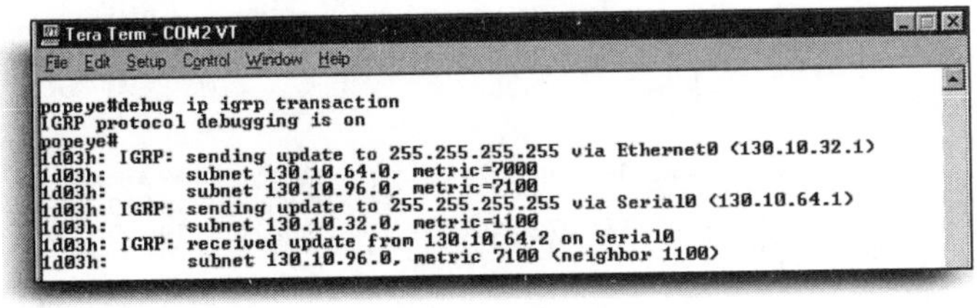

FIGURE 11.13
The debug ip igrp transaction command provides information on update messages sent and received and the metric value used.

SEE ALSO

➤ *For background information on IGRP, see page 93.*

➤ *For an overview of Exterior Gateway Protocols, see page 95.*

Dynamic Routing Versus Static Routing

The previous two sections of this chapter enabled the router for dynamic routing. The selected routing protocol (RIP or IGRP) builds a routing table using information received from neighboring routers. You can also configure your routers for *static routing* where you specify the routes in a static routing table. Static routing also requires that you update the routing tables manually.

Static routing doesn't require the use of a routing protocol. You are in charge of the routing tables. However, static routing should probably only be used in cases where the internetwork paths are fairly simple and there is only one route between the network or networks serviced by your router and another router's networks. Static routing tables cannot react to route changes because of lines going down.

Let's keep this simple and use two routers that support networks that have not been subnetted (several different Class C networks). For example, let's say you have two routers connected as shown in Figure 11.14. You want to set up a static route from the router at Branch Office A to the LAN at Branch Office B (Class C network address 194.10.30.0).

FIGURE 11.14
A small internetwork can be configured for static IP routing.

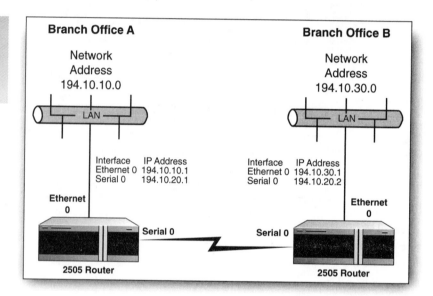

FIGURE 11.14
A small internetwork can be configured for static IP routing.

At the configuration prompt (on the Branch Office A router), you would type the command ip route 194.10.30.0 255.255.255.0 194.10.20.2. This tells your router (at Branch Office A) to build a static routing table where network 194.10.30.0 (the LAN at Branch Office B) is reached by the serial connection between the two routers, with the interface on the Branch Office B router configured with the IP address 194.10.20.2. Figure 11.15 shows how this command would look on the router console.

You would have to provide paths for all the routes served by remote routers for your Branch Office A router. And because you have a router at Branch Office B, you would have to use the ip route command to configure its static routing table to LANs serviced by other routers (such as the Branch Office A router).

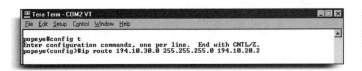

FIGURE 11.15
You configure static
routes using the ip
route command fol-
lowed by the destination
network and the IP
address of the router
interface on the router
that serves the particular
network.

As you can see, building your own routing tables statically requires a
lot of up-front work. You would also have to update the tables on all
the routers involved if any of the routes changed.

Static routing does provide you with complete control over the paths
that packets are routed on. However, on large, dynamic internetworks, dynamic routing is probably the way you will want to go
when configuring your routers.

Using Telnet

One big plus of configuring IP on your router interfaces is that you
can Telnet (connect to) another router using the IP address of one of
its interfaces. For example, you have been working with two 2505
routers connected by a serial cable. The router that you are connected to via a serial connection has an IP address of 130.96.1 on its
Ethernet 0 port and 130.10.64.2 on its Serial 0 port. You can use
either of these IP addresses to gain entry (Telnet) to the other router.
After connecting to the router, you must provide the virtual terminal
password that was configured on the router.

Using Telnet to connect to another router

1. At the user or privileged prompt, type telnet [ip address],
   where ip address is the IP address of one of the interfaces on
   the other router. To Telnet to the Olive router, directly connected via a serial connection to our Popeye router, type telnet
   130.10.96.1 (the IP address of its Ethernet 0 port), and then
   press **Enter**.

2. You are connected to the other router and asked to provide the
   virtual terminal password. Type the virtual terminal password,
   and then press **Enter**.

You are now logged on to the other router (see Figure 11.16).

FIGURE 11.16
You can Telnet to a remote router to view its configuration or to configure the router.

If you know the enable password, you can enter the Privileged mode on this router and even change the configuration of the router remotely. When you have finished working on the remote router, type quit at the prompt. You are logged off the remote router and returned to the prompt for your local router.

Telnet is a great tool for connecting to remote routers and monitoring or configuring them. It's as if you are sitting at the console computer directly connected to that router.

SEE ALSO
➤ *For information on setting the virtual terminal password when first configuring the router, see page 129.*

chapter

12

Routing Novell IPX

Introducing IPX/SPX

Novell NetWare is a popular network operating system (NOS) that has provided file and print server functionality to LANs since the early 1980s. NetWare has its own proprietary network protocol stack called *IPX/SPX*. IPX is similar to TCP/IP in that the protocols that make up the IPX/SPX stack don't directly map to the layers of the OSI model. IPX/SPX gained a strong foothold in early local area networking because it was strong on performance and did not require the overhead that is needed to run TCP/IP. For many years, NetWare was the leading NOS of choice and can provide client machines with access to LAN and WAN resources.

Novell NetWare is an excellent example of a pure client/server–based NOS. Computers on the network are either clients (who receive services) or servers (who provide services).

IPX/SPX is a routable protocol and so important to our discussion of routing and Cisco routers in particular. Figure 12.1 shows the IPX/SPX stack mapped to the OSI model. The next two sections discuss the protocols in the IPX/SPX stack and how IPX addressing works.

FIGURE 12.1
The IPX/SPX protocol is a routable stack made up of several protocols.

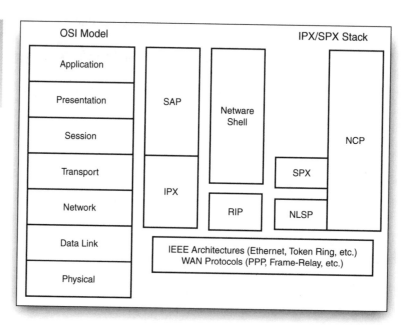

212

SEE ALSO

➤ *For a quick review of IPX/SPX in relation to other networking protocols (such as TCP/IP and AppleTalk), see page 48.*

➤ *For a quick review of the OSI model, see page 34.*

Routing-Related IPX/SPX Protocols

As with TCP/IP, a number of different protocols with different duties make up the IPX/SPX stack. For example, the *NetWare Core Protocol (NCP)* handles network functions at the Application, Presentation and Session layers of the OSI model. The *NetWare VLMs (Virtual Loadable Modules)* establish and maintain network sessions between the client and server. More important to this discussion of routing are the IPX/SPX protocols that are involved in the routing process:

- *SPX (Sequence Packet Exchange)*—A connection-oriented transport protocol that provides the upper-layer protocols with a direct connection between the sending and receiving machines. SPX uses virtual circuits to provide the connection between computers and will display a connection ID in the SPX datagram header (SPX is similar to TCP in the TCP/IP protocol).

- *IPX (Internet Package Exchange Program)*—A connectionless transport protocol, IPX provides the addressing system for the IPX/SPX stack. Operating at the Network and Transport layers of the OSI model, IPX directs the movement of packets on the internetwork using information that it gains from the IPX Routing Information Protocol (RIP).

- *RIP(Routing Information Protocol)*—A routing protocol that uses two metrics, *clock ticks* (1/18 of a second) and *hop count*, to route packets through an IPX internetwork. IPX RIP (like TCP/IP RIP) is a distance vector-routing protocol that builds and maintains routing tables between IPX-enabled routers and NetWare servers.

- *SAP (Service Advertisement Protocol)*—A protocol that advertises the availability of various resources on the NetWare network. NetWare servers broadcast SAP packets every 60 seconds, letting client machines on the network know where file and print

NetWare derived from XNS

In the 1960s, a bunch of geniuses at the Xerox Palo Alto Research Center developed the *XNS (Xerox Network Systems)* network operating system. NetWare is based heavily on this early networking protocol stack. This group of computer scientists and engineers also developed a networked computer that had a graphical user interface and used both a mouse and keyboard as input devices. The technology developed at Palo Alto predates both the IBM PC and the Apple Macintosh. A lot of great ideas came out of this one think tank. So, why doesn't Xerox own the computer world today? Good question.

services can be accessed (each type of service is denoted by a different hexadecimal number in the SAP packets).

- *NLSP (NetWare Link Services Protocol)*—A Novell-developed link-state routing protocol that can be used to replace RIP (and SAP) as the configured routing protocol for IPX routing. The RIP/SAP relationship will be discussed further in the "Configuring IPX Routing" section of this chapter.

As you can see from the discussion of TCP/IP in Chapter 10, "TCP/IP Primer," IPX/SPX is a comparable stack (although it does operate somewhat differently). It has several different protocols that operate at the lower layers of the OSI model (Networking and Data Link) and are involved in the routing process. Before you learn how these protocols interact to make routing of the IPX/SPX packets a reality, you'll learn how IPX/SPX provides an addressing system that defines networks and clients on the network.

Understanding IPX Addressing

IPX addressing uses an 80-bit (10 byte) system (remember, TCP/IP used a 32-bit system), which is comprised of both network and node information, making it a hierarchical addressing system like IP addresses. IPX addresses appear in hexadecimal format and are broken down into two parts. The first part of the address, which can be up to 16 hexadecimal characters in length (this part of the address is 32 bits), is the *IPX network number*. The remaining 12 hexadecimal digits in the address make up the node address (which makes up the remaining 48 bits of the address). Figure 12.2 shows a typical IPX address for a node on a Novell network.

The question then arises as to where the network number comes from and where you get the node address information. I'll discuss the network number first.

When the first NetWare server is brought online in a Novell LAN, a network number is generated during the server software installation. This hexadecimal number becomes the network number for the LAN, no matter how many additional NetWare servers (additional file and print servers) are added to the LAN. So, all client machines (and additional servers) on the LAN will be assigned the same network number (such as 763B20F3, shown in Figure 12.2).

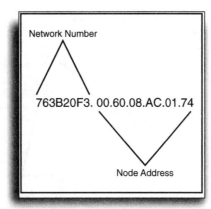

FIGURE 12.2
The IPX addresses consist of a network number and a node address.

When another new LAN (a separate network entity from the first LAN brought online) is brought into service, its network number will be provided by the first NetWare server brought online on that particular LAN. So, IPX networks are differentiated by their network numbers (whereas IP networks were differentiated by their subnet masks and the subnet bits in the IP addresses). Any routers that play a part in routing packets from a particular LAN will be configured with the network number for that NetWare LAN. This means that the Ethernet 0 interface on the router is connected to a particular NetWare LAN, so it will use that LAN's network number in its interface configuration.

Dealing with the node address for IPX clients is a real no-brainer. It is actually dynamically assigned to the nodes on the network and consists of the MAC address on their network interface card. So, an IPX address is the network number followed by the computer's MAC address. Figure 12.3 shows two nodes and a server on the same NetWare LAN.

SEE ALSO

➤ *For information on MAC hardware addresses, see page 41.*

➤ *For a quick review of network interface cards, see page 13.*

So, how do I get the network number?

If you aren't the NetWare LAN administrator, you are, obliviously, going to have to ask the person in charge of the IPX network to give you the network number so that you can correctly configure your router interfaces. If you are the NetWare administrator, load the monitor utility on the server (type `load monitor` at the server prompt, and then press **Enter**) and then open the Network information screens from the Monitor window.

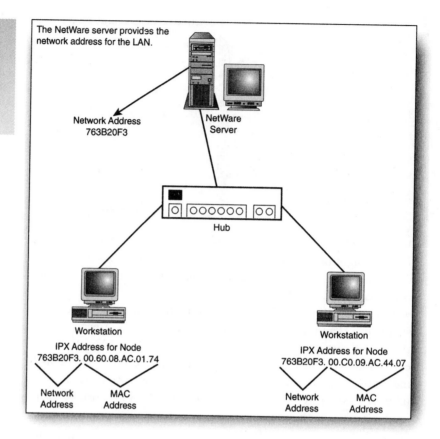

FIGURE 12.3
The IPX addresses for clients on the network will consist of the network number and the client's MAC address.

The NetWare server provides the network address for the LAN.

Network Address
763B20F3

NetWare Server

Hub

Workstation
IPX Address for Node
763B20F3. 00.60.08.AC.01.74

Network Address   MAC Address

Workstation
IPX Address for Node
763B20F3. 00.C0.09.AC.44.07

Network Address   MAC Address

Understanding SAP

One other aspect of NetWare that I must discuss before I can turn to the configuration aspects of IPX on a router is the part that SAP broadcasts play in IPX networking. Novell servers broadcast SAP announcements every 60 seconds. These broadcasts consist of all the services provided by the server making the SAP announcement and any other services that the server has learned about that are provided by other NetWare servers. The information that a particular server has gathered about other servers and the services they offer is logged in the server's SAP table.

When a particular server broadcasts a SAP advertisement, it is actually broadcasting its entire SAP table and is providing the SAP information to any server (or router) on the network that cares to listen (and all servers do). This means that the SAP information is shared among the servers.

Cisco routers that have interfaces configured for IPX will also build SAP tables and broadcast their SAP information to the networks that the router's interfaces are connected to. Cisco routers don't, however, forward SAP broadcasts from one Novell LAN to another but broadcast their own SAP table (which is a summary of the services offered by each LAN connected to a different router interface). The router provides a summary of all the different LAN SAP tables to each of the different networks. Figure 12.4 shows how the Cisco router would collect the SAP tables from the different networks.

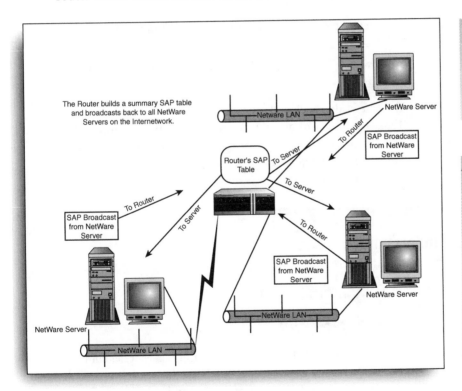

FIGURE 12.4
SAP broadcasts are sent from servers to the router and from the router to the servers.

Client/server communications

When clients on a Novell network want a particular service, they use a broadcast message called a GNS (Get Nearest Server request) to advertise their particular need. A server on the network receiving the GNS will check its SAP table to see where that particular resource (such as a file or printer) is kept. The Server will then send a GNS response to the client, letting it know which server hosts that particular service.

Configuring IPX Routing

Now that you have a feel for how IPX addresses work and the IPX/SPX protocols that are involved in routing, you can configure a router for IPX routing. First, you must start the IPX routing process, and then individual interfaces can be configured.

Enabling IPX Routing

1. At the privileged prompt, type `config t`, and then press **Enter**. This places you in the Global Configuration mode and you are configuring from the console terminal ("t").

2. Type `ipx routing` at the configuration prompt, and then press **Enter**. The configuration command is entered (see Figure 12.5).

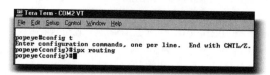

FIGURE 12.5
Enabling IPX routing only takes one global command in the Configuration mode.

3. To complete the process and exit the Configuration mode, press **Ctrl+Z**.

4. You may have to press **Enter** again to return to the privileged mode prompt.

You can easily check and see whether IPX routing has been enabled. Type `show protocol` at the prompt and then press **Enter**. A list of the network protocols enabled for routing will appear (see Figure 12.6). Information related to the protocols is also provided for the interfaces on the router.

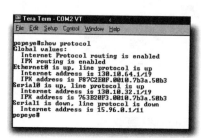

FIGURE 12.6
List the enabled network protocols with the show protocol command.

When you turn on IPX routing using the `ipx routing` command, this also automatically configures IPX RIP as the routing protocol. As mentioned before, RIP uses hop counts and clock ticks as the metric (the RIP used for IP routing used only hop counts). The way in which the two metrics work together is pretty straightforward, if two paths to a particular destination are found (using a router's IPX routing table) that have the same hop count (say, five hops). The more recent of the entries in the routing table, the path with the least number of clock ticks, will be used as the route for the packets. The reverse is also true; when paths have the same tick count, the path with the fewest number of hops is chosen.

Figure 12.7 shows an IPX internetwork where two paths exist between two computers (one sending, one receiving). The paths have the same number of hops (2). If you look at the ticks for the IPX route via Network 2 (a serial connection between router A and one of its neighbors), however, it has only 3 ticks, making it the path that router A will use to forward the packets.

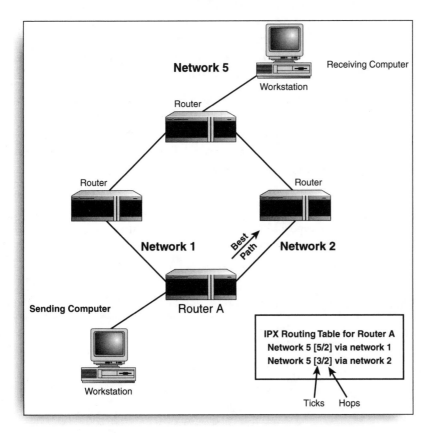

Network 5

Receiving Computer

Workstation

Router

Router

Router

Network 1

Best Path

Network 2

Sending Computer

Router A

IPX Routing Table for Router A
Network 5 [5/2] via network 1
Network 5 [3/2] via network 2

Workstation

Ticks   Hops

FIGURE 12.7
IPX rip uses hop count and tick count as its metrics.

What's the node address?

The format for the command that turns on IPX routing is `ipx routing node`, where *node* is the MAC address of the interface. If you don't enter a node number (MAC address), it is entered automatically for you. Because serial interfaces don't have MAC addresses, they actually "borrow" the MAC address of one of the Ethernet ports on the router for IPX routing. You learn more about this in the section "Configuring Router Interfaces with IPX."

Configuring Router Interfaces with IPX

After IPX routing has been globally enabled, you can configure the router interfaces that you will route IPX on. The interfaces must be configured for a particular IPX network (dictated by the network number generated by the first Novell server up and running on that LAN). Because the node numbers are supplied by the MAC addresses of the interfaces, you don't have to worry about that.

It would seem that configuring IPX is easier than dealing with IP routing. But hold on, IPX throws its own curve at you related to the encapsulation type set on LAN interfaces on the router.

LAN Interfaces

All data on a network is encapsulated in a particular frame type as it moves over the network media as a bit stream. Encapsulation is pretty straightforward with LAN protocols: Ethernet networks use an Ethernet frame, Token Ring networks use a Token Ring frame, FDDI networks use an FDDI frame.

Well unfortunately, NetWare supports more than one frame type for the popular LAN architectures—Ethernet, Token Ring, and FDDI. And if you don't configure your interfaces with the correct frame type or types, they aren't going to talk to nodes on the network or other routers on the internetwork.

NetWare actually supports four different frame types for Ethernet. Because Ethernet networks are so common, Table 12.1 describes each frame type and where you might run into it. The Cisco IOS command (the word you use to set the Ethernet frame type on an interface) is also supplied.

Table 12.1 Ethernet Frame Types

Novell Ethernet Frame Type	Where You Find It	Cisco IOS Command
Ethernet 802.3	Default Frame Type for early versions of NetWare (versions 2–3.11). This is the default frame type chosen when you enable IPX routing on the router.	novell-ether
Ethernet 802.2	Default Frame Type for NetWare versions 3.12–5.	sap

Novell Ethernet Frame Type	Where You Find It	Cisco IOS Command
Ethernet II	Used in networks running TCP/IP and/or DECnet.	arpa
Ethernet SNAP	Used in networks running TCP/IP and/or AppleTalk.	snap

NetWare supports multiple Token Ring and FDDI frames

Not only does Novell support more than one Ethernet frame type, but it also supports multiple Token Ring and FDDI frames. For Token Ring, it supports standard Token Ring and Token Ring Snap. For FDDI, it supports FDDI SNAP, FDDI 802.2, and FDDI RAW (FDDI frames that don't meet the IEEE specs).

You can specify multiple frame types (encapsulations) on a particular router interface, but each encapsulation must use a separate network number. You are, in effect, using different "virtual" networks to route the different frame types over an interface (when you check the network number on a NetWare server as described in the earlier sidebar, there is actually a different network number provided for each of the different Ethernet frame types).

So, configuring a LAN interface for IPX means that you must supply the network number and the encapsulation type (or types) for the interface. The node address is a given because it is the MAC address of the interface.

Configuring IPX on LAN Interface

1. At the Privileged prompt, type config t, and then press **Enter**. This places you in the global configuration mode and you are configuring from the console terminal ("t").

2. To configure an Ethernet port for IPX (such as Ethernet 0), type interface ethernet 0 at the configuration prompt, and then press **Enter**. The configuration prompt changes to config-if, letting you know that you can now enter the IPX information for the interface.

3. Type ipx network : ipx network "*network number*" encapsulation "*frame type*", where *network number* is the NetWare network number provided to you by the NetWare administrator. You must also provide the encapsulation type in this compound command. Suppose you are connecting an Ethernet interface to a Novell network that is running Novell IntraNetWare 4.11. This NOS uses the Ethernet 802.3 frame (the Cisco IOS command is sap). Therefore, a complete command would be ipx network f87c2e0f encapsulation sap (see Figure 12.8). Press **Enter** to execute the command.

FIGURE 12.8
You must provide the network number and the encapsulation type to configure a LAN interface for IPX.

4. To complete the process and exit the Configuration mode, press **Ctrl+Z**.

5. You might have to press **Enter** again to return to the Privileged mode prompt.

Now you can take a look at the IPX configuration for a particular interface. For example, to check out my Ethernet 0 interface (after configuring it for IPX), I would type show ipx interface Ethernet 0 and then press **Enter**. Figure 12.9 shows the IPX information for Ethernet 0 on a 2505 router.

FIGURE 12.9
You can check the network number and encapsulation on a router interface.

```
popeye#show ipx interface ethernet 0
Ethernet0 is up, line protocol is up
  IPX address is F87C2E0F.0010.7b3a.50b3, SAP [up]
  Delay of this IPX network, in ticks is 1 throughput 0 link delay 0
  IPXWAN processing not enabled on this interface.
  IPX SAP update interval is 1 minute(s)
  IPX type 20 propagation packet forwarding is disabled
  Incoming access list is not set
  Outgoing access list is not set
  IPX helper access list is not set
  SAP GNS processing enabled, delay 0 ms, output filter list is not set
  SAP Input filter list is not set
  SAP Output filter list is not set
  SAP Router filter list is not set
  Input filter list is not set
  Output filter list is not set
  Router filter list is not set
  Netbios Input host access list is not set
  Netbios Input bytes access list is not set
  Netbios Output host access list is not set
  Netbios Output bytes access list is not set
  Updates each 60 seconds, aging multiples RIP: 3 SAP: 3
  SAP interpacket delay is 55 ms, maximum size is 480 bytes
  RIP interpacket delay is 55 ms, maximum size is 432 bytes
  IPX accounting is disabled
  IPX fast switching is configured (enabled)
  RIP packets received 0, RIP packets sent 170
  SAP packets received 0, SAP packets sent 4
popeye#
popeye#
```

You can view all the IPX-enabled interfaces

To view all the interfaces on a router enabled for IPX, type show ipx interface and then press **Enter**. All the enabled interfaces will be listed with their network number and encapsulation type.

SEE ALSO

➤ *For an overview of the Cisco IOS and the different IOS modes, see page 142.*

WAN Interfaces

Serial interfaces (using WAN protocols) are configured exactly the same way that you configure a LAN interface for IPX. However, because WAN protocols use their own encapsulation types (they use the frame type supported by the WAN protocol that they are configured for), you don't have to provide an encapsulation type with the IPX network number as you do for LAN interfaces. The encapsulation type for WAN interfaces is set with a separate command where you have to provide a WAN encapsulation method such as PPP or Frame-Relay. The default is HDLC (you will learn how to set different WAN encapsulations like HDLC, Frame-Relay, and PPP in Chapter 15, "Configuring WAN Protocols").

Figure 12.10 shows the configuration parameters for a Serial O interface on a 2505 router. One thing that you must remember when configuring serial interfaces is that two connected serial interfaces (two routers connected to their serial interfaces by a Frame-Relay connection) must inhabit the same IPX network. This isn't unlike IP routing where connected serial interfaces had to be on the same IP subnet.

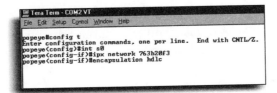

FIGURE 12.10
The IPX configuration of a serial interface.

SEE ALSO
➤ *For a quick review of WAN protocols such as HDLC and PPP, see page 65.*

Monitoring IPX Routing

After you've configured your router or routers to route IPX, you can view the IPX routing tables that are built by the routers. These tables show the networks that the router is directly connected to and other networks that the router has learned about from other routers. You can enter this command in the User or Privileged mode: type show ipx route. Then press **Enter**.

Figure 12.11 shows the IPX routing table for a 2505 router connected to another 2505 router via a serial connection. Notice that two networks (763B20F3 and F87C2E0F) are directly connected to the router (denoted with a capital C). Also notice that Network

B86C033F (connected to the Ethernet 0 interface on the other router) is shown in the routing information and can be reached in 7 ticks and 1 hop (7/1).

FIGURE 12.11
You can view the IPX routing table for a router.

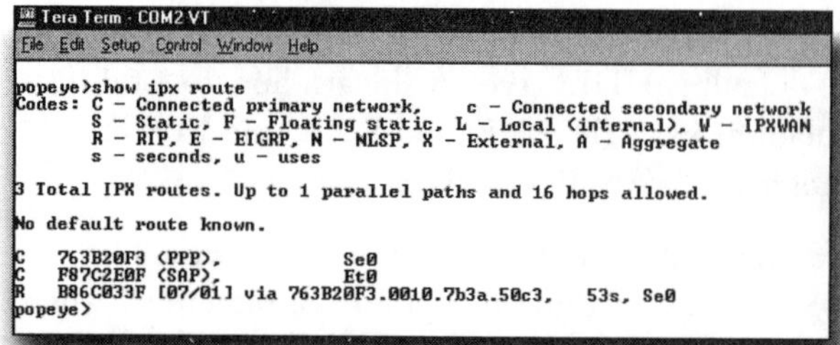

This network is in the routing table because this router received IPX routing information from the other router that it is connected to. This is how IPX routing tables and routing tables in general, no matter the protocol, are built. Connected routers share information about the internetwork topology.

A couple of other commands that you may find useful when monitoring IPX routing are show ipx traffic and debug ipx routing activity. The show ipx traffic command enables you to view the number and type of IPX packets that have been sent and received by your router. Figure 12.12 shows the syntax for this command and its results.

FIGURE 12.12
show ipx traffic enables you to view the IPX packets sent and received.

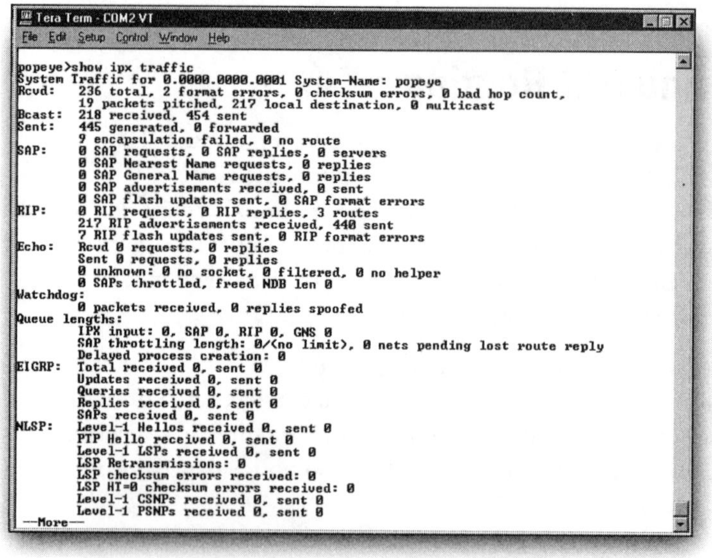

The `debug ipx routing activity` command is a little different in that it doesn't provide a static table of information like the `show ipx route` and `show ipx traffic` commands (those commands are like snapshots of the current status of the router). It actually lets you see the RIP and SAP broadcasts as your router sends and receives them. You must execute this command in the Privileged mode.

```
Tera Term - COM2 VT
File  Edit  Setup  Control  Window  Help

popeye#debug ipx routing activity
IPX routing debugging is on
popeye#
1d02h: IPXRIP: positing full update to 763B20F3.ffff.ffff.ffff via Serial0 (broadcast
)
1d02h: IPXRIP: src=763B20F3.0010.7b3a.50b3, dst=763B20F3.ffff.ffff.ffff, packet sent
1d02h:       network F87C2E0F, hops 1,  delay 7
1d02h: IPXRIP: update from 763B20F3.0010.7b3a.50c3
1d02h:       B86C033F in 1 hops, delay 7
1d02h: IPXRIP: positing full update to F87C2E0F.ffff.ffff.ffff via Ethernet0 (broadca
st)
1d02h: IPXRIP: src=F87C2E0F.0010.7b3a.50b3, dst=F87C2E0F.ffff.ffff.ffff, packet sent
1d02h:       network B86C033F, hops 2,  delay 8
1d02h:       network 763B20F3, hops 1,  delay 2
```

FIGURE 12.13
The debug command enables you to view RIP and SAP broadcast updates as they come in.

After you turn on debugging, you will find that you really can't do a whole lot else on the router because incoming broadcasts keep interrupting your commands. This next command is pretty much worth the price of this book: `no debug ipx routing activity`. This command shuts off the IPX debugging. Never turn it on if you can't remember how to turn it off.

chapter 13

Routing AppleTalk

Understanding AppleTalk •

Configuring AppleTalk Routing •

Monitoring AppleTalk routing •

Understanding AppleTalk

AppleTalk is a routable network protocol stack that provides network connectivity for peer computers (typically Apple Macintosh computers) that want to share files and other network resources such as printers. AppleTalk has its own strategy for network addressing and the grouping of computers into logical workgroups, called *zones*.

Because there always seems to be at least a few Apple computers at every company or institution for multimedia and desktop publishing tasks, it makes sense to be able to route AppleTalk on a Cisco router and allow these computers to share information over an internetwork.

Macintosh computers come equipped with a built-in network interface that can be attached to a hub or other connectivity device using an Apple shielded twisted-pair cable (You have been able to network Macs since they arrived on the scene. The new PowerMacs and G3 computers ship with built-in Ethernet ports). Macintoshes that are integrated into other network architectures can be outfitted with an additional network interface card for that particular architecture (such as an EtherTalk card). AppleTalk supports Ethernet (EtherTalk), Token Ring (TokenTalk), and FDDI (FDDITalk).

Figure 13.1 shows the protocols in the AppleTalk stack that reside at the lower levels of the OSI model. These protocols are used by computers and routers on the internetwork to exchange information such as the location of resources (a server or printer) These protocols are discussed in the following list:

- *DDP (Datagram Delivery Protocol)*—A Network layer protocol that provides a connectionless datagram delivery system similar to UDP in the TCP/IP stack.

- *AARP (AppleTalk Address Resolution Protocol)*—A Network layer protocol that resolves AppleTalk network addresses with hardware addresses. AARP sends broadcasts to all stations on the network to match hardware addresses to logical destination addresses for packets.

- *ZIP (Zone Information Protocol)*—A Network and Transport layer protocol that is used to assign logical network addresses to nodes on the network. This protocol is discussed in more detail in the next section.

- *RTMP (Routing Table Maintenance Protocol)*—A Transport layer protocol that is responsible for establishing and maintaining routing tables on routers that are enabled to route AppleTalk. Routers periodically broadcast routing table information to neighboring routers providing the hops to and the location of AppleTalk networks on the internetwork.

- *NBP (Name Binding Protocol)*—A Transport layer protocol that maps lower layer addresses to AppleTalk names that identify a particular network resource such as a printer server that is accessible over the internetwork.

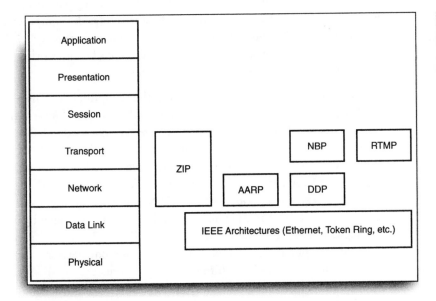

FIGURE 13.1
The routing-associated protocols of the AppleTalk stack mapped to the OSI model.

SEE ALSO

➤ *For general information on AppleTalk in relation to other networking architectures and a look at the AppleTalk protocol stack, see page 49.*

AppleTalk Addressing

AppleTalk uses a 24-bit addressing system that identifies the network segment that the node exists on and the node address itself, which identifies the actual workstation or server.

AppleTalk phase 1 versus AppleTalk phase 2

There have actually been two different phases of AppleTalk: 1 and 2. AppleTalk phase 1 limited the assignment of network numbers to a physical network segment to one network number per physical network. The number of nodes on that network was limited to 127, and the number of servers was limited to 127, making the total number of possible computers 254. AppleTalk phase 2 supplies you with the ability to assign multiple network numbers to the physical network wire and place an unlimited number of nodes and servers on that wire. Phase 2 also allows multiple zones per network. Our discussion of AppleTalk in this chapter will assume the use of AppleTalk phase 2 (which is the appropriate addressing scheme for properly configuring Cisco routers for the routing of AppleTalk).

Dynamic addressing versus static addressing

As already noted, Macintosh computers dynamically generate a network node number on the network. In stark contrast is Novell NetWare (running IPX/SPX) where the node address is assigned statically using the computer's MAC hardware address.

The network address is 16 bits long and the node address portion of the AppleTalk address is 8 bits. Because the number of bits is always fixed for network and node address, you cannot subnet AppleTalk networks as you can with IP addressing. Written in dotted decimal format, the AppleTalk address for particular node would take the format: network.node.

Network addresses are assigned to the various AppleTalk networks by the network administrator and can be a single number designating one network on the network wire or it can be a range of network numbers specifying a number of networks on the same wire. For example, a network address designated as 10-10 means that only one network (network 10) exists on the physical wire that the computers, various hubs, and printers are connected to. A range such as 100-130 would designate multiple networks inhabiting the same network wire. This would be referred to as a *cable range*.

When multiple network numbers inhabit the same AppleTalk network segment this segment is called an *extended segment*. Those with only one network number are called *nonextended*. Each extended network segment can have 253 node numbers associated with each of the network numbers assigned to that particular physical network. Figure 13.2 shows an AppleTalk internetwork with a large LAN made up of extended segments and a LAN that is a nonextended segment. The fact that multiple network addresses can be assigned to the segment (with each network number limited to 253 nodes) makes it possible to put a large number of nodes on any one network segment. Remember that the 8-bit node address limits the number of nodes available, so increasing the number of network addresses available on the network segment increases the number of nodes you can place on it.

AppleTalk node addresses are very easy for the network administrator to deal with because they are dynamically assigned. When a Macintosh comes online with the network, the computer will send out a ZIP broadcast to determine the network number or range of network numbers available on the wire. It will also generate a random node number. The node determines whether the node number is already in use by issuing an *AARP broadcast*.

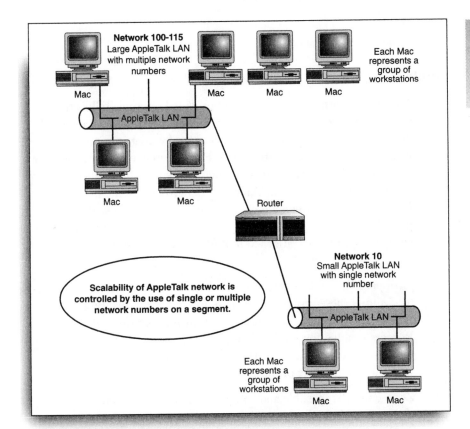

FIGURE 13.2
Extended AppleTalk segments connected by a router.

If the chosen node address on the network number is already taken, the computer will generate another random node address and send out a new AARP broadcast. If the computer finds that all the node numbers are used up on a particular network number, it will choose a new network number and then continue to attempt to take possession of random node addresses on that network (in cases where extended segments have been configured).

After the computer finds a network number and an appropriate node number combination that is available, it will use that address (network.node) as its permanent network address. For example, a computer on network 10 that takes possession of node number 200 would have the permanent address of 10.200.

SEE ALSO
➤ *For information on IP subnetting, see page 180.*

➤ *For information on IP subnetting, see page 180.*

AppleTalk Zones

Another network management tool provided by AppleTalk is the ability to divide the AppleTalk network into zones. *Zones* are logical groupings of users, similar to the concept of workgroups in Microsoft peer-to-peer networking. For example, you may have your desktop publishing staff spread throughout your building; let's say you have Mac users in the Marketing department, some in the Publications department, and so on. You can group these desktop publishers into a logical networking group (known as a *logical zone*) even though they are attached to different segments of the physical AppleTalk network.

Grouping all the desktop publishing staff into the logical zone "desktop" allows these groups to advertise for and access printing and other network services that are spread throughout the building. Routers enabled for AppleTalk will actually build zone tables that can forward broadcast messages from segment to segment on the network, if they are part of the same logical zone.

Zone names are flexible and contain alphanumeric and numeric characters. Marketing1 would be a legal zone name as would destkopA1. Figure 13.3 illustrates the concept of combining AppleTalk LAN segments into the same zone.

Configuring AppleTalk Routing

When you enable AppleTalk on your routers and then appropriately configure the router interfaces, the routers will build routing tables that contain network path information much like IP networks. These routing tables allow routers on the internetwork to forward packets on to the appropriate router as the packets move from the sending node to the receiving node.

Before you can configure the router interfaces for AppleTalk routing, you must use a global configuration command to turn AppleTalk routing on.

Reserved node numbers

AppleTalk does reserve certain node numbers from the pool of 255 numbers—0, 254, and 255. The node number 0 is reserved for temporary use by nodes attempting to determine which network they reside on. Node numbers 254 and 255 are used in broadcast messages to the network, so they cannot be assigne

Learning more about AppleTalk networking

AppleTalk is actually a very sophisticated network protocol stack and as robust and complex as TCP/IP or IPX/SPX. Although you will probably run into AppleTalk less frequently than these other two network protocol stacks, it is still a very viable protocol because Apple computers are common in the desktop publishing and multimedia realms. Because this book is about routers and how they work, the coverage of AppleTalk is limited to broad principles and its addressing system in relation to routing. For more general information on AppleTalk, check out Apple Computer's article library at `http://til.info.a pple.com`. Additional documentation on AppleTalk and the Cisco IOS can be found at `www.cisco.com`.

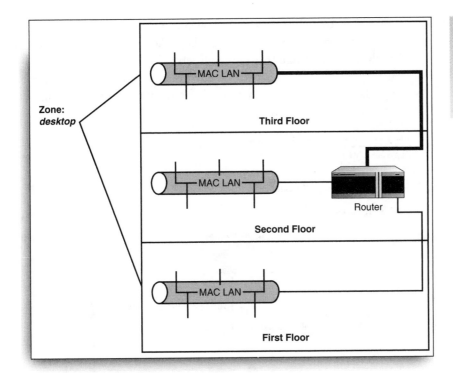

FIGURE 13.3
AppleTalk zones can be used to "join" network segments into one logical workgroup.

Enabling AppleTalk Routing

1. At the Privileged prompt type config t, and then press **Enter**.

2. Type appletalk routing, and then press **Enter** (see Figure 13.4).

3. To end the configuration session, press **Ctrl+Z**.

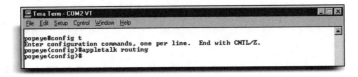

FIGURE 13.4
AppleTalk routing must be enabled on the router before interfaces can be configured.

4. Press **Enter** to return to the Privileged prompt.

When you use the appletalk routing command, RTMP is configured automatically as the AppleTalk routing protocol, so it doesn't have to be configured separately (as RIP and other IP routing protocols did).

Now that AppleTalk routing has been enabled, the interfaces that will be involved in routing AppleTalk packets can be configured. Both the cable range (the range of networks on each segment) and the AppleTalk zones that will be used must be configured on each interface. Figure 13.5 shows two different sites connected using 2505 routers.

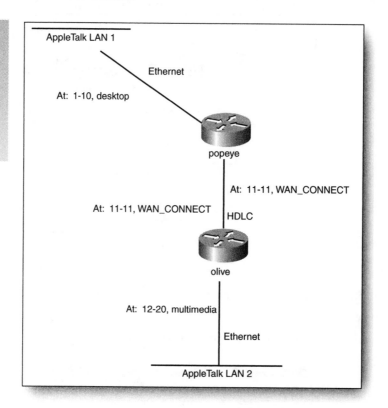

AppleTalk LAN 1

Ethernet

At: 1-10, desktop

popeye

At: 11-11, WAN_CONNECT

At: 11-11, WAN_CONNECT

HDLC

olive

At: 12-20, multimedia

Ethernet

AppleTalk LAN 2

Each LAN uses a cable range (providing a greater number of node addressing possibilities) and the WAN connection uses one network address (which much be configured on the serial port of each connected router). For convenience, the WAN connection is also provided a zone name: WANCONNECT.

Table 13.1 summarizes the configuration information for the AppleTalk network shown in Figure 13.5. We will use this configuration information as examples when we configure the LAN and WAN interfaces for AppleTalk in the next two sections of this chapter.

Table 13.1 AppleTalk Network Configuration Information

Router	Interface	Cable Range	Zone
Popeye	Ethernet 0	1–10	Desktop
	Serial 0	11	WANCONNECT
Olive	Ethernet 0	12–20	Multimedia
	Serial 0	11	WANCONNECT

Configuring LAN Interfaces

Configuring LAN interfaces for AppleTalk is very similar to configuring LAN interfaces for IP or IPX. Network and zone information must be supplied in the Configuration mode for the interface you want to configure.

Configuring a LAN interface for AppleTalk

1. At the privileged prompt type `config t`, and then press **Enter**. You will be placed in the Global Configuration mode.

2. Type `interface ethernet 0` (remember you can abbreviate your commands), and then press **Enter**.

3. At the config-if prompt type `appletalk cable-range 1-10`, and then press **Enter**. (Use the cable range you have determined for your AppleTalk LAN.) This specifies the cable range for the LAN that is connected to the LAN interface on the router.

4. To specify the zone for the interface, type `appletalk zone desktop`. Desktop is the name I am using as a sample LAN zone; you would enter the name of your zone. Then press **Enter** (see Figure 13.6).

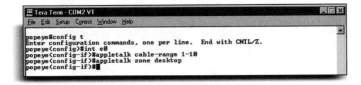

FIGURE 13.6
LAN interfaces must be configured with network and zone information.

Configuring other LAN types

The example given for configuring AppleTalk on a LAN interface uses an Ethernet interface. AppleTalk also supports Token Ring and FDDI. So if you were configuring a Token Ring interface (the first one on the router) for the routing of AppleTalk, you would supply the network and zone information for the Token Ring 0 interface.

5. To end the configuration press **Ctrl+Z**.

6. Press **Enter** to return to the privileged prompt.

This procedure would be repeated for each LAN interface you want to enable to support AppleTalk routing. Remember to provide the correct network range and zone information for each interface. Inadvertently using the same cable range twice would be similar to using the same IP address on two different router interfaces; you won't get the routing that you expect between the networks.

Configuring WAN Interfaces

Configuring WAN interfaces is very straightforward. You must configure the serial ports involved on each router for the appropriate WAN protocol. You must also configure these interfaces with the appropriate network and zone information. Two routers connected via their serial interfaces will have the serial interfaces configured so that they are on the same network and same zone (similar to IP addressing, where both routers must have the connected serial interfaces on the same IP subnet).

Configuring a WAN interface for AppleTalk

1. At the privileged prompt type `config t`, and then press **Enter**. You will be placed in the Global Configuration mode.

2. Type `interface serial 0` (remember you can abbreviate your commands), and then press **Enter**.

3. At the config-if prompt type `appletalk cable-range 11`. Use the network number you have determined for your WAN connection. Then press **Enter**.

4. To specify the zone for the interface, type `appletalk zone wan-connect` (`wanconnect` is used to provide a zone name for the serial connection and also used as a reminder that this is a WAN connection). Then press **Enter** (see Figure 13.7).

5. To end the configuration press **Ctrl+Z**.

6. Press **Enter** to return to the privileged prompt.

SEE ALSO

➤ *For information on configuring a number of the commonly used WAN protocols on a Cisco router, see page 259.*

```
Tera Term - COM2 VT
File Edit Setup Control Window Help
popeye#config t
Enter configuration commands, one per line.  End with CNTL/Z.
popeye(config)#int s0
popeye(config-if)#appletalk cable-range 11-11
popeye(config-if)#appletalk zone wanconnect
popeye(config-if)#
```

FIGURE 13.7
WAN interfaces must be configured with network and zone information.

Monitoring AppleTalk Routing

After AppleTalk has been enabled on the router and the appropriate router interfaces have been configured, you can view the AppleTalk routing tables on a router and view the configuration of the various interfaces. You can also view statistics related to the AppleTalk traffic on the network including packets sent and received by the router.

To take a look at the routing table for a particular router, type show appletalk route at the user or privileged prompt and then press **Enter**. Figure 13.8 shows the routing table for a 2505 router that has its Ethernet 0 interface connected to an AppleTalk LAN and a serial connection to another 2505 router via its Serial 0 interface. The network ranges marked with a C are directly connected to the router. The network range (12–20) marked with an R is another AppleTalk LAN reached via the serial connection to the other router (refer to Figure 13.5 for a diagram showing how these AppleTalk networks are connected).

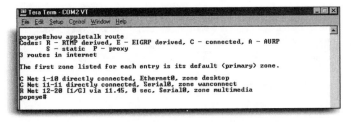

```
Tera Term - COM2 VT
File Edit Setup Control Window Help
popeye#show appletalk route
Codes: R - RTMP derived, E - EIGRP derived, C - connected, A - AURP
       S - static  P - proxy
3 routes in internet

The first zone listed for each entry is its default (primary) zone.

C Net 1-10 directly connected, Ethernet0, zone desktop
C Net 11-11 directly connected, Serial0, zone wanconnect
R Net 12-20 [1/G] via 11.45, 0 sec, Serial0, zone multimedia
popeye#
```

FIGURE 13.8
Use the show appletalk route command to view the AppleTalk routing table on your router.

Several show related commands are useful for monitoring the AppleTalk setup on the router. You can view information related to a particular interface or use a broader command that shows AppleTalk configuration information for all enabled interfaces. You can also view AppleTalk zones and their associated network ranges. Table 13.2 provides a summary of some of these commands. These commands can be used at the user or privileged prompt.

show commands provide a lot of information

If you've been going through the chapters in this book in order, you probably noticed that the show commands listed in Table 13.2 are similar to show commands that you used to view information on a router's IP configuration and IPX/SPX configuration information. Learning several of the different show commands, enables you to sit down at any router and quickly get a good picture of how that router has been configured for any network protocol.

Table 13.2 show appletalk Commands

Command	Shows
Show appletalk interface brief	Provides a short summary of all the interfaces on the router and their AppleTalk configurations
Show appletalk interface	Provides more detailed information on the router interfaces and their AppleTalk configurations
Show appletalk interface e0	Enables you to view detailed AppleTalk configuration information for a specified router interface
Show appletalk zone	Provides zone and network information for the zone available on the internetwork.
Show appletalk global	Provides information on the number of networks and zones available on the internetwork and the time interval for ZIP queries and RTMP updates.

Figure 13.9 shows the results of the show appletalk interface brief command. Figure 13.10 shows the results of the show appletalk zone command and Figure 13.11 provides a view of the results of the show appletalk global command.

FIGURE 13.9
Use the show appletalk interface brief command to take a look at the interface configurations on the router.

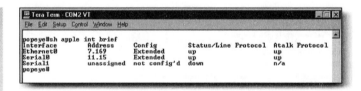

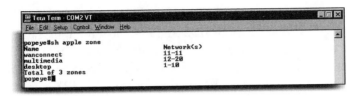

FIGURE 13.10
Use the show
appletalk zone
command to take a look
at the zone and network
information on the inter-
network.

```
popeye#sh apple zone
Name                            Network(s)
wanconnect                      11-11
multimedia                      12-20
desktop                         1-10
Total of 3 zones
popeye#
```

FIGURE 13.11
Use the show
appletalk global
command to view the
overall AppleTalk config-
uration on the router.

```
popeye#sh apple global
AppleTalk global information:
    Internet is incompatible with older, AT Phase1, routers.
    There are 3 routes in the internet.
    There are 3 zones defined.
    Logging of significant AppleTalk events is disabled.
    ZIP resends queries every 10 seconds.
    RTMP updates are sent every 10 seconds.
    RTMP entries are considered BAD after 20 seconds.
    RTMP entries are discarded after 60 seconds.
    AARP probe retransmit count: 10, interval: 200 msec.
    AARP request retransmit count: 5, interval: 1000 msec.
    DDP datagrams will be checksummed.
    RTMP datagrams will be strictly checked.
    RTMP routes may not be propagated without zones.
    Routes will not be distributed between routing protocols.
    Routing between local devices on an interface will not be performed.
    IPTalk uses the udp base port of 768 (Default).
    AppleTalk EIGRP is not enabled.
    Alternate node address format will not be displayed.
    Access control of any networks of a zone hides the zone.
popeye#
```

You can also turn on AppleTalk RTMP debugging and view the
RTMP routing updates sent and received by the router. Type debug
apple routing at the privileged prompt and press **Enter**. Figure
13.12 shows the results of this command. To turn off debugging,
type no debug apple routing, and then press **Enter**. Otherwise, you
will find it hard to enter any commands at the prompt.

FIGURE 13.12
The results of debug
apple routing.

```
popeye#debug apple routing
AppleTalk RTMP routing debugging is on
AppleTalk EIGRP routing debugging is on
popeye#
6d19h: AT: RTMP from 11.45 (new 0,old 1,bad 0,ign 0, dwn 0)
6d19h: AT: src=Ethernet0:7.169, dst=1-10, size=22, 2 rtes, RTMP pkt sent
6d19h: AT: src=Serial0:11.15, dst=11-11, size=16, 1 rte, RTMP pkt sent
6d19h: AT: Route ager starting on Main AT RoutingTable (3 active nodes)
6d19h: AT: Route ager finished on Main AT RoutingTable (3 active nodes)
6d19h: AT: RTMP from 11.45 (new 0,old 1,bad 0,ign 0, dwn 0)
6d19h: AT: src=Ethernet0:7.169, dst=1-10, size=22, 2 rtes, RTMP pkt sent
6d19h: AT: src=Serial0:11.15, dst=11-11, size=16, 1 rte, RTMP pkt sent
6d19h: AT: Route ager starting on Main AT RoutingTable (3 active nodes)
6d19h: AT: Route ager finished on Main AT RoutingTable (3 active nodes)
6d19h: AT: RTMP from 11.45 (new 0,old 1,bad 0,ign 0, dwn 0)
6d19h: AT: src=Ethernet0:7.169, dst=1-10, size=22, 2 rtes, RTMP pkt sent
6d19h: AT: src=Serial0:11.15, dst=11-11, size=16, 1 rte, RTMP pkt sent
6d19h: AT: Route ager starting on Main AT RoutingTable (3 active nodes)
6d19h: AT: Route ager finished on Main AT RoutingTable (3 active nodes)
6d19h: AT: RTMP from 11.45 (new 0,old 1,bad 0,ign 0, dwn 0)
6d19h: AT: src=Ethernet0:7.169, dst=1-10, size=22, 2 rtes, RTMP pkt sent
6d19h: AT: src=Serial0:11.15, dst=11-11, size=16, 1 rte, RTMP pkt sent
6d19h: AT: Route ager starting on Main AT RoutingTable (3 active nodes)
6d19h: AT: Route ager finished on Main AT RoutingTable (3 active nodes)
6d19h: AT: RTMP from 11.45 (new 0,old 1,bad 0,ign 0, dwn 0)
6d19h: AT: src=Ethernet0:7.169, dst=1-10, size=22, 2 rtes, RTMP pkt sent
6d19h: AT: src=Serial0:11.15, dst=11-11, size=16, 1 rte, RTMP pkt sent
6d19h: AT: Route ager starting on Main AT RoutingTable (3 active nodes)
6d19h: AT: Route ager finished on Main AT RoutingTable (3 active nodes)
```

As you can see, AppleTalk provides a routing environment every bit as robust as IP or IPX. And in some ways AppleTalk provides features, such as zones and extended networks, that enable you to easily create complex internetworks of LAN computers at different locations. However, IP still rules the day (and IPX comes in second) so your opportunity to implement AppleTalk routing in the workplace may prove to be very limited.

part

IV

ADVANCED CONFIGURATION AND CONFIGURATION TOOLS

chapter

14

Filtering Router Traffic with Access List

Understanding Access Lists

So far in this book, you've had a chance to look at how three different LAN protocols (TCP/IP, IPX/SPX, and AppleTalk) are configured on a Cisco router. Interfaces have been configured and connectivity issues relating to creating an internetwork that supports these protocols have been discussed.

But whatyou've basically done is configure your routers so that the doors to your internetwork are hanging wide open. Data packets and broadcast packets have the run of your routers and can enter and leave from any router port they want; you basically have configured a Wild West boomtown without a sheriff. An important part of managing routers and internetwork access is shutting the door on some packets and being a little more selective about what interfaces and routes are available to the data traffic from certain nodes and LANs on your internetwork.

This is where an Access list comes in.

The *Access list* is a list of conditions called `permit` and `deny` *statements* that help regulate traffic flow in to and out of a router (and can even control user access to a router via Telnet). A `permit` statement basically means that packets meeting a certain conditional statement won't be filtered out. This means that these packets are "permitted" to continue their journey across the interface. A `deny` statement (by some criterion such as IP address or IPX network address) specifies the packets to be filtered out, or discarded.

Access lists can be used to deny the flow of packets in to a particular router interface or out of a particular router interface. They can also be used to restrict the access capability of certain users and devices to the routers on the internetwork.

How Access Lists Work

As already mentioned, Access lists are a series of conditional statements that can restrict entry of packets from the internetwork to your router based on particular criteria. Each statement in the Access list is read in order, which means that packets coming into a particular router interface are compared to the list criteria from the top to the bottom of the list.

Access lists—a science unto themselves

Working with Access lists gives you a huge amount of control over the data flow on your internetwork. Understanding all the idiosyncrasies of Access lists is a huge task. This chapter gets you started on this subject and covers standard Access lists (you also spend more time working with IP Access lists because IP is the most routed protocol in the world). Extended Access lists can also be built for network protocols such as IP and IPX. For more information, check out www.cisco.com or talk to your local Cisco training group (training information is also available on the Cisco Web site). They provide hands-on classes that can help you with a number of advanced subjects related to routers and the Cisco IOS.

Packets denied are dropped. Packets that are permitted are forwarded as if no Access list existed. If a packet entering the router doesn't match the first statement in the Access list (which can be a deny or permit statement) the packet is then compared to the next statement in the list.

This process of matching the packet to the permit and deny statements continues until the packet matches a criteria in the Access list and is either forwarded or dropped. Figure 14.1 illustrates the process of a packet being matched to the deny and permit statements in an Access list.

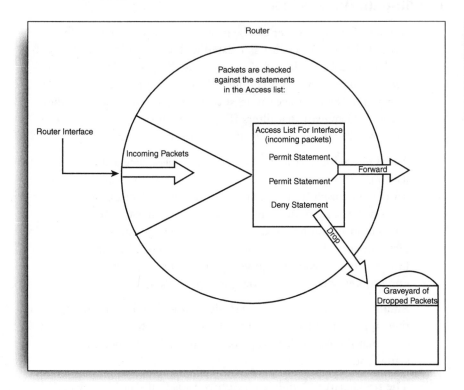

Router

Packets are checked
against the statements
in the Access list:

Router Interface

Incoming Packets

Access List For Interface
(incoming packets)

Permit Statement

Permit Statement

Deny Statement

Forward

Drop

Graveyard of
Dropped Packets

FIGURE 14.1
Packets are either forwarded or dropped based on the statements in the Access list.

A packet that is forwarded from an incoming interface (based on the Access list grouped to that interface) may then face another Access list that is grouped to an outgoing interface on the same router. This means packets can be filtered when received by an interface and then filtered again as it is switched to the departure interface.

For example, you may have a case where you don't want packets entering a router, so you block those packets from entering a particular interface, such as an Ethernet interface that is connected to a LAN. Or you may want to filter the packets as they depart the router. You don't want the packets to leave by a particular serial interface that is connected to another router by a slow WAN connection. You can then assign a filter to this interface, which won't allow packets (addressed in a particular way) to depart from that interface.

Building an Access List

Any interface the router can be grouped to Access lists. But there can only be one Access list associated with the interface for each network protocol that the interface supports. For example, on a router's Ethernet 0 port (which is configured for IP and IPX) an Access list grouped to the interface can exist that filters IP traffic and another Access list can exist that filters IPX traffic. However, you could not have two lists that filter IP traffic grouped to the same interface.

A real plus with Access lists is that you can associate a single Access list to more than one interface on a router. So, for example, the same list could be used by an Ethernet 0 interface and an Ethernet 1 interface on the same router. And you specify whether the Access list is set to filter incoming packets on the interface or outgoing packets. In fact, the same Access list could be grouped to one interface where it filters incoming packets and grouped to another interface on the same router where it filters outgoing packets.

Building an Access list is fairly straightforward; you build the list and then apply it to a particular interface on the router. Be advised, however, that the Access list must contain at least one functioning permit statement.

The tricky part of building an Access list is that you have two conditional statements: deny and permit. You have to determine how you will use these statements to actually limit traffic on the router (without permitting traffic you don't want and restricting traffic you do want).

For example, your strategy might be to use the `permit` statement to allow access to the router for packets originating on certain LANs on your network (by specifying a separate `permit` statement that points out each network address that will be permitted). This means that you have several `permit` statements in the Access list. You can then place a `deny` statement at the end of the Access list that denies entry to all other networks (which is done in different ways depending on the type of traffic, such as IP packets, that you are filtering).

Or you can use the `deny` statement to deny entry to certain node or network addresses and then place `permit` statements near the end of the Access list that allow a number of different networks to move their packets through the interface on your router. Whichever strategy you use, you certainly can't permit a particular network address access to the router through an interface and then deny these same addresses in a later statement. After they hit that `permit` statement those packets are forwarded, so they are gone even before they are compared to the `deny` statement.

Creating good Access lists is really a journey in the realm of logic, where you must carefully craft `deny` and `permit` statements that forward packets that you want to have routed and drop packets that you don't want routed. And each conditional statement in the Access list must be built so that it doesn't countermand another statement in the list. You certainly don't want the Access list to inadvertently `deny` the forwarding of packets by your router, when your router is the only path for these packets as they move to their final destination. Let's look at some specific network protocols and how basic Access lists are created for each. This will help shed some light onto the logic of Access lists.

> **Access lists are a combination of deny and permit statements**
>
> You will find that Access lists for interfaces on a router that is part of a fairly good size internetwork will have to weave a filtering web using both `deny` and `permit` statements. And after specific nodes and networks have been dealt with in the Access list, a `deny all` statement (using a wildcard statement based on the network protocol addressing system) is typically placed at the very bottom of the Access list. This denies packets that don't meet any of the conditions you have set in your `deny` and `permit` statements.

Working with IP Access Lists

Standard IP Access lists examine the source IP address of packets that are to be filtered on a particular router interface. You use the source IP address as the match criteria for the various `deny` and `permit` statements that you place in the Access list.

When designing an Access list that will be used on an interface (such as Ethernet 0 or Serial 1) you must also decide whether the Access list controls the entry of packets on that interface or whether the Access list controls the departure of packets from that interface (which will be forwarded out onto the internetwork). Whether the Access list is for incoming or outgoing packets will have to be specified when the Access list is grouped to the interface. Figure 14.2 shows an IP Access list. I will discuss the commands for creating an Access list in the sections that follow.

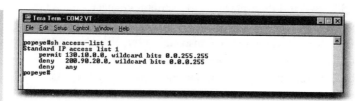

FIGURE 14.2
An IP Access list that permits packets from one network and then denies all others.

IP extended access lists

Although our basic discussion of Access lists will examine the use of Standard Access lists for protocols such as IP, you can further fine-tune your network traffic with extended Access lists. In the case of IP, extended Access lists enable you to filter packets based on not only the source IP address, but also the destination address of the packet and particular IP protocols such as UDP and ICMP.

Let's take a look at a simple internetwork and use the IP addresses that it provides to create Access lists for some of the routers on the internetwork. Figure 14.3 supplies the information that you will use to create your Access lists.

First, to keep things simple, you will create an Access list for the Serial 0 interface on Router A. You want the data sent from workstation 1A to nodes on the 130.10.0.0 network to be able to use the leased line that connects Router A to Router C as a route. However, you don't want any of the other LANs such as the LAN (200.90.20.0) serviced by router B to use this WAN connection as a possible route (because router B is directly connected to router C). So your list will permit packets from workstation A1 and deny all other packets (from the other LANs).

The first step in the process is to create the Access list. The second step in the process is to group the Access list to an interface. However, before you actually create the list, you need to look at one more conceptual item related to IP Access lists—wildcard masks.

SEE ALSO

➤ *For a review of IP addressing, see page 174.*

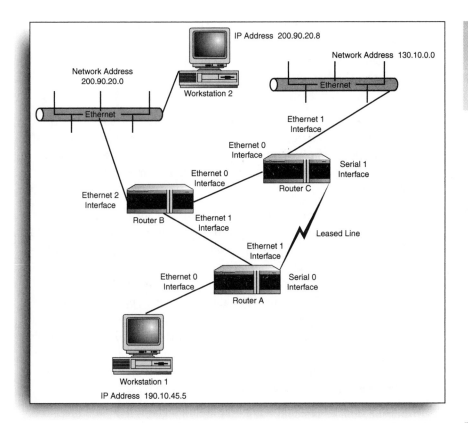

FIGURE 14.3
A simple internetwork
crying out for some
Access lists.

IP Wildcard Masks

Because the IP addresses used by in basic IP Access lists can be referring to node addresses, subnet addresses, or major network
addresses, there must be some mechanism to let the router know
which bits in the source IP address of packets that it received should
be checked against the IP address provided in the Access list. For
example, if the major network address 200.90.20.0 is used in a deny
or permit statement, you want to make sure that the bits in the first
three octets are used by the router when it enforces the statement in
the Access list on packets that are being processed by one of its interfaces (the interface that the Access list has been grouped to).

You do this with a *wildcard mask*. Bits that you want to have checked
in an address must have a wildcard mask value of 0. Bits in the
address that you don't want checked are assigned a wildcard mask bit

**Wildcard masks are not
subnet masks**

Don't confuse wildcard
masks with subnet masks.
Wild card masks are only
used in Access lists and
their purpose is to let the
router know which bits it
needs to check in the
source IP address of packets to determine whether
they should be filtered by
the Access list.

value of 1. So, for your major network address 200.90.20.0, where you want all the bits in the first, second, and third octets to be checked by the router, the wildcard mask would be 0.0.0.255 (the binary equivalent of these decimal values would be 00000000 00000000 00000000 11111111).

In the case of a node address (such as 190.10.45.5) where you want all the bits in each octet checked against your entry in the Access list (this would be checked on each packet processed by the interface), you would use a wildcard mask of 0.0.0.0. This means "check all the bits in each octet."

As you can see, when you are working with major network addresses and node addresses, coming up with the wildcard mask is easy. To do this, you would use all zero bits—which equal a decimal value of 0— for octets to be checked, and all 1s or a decimal value of 255 for octets not to be checked. However, when you are dealing with networks that have been subnetted, and you want to permit or deny certain subnets and ignore others (from your range of subnets found on your network), you must construct a mask that tells the router which bits to check in the IP addresses of packets it must process. Let's say that you have subnetted your network (a Class B network) into six subnets as shown in Table 14.1.

Wildcard mask keywords

In the case of a node address where you want all the address bits checked against the entry in the Access list, you use a wildcard mask of 0.0.0.0. However, you can replace this wildcard mask with the keyword "host," which provides the router with the same mask bits as does the wildcard mask of all zeros. In cases where you want to specify that a `permit` or `deny` statement act on all IP addresses not given in other `deny` or `permit` statements in the Access list, you can use the keyword "any." This is useful if you want a `deny any` statement, which denies all IP addresses except for those placed in `permit` statements in the Access list.

Table 14.1 IP Address Ranges for Six Subnets on 130.10.0.0

Subnet #	Subnet Address
1	130.10.32.0
2	130.10.64.0
3	130.10.96.0
4	130.10.128.0
5	130.10.160.0
6	130.10.192.0

You want to create a `deny` statement that will deny packets from subnets 1, 2, and 3 (a subnet range of 130.10.32.0 through 130.10.96.0). This statement would read as `deny 130.10.32.0 0.0.31.255`. The IP address of the first subnet follows the `deny` statement, and the wildcard mask follows the IP address. The big question is how did you come up with the wildcard mask?

For packets to be acted on by the deny statement in the Access list, their first octet must match the decimal value 130 so the wildcard mask for that octet in binary will be 00000000—0 in decimal (meaning all the bits in the first octet of the packet must match the binary value of 130 (10000010). And the second octet must match the binary equivalent of 10 (00001010), so again, its wildcard mask will be 00000000 (0 in decimal). So, this means that so far your wildcard mask is 0.0.

Now things become complicated because you are at the third octet where bits have been borrowed for subnetting. Subnet 1 has a third octet value of 32; the binary equivalent of 32 is 00100000. So you have to make sure the third bit is checked (reading the 8 bits from left to right) in packets that are being considered by the router to have the Access list applied to them.

In the second subnet the third octet value is 64 (01000000), so you have to make sure that the second bit in the third octet of the packet is checked. In subnet 3 the subnet value in decimal is 96 (binary value of 01100000), so you need to have the second and third bits checked in a packet to find packets that are in subnet 3.

This means that your wildcard mask from left to right will read 00011111 because you need to check the first bit in the octet (128 to make sure it is off) and you need to check the second and third bit to make sure they are on or off—the 64 and 32 bits. The rest of the bits, 4 through 8, don't need to be checked, so in a wildcard mask these bits are set to 1 (meaning don't check). These bits then have the value 16+8+4+2+1=31. So your wildcard mask for the Access list deny statement will read: 0.0.31 for the first three octets in the wildcard mask.

Now you must determine the value for the last octet in the wildcard mask. This octet gives us 8 bits of information relating to node addresses, which you don't want to have checked (the only octet of importance to your router when checking packets against the Access list is octet 3. Octet 4 doesn't have to be checked, so you use a wildcard mask value of 255, which in binary is 11111111). Your complete wildcard mask to filter out (deny) packets from the subnet range 130.10.32.0 through 130.10.96.0 will be: 0.0.31.255.

Remember that wildcard masks aren't subnet masks. The only similarity is that you must convert decimal values to binary values to determine the use of 1s and 0s in the wildcard mask. Now you can create an Access list.

Creating the Access List

So, you will create an Access list that permits packets from workstation A1 (190.10.45.5) to be forwarded out of Serial 0 on Router A but denies packets from all other IP networks. When you create the list you need to assign the list a number from 1 to 99. After the list has been created you will then group it to a particular router interface and at that point make sure to let the router know whether the Access list is filtering packets in or out of the specified interface.

Creating a standard IP Access list

1. At the Privileged prompt type `config t`, and then press **Enter**. You are placed in the Global Configuration mode.

2. To create the first line in the Access list type `access-list [list #] permit or deny [ip address] wildcard mask`; where the `list #` is a number from 1–99. The statement can only contain deny or permit (not both) and the IP address is the IP address of a particular workstation or network on the internetwork. In your case, you want to block packets from workstation A1 (190.10.45.5), so the command would be `access-list 1 permit 190.10.45.5 0.0.0.0`. Then press **Enter** to continue.

3. To deny all other network packets, type `access-list 1 deny any` (see Figure 14.4).

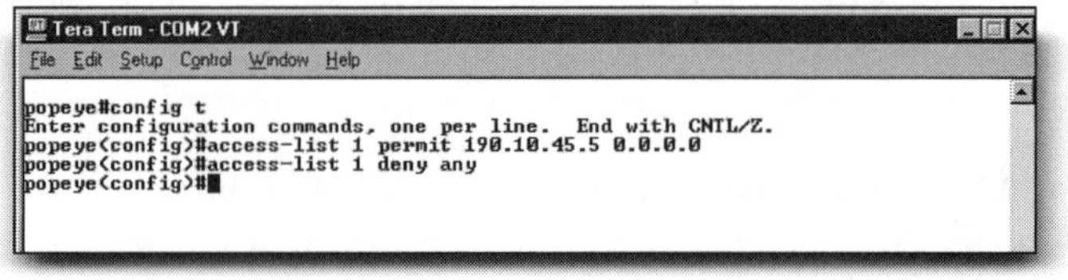

FIGURE 14.4
The Access list is built in the Configuration mode.

```
popeye#config t
Enter configuration commands, one per line.  End with CNTL/Z.
popeye(config)#access-list 1 permit 190.10.45.5 0.0.0.0
popeye(config)#access-list 1 deny any
popeye(config)#
```

4. Press **Ctrl+Z** to end the configuration session.

5. Press **Enter** to return to the privileged prompt.

You can view your Access list using the show command. Type show access-list 1 at the prompt and then press **Enter**. Figure 14.5 shows the results of this command.

FIGURE 14.5
The results of the show access-list command.

Grouping the Access List to an Interface

Now that you have an Access list you can group it to a particular interface on a router. In this case you would want to group this list (which would be created on Router A) to the router's serial 0 interface. You also want the interface to check the packets when they are being prepared to move out of the interface.

Grouping the list to interface serial 0

1. At the privileged prompt type config t, and then press **Enter**. You are placed in the global configuration mode.

2. To enter the Configuration mode for serial 0, (or any other interface) type: interface serial 0, and then press **Enter**.

3. At the config-if prompt type ip access-group 1 out (see Figure 14.6). Then press **Enter**.

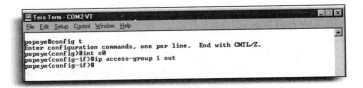

FIGURE 14.6
You must group the Access list to the interface and specify whether the list is used on incoming or outgoing packets.

4. Press **Ctrl+Z** to end the configuration session.

5. Press **Enter** to return to the privileged prompt.

Now that the list has been grouped to the interface, the router can use it to filter packets routing to that interface. You can add additional deny and permit statements to the Access list. These new statements are added using the same command that you used in the steps

Deleting an Access list

If you find that an Access list isn't working properly (after monitoring traffic on the interface) or you want to start from scratch and build an Access list with the same number, use the command no access-list 1 (or specify the number of your Access list).

revolving around building your initial Access list. New statements for the list are added at the bottom of the list just above the deny any statement (this statement is kind of like a failsafe statement used to block any IP addresses that you missed in your other deny statements).

Creating IPX Standard Access Lists

Standard IPX Access lists can deny or permit packets based on their IPX source and destination address. IPX Access lists are numbered from 800–899 (this is the range reserved for IPX Access lists) and are structured similarly to IP Access lists except they use IPX addressing to specify the incoming or outgoing packets that are to be filtered on the router interface.

A typical conditional statement in the Access list would appear as access list 800 deny [source network address] [destination network address]. The number 800 (from the IPX Access range of 800–899) tells the router that the Access list is an IPX list. The source network address would be the IPX network (the network number is provided by the first NetWare server on that network) that serves as the source of the packets. The destination network address would be the IPX network address of the network that is the intended recipient of the packets.

In IPX Access lists, the value -1 serves as a wildcard that refers to all IPX networks and is useful in permit or deny all statements (referring to all networks that aren't listed in more specific deny and permit statements).

Figure 14.7 shows a simple IPX internetwork. Let's say that you want to build an Access list that will deny packets from network 763B20F3 that are sent to network 02B2F4 via Router C's Ethernet 0 interface.

As with IP Access lists, you must complete two steps. Create the Access list and then group it to the appropriate router interface.

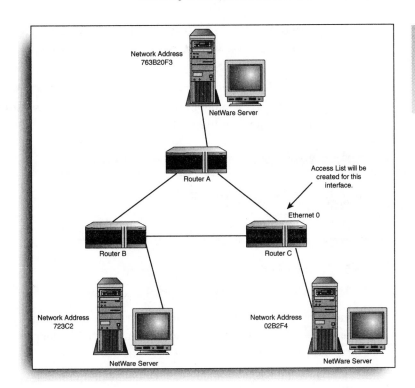

FIGURE 14.7
A NetWare internetwork connected by three routers.

Creating and grouping an IPX Access list

1. At the privileged prompt type `config t`, and then press **Enter**. You are placed in the Global Configuration mode.

2. To begin the IPX Access list type `access-list 800` (use any number between 800 and 899 for an IPX list) followed by the source address for the packets, followed by the destination address for the packets. In the case of your sample network (see Figure 14.6) the command would be `access-list 800 deny 763B20F3 02B2F4` (source network address followed by destination address). Then press **Enter**.

3. Add additional `permit` or deny statements as needed. In this case we will add a `permit all` statement for all other IPX networks on our network. Type `access-list 800 permit -1 -1` (permit packets from any network going to any other network). Press **Enter** to continue.

4. To group the list to the Ethernet 0 interface on the router, type interface Ethernet 0 at the config prompt, and then press **Enter**.

5. At the config-if prompt type ipx access-group 800 in (you are filtering packets coming into the interface). Then press **Enter**. Your list is shown in Figure 14.8.

6. Press **Ctrl+Z** to end the configuration session.

7. Press **Enter** to return to the privileged prompt.

You can view your IPX Access list using the show command. Type show access-list 800 (or the number you assigned to your Access list) and press **Enter**.

The Cisco IOS also provides you with the capability to create extended IPX access lists (as it does for IP Access lists) where you can further filter traffic on the network. Extended lists provide you with the capability to filter by network/node source and destination addresses and filter by particular IPX/SPX protocols such as SAP and SPX. Information on Extended list commands can be found on the Cisco IOS Command CD-ROM that is provided with your router.

SEE ALSO
➤ For a review of IPX addressing, see page 214.

Creating AppleTalk Standard Access Lists

Access lists can also be built for routers that route AppleTalk traffic. The list numbers reserved for AppleTalk Access lists by the Cisco IOS are 600–699. These Access lists can filter packets based on cable ranges (the network address ranges for a particular physical segment of the AppleTalk internetwork). For example a permit statement for an interface may read as: access-list 600 permit cable-range 100-110.

AppleTalk Access lists can also be built using AppleTalk zone designations in `permit` or `deny` statements. Using zone designations may serve as a better way to identify parts of your AppleTalk network in `deny` and `permit` statements because Zones can often include more than one cable range. For example, let's say that you have an interface on a router where you want to deny traffic from a particular AppleTalk zone. Figure 14.9 shows a portion of an AppleTalk internetwork.

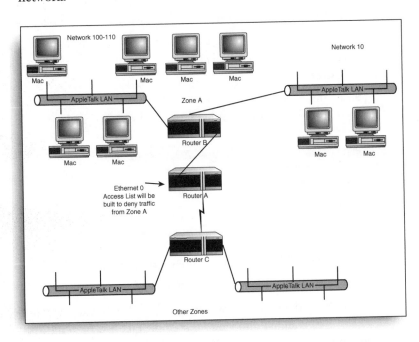

FIGURE 14.9
Access lists can be built to deny or permit traffic from AppleTalk cable ranges and AppleTalk zones.

You want to create an Access list that will deny packets from Zone A (which includes network 100–110 and network 10) on the Ethernet 0 interface of Router A. You also want to make sure that the list allows packets from other zones that might be connected to your network.

Creating and grouping an AppleTalk Access list

1. At the Privileged prompt type `config t`, and then press **Enter**. You are placed in the Global Configuration mode.

2. To begin the AppleTalk Access list type `access-list 600` (use any number between 600 and 699 for an AppleTalk list) followed by the zone designation for the packets you want to filter. For the

AppleTalk uses object names

AppleTalk networks also use object names to refer to servers and other resources on the network. Access list `deny` and `permit` statements can be created using the object keyword followed by the name of the object such as `PrintServer`. Check your router documentation (on the CD-ROM) and `www.cisco.com` for more information on AppleTalk and the Cisco IOS.

sample network (see Figure 14.8) the command would be access-list 600 deny zone ZoneA (the command word zone specifies that you want to set up the statement using a zone name, in this case ZoneA). Then press **Enter**.

3. Add additional permit or deny statements as needed. In your case you will add a permit all statement for all the other zones that are on the internetwork. Type access-list 600 permit additional-zones (this permits packets from any other zone connected to your internetwork). Press **Enter** to continue.

4. To group the list to the Ethernet 0 interface on the router, type interface Ethernet 0 at the config prompt, and then press **Enter**.

5. At the config-if prompt type appletalk access-group 600, and then press **Enter**. Your list is shown in Figure 14.10.

FIGURE 14.10
An AppleTalk Access list under construction that has been grouped to a router's Ethernet 0 interface.

6. Press **Ctrl+Z** to end the configuration session.

7. Press **Enter** to return to the privileged prompt.

You can use the show access-list 600 (specify the number of your Access list) command to view your AppleTalk list. Dealing with AppleTalk Access lists is actually a little more difficult than IP and IPX lists because of the use of zones and cable ranges to specify network grouping and networks. Considering that you might only deal with small numbers of Macintoshes on a corporate internetwork, the need for filtering might be minimal.

SEE ALSO

➤ *For a review of AppleTalk addressing, see page 229.*

chapter

15

Configuring WAN Protocols

Understanding Serial and WAN Interfaces

Most of the discussion so far has been related to connecting LANs to Cisco routers (such as Ethernet LANs using IP, IPX, or AppleTalk as the network protocol), but these routers also enable you to connect routers using a variety of WAN technologies and WAN protocols. The serial interfaces on the router provide the connectivity to the different WAN technologies discussed in Chapter 3, "Wide Area Networking." Routers connecting remotely to other routers using ISDN will typically be outfitted with an ISDN interface.

In this chapter, you will look at the Cisco IOS commands that enable you to configure the different WAN protocols on your router or routers. WAN connectivity in general has become much more cost-effective in recent years. Whereas companies once might have used a Switched 56K line connection because of its relative low cost, they now can now use Frame Relay over a T1 line for roughly the same cost.

The type of connection you use will, no doubt, center on cost and line speed. Do your homework before you make the final decision on any WAN connection.

Typically, routers function as Digital Terminal Equipment (DTE) and so a DTE cable would be connected to the serial port on the router and then to a CSU/DSU device (referred to as the Digital Communication Equipment, or DCE) that is then hooked to the line supplied by the phone company. The CSU/DSU device supplies the clock rate for the synchronous transmission.

You can quickly check the encapsulation (the WAN protocol set) for a serial interface using the show interface serial [*interface number*] command. The *interface number* would be the serial interface you want to examine. For example, to examine serial 0, the command would be show interface serial 0 (remember that you can abbreviate your commands). Figure 15.1 shows the results of this command. Note that the interface is currently configured for PPP.

Is Frame Relay really cost effective?

A local phone company representative quoted me a cost of less than $300 per month for Frame Relay over a T1, which is extremely cheap compared to the cost of this connection a couple of years ago. If you're still using a switched 56K line, check current pricing for Frame Relay over a T1 line. You might be surprised at how affordable Frame Relay has become.

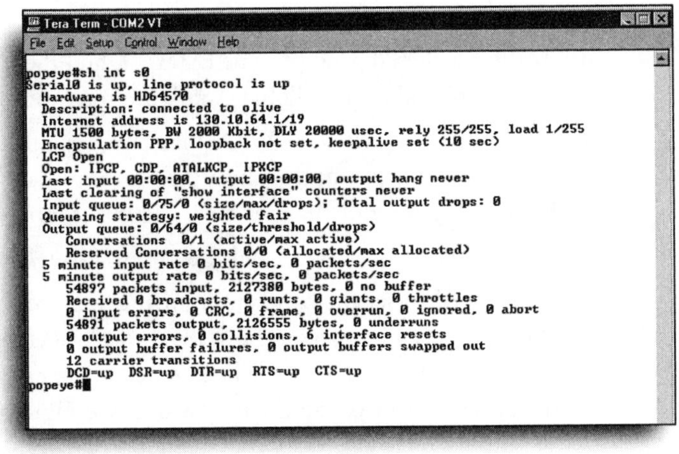

FIGURE 15.1
The show interface command can be used to quickly examine the WAN encapsulation for a serial interface on the router.

Turning a router into a DCE

You can actually make a router act like a DCE device. In fact, this book was written with two 2505 routers connected with V.35 cables where one router was configured as the DTE and one was configured as the DCE. A V.35 DTE cable was used on the DTE and a V.35 DCD cable was used on the DCE. These two cables where then hooked together (one is female the other male) making the routers think they were connected by a WAN connection. The DCE router had to be configured to provide the clocking that normally is provided by the CSU/DSU device. The clock rate (at the config-if prompt for the serial interface being configured) command was used to set the clock-rate on the router. Clock-rate is actually set in bits per second and can range from 1,200 to 8,000,000 depending on the connection. You can check the type of cable attached to your router (DTE or DCE) using the show controller serial [*interface number*] command.

SEE ALSO

➤ *For an overview of packet-switching protocols such as X.25 and Frame Relay, see page 62.*

➤ *For an overview of other WAN protocols such as HDLC and PPP, see page 65.*

➤ *For an overview of serial interfaces, see page 104.*

Configuring High-Level Data Link Control (HDLC)

HDLC is a point-to-point WAN protocol that serves as the default WAN protocol on Cisco routers. It is already enabled by default. If it isn't enabled on the router, a simple encapsulation command turns HDLC on. One other parameter that you might have to provide when configuring HDLC is bandwidth. This is the throughput of the line that you have leased from the phone company (for example, a 56K line would have a bandwidth of 56). Bandwidth is measured in kilobits/second and is a necessary parameter if you are using IGRP as your routing protocol because IGRP uses bandwidth as one of its metrics.

If HDLC isn't the current WAN protocol for a particular interface, it is quite easy to enable it on a serial interface.

Configuring HDLC on a serial interface

1. At the privileged prompt, type config t, and then press **Enter**. You are placed in the Global Configuration mode.

2. To configure a particular WAN interface, type the name of the interface at the prompt, such as interface serial 1. Then press **Enter**. The prompt changes to the config-if mode.

3. Type encapsulation HDLC, and then press **Enter**.

4. If you need to set the bandwidth for the interface, type bandwidth [kilobits/second], where the kilobits/second is the speed of the line. For instance, for a 56K line you can type bandwidth 56, and then press **Enter** to input a bandwidth (see Figure 15.2).

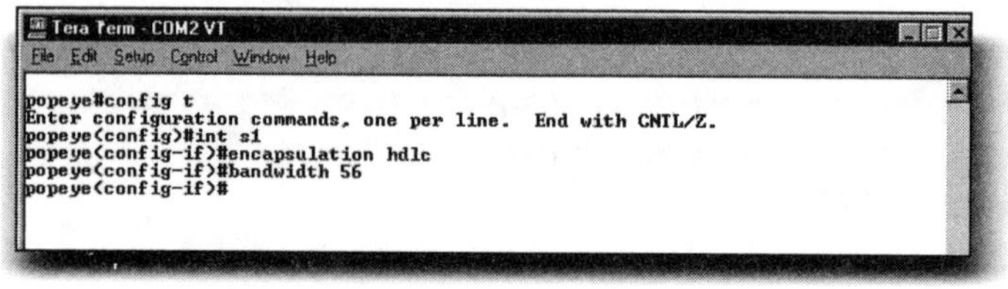

FIGURE 15.2
HDLC is set as the WAN protocol using the encapsulation command. Use the bandwidth command to set the bandwidth if needed.

5. To end the configuration of the interface, press **Ctrl+Z**.

6. Press **Enter** again to return to the privileged prompt.

Configuring PPP

Configuring high-end routers

Routers that use modular interface slots specify their interfaces in a slightly different way. For example a Cisco 7200 series router denotes a serial interface with the configuration command interface serial slot/port. The slot is the modular interface slot on the router and the port is the port number on that slot.

Point-to-Point Protocol (PPP) is the TCP/IP stack's point-to-point protocol and can be used for connections between routers using leased lines (in much the same way as HDLC). PPP is an open system protocol and works with IP, IPX, or AppleTalk routing.

Configuring PPP is very straightforward using the encapsulation command. You can also set the bandwidth for the connection as was done for HDLC in the previous section.

Configuring PPP on a serial interface

1. At the privileged prompt, type config t, and then press **Enter**. You are placed in the Global Configuration mode.

2. To configure a particular WAN interface, type the name of the interface at the prompt, such as interface serial 0. Then press **Enter**. The prompt changes to the config-if mode.

3. Type encapsulation PPP, and then press **Enter**.

4. If you need to set the bandwidth for the interface, type bandwidth [*kilobits/second*], where the *kilobits/second* is the speed of the line. For instance, for a 56K line you can type bandwidth 56, and then press **Enter** to input a bandwidth (see Figure 15.3).

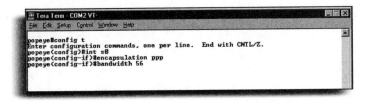

FIGURE 15.3
PPP is set as the WAN protocol for a serial interface using the encapsulation command.

5. To end the configuration of the interface, press **Ctrl+Z**.

6. Press **Enter** again to return to the privileged prompt.

To check your PPP connection to another router, you can use the ping command to make sure that both ends of the WAN line are communicating. For example, I have two routers connected or a WAN connection via their serial 0 interfaces. PPP is the encapsulation type. If I know that IP address of the serial interface on the other end of the WAN connection, I can check the line by typing ping [*ip address*]. Figure 15.4 shows the results of the ping command. The destination address was a serial interface on another router with the IP address of 130.10.64.2 (this wouldn't be a possibility if I had configured my serial ports as IP unnumbered).

FIGURE 15.4
You can ping a serial interface to check your WAN connection.

Configuring X.25

The X.25 protocol, developed in the 1970s, seems older than the hills now (when compared to Frame-Relay and other more recent and efficient additions to the packet-switching protocol family), but is still employed by companies and institutions for WAN connections. X.25 provides connections between DTEs (such as your router) and DCEs (such as a CSU/DSU).

X.25 uses the *X.121* telephone standards addressing scheme (also known as International Data Numbers) that is comprised of one to 14 decimal digits. This number identifies the local X.121 address for your serial interface and must be configured on the router that is being enabled for X.25.

Depending on the type of X.25 switch your router will connect to, you might also have to set the size of the input and output packets that are moved in to and out of the router over the X.25 connection (the default size is 128 bytes). And again, depending on the type of X.25 switch that serves as your entrance to the X.25 packet-switched cloud, you might also have to set the input and output window size for packets that is used by X.25 flow control (the default window size is 2 packets). All this information should be provided by your connection service provider.

Configuring X.25 on a serial interface

1. At the privileged prompt type `config t`, and then press **Enter**. You are placed in the Global Configuration mode.

2. To configure a particular WAN interface, type the name of the interface at the prompt, such as `interface serial 1`. Then press **Enter**. The prompt changes to the config-if mode.

3. Type `encapsulation x25`, and then press **Enter**.

4. To set the X.121 address for the router interface, type `x25 address [data link address]`. The `data link address` is the decimal address number (provided by your X.25 provider). For example, you can use the command `x25 address 347650001` (where `347650001` is the X.121 decimal address). Press **Enter** to continue.

5. To set the input packet size, type `x25 ips [bits]`, where `bits` is the size of a legal incoming packet. For a packet size of 256, the command would read `x25 ips 256`. Press **Enter** to continue.

6. Output packet size might also have to be set; type `x25 ops [bits]`. To set an outgoing packet size of 256 the command would read `x25 ops 256`. Press **Enter** to continue.

7. To set the window size (based on number of flow control packets) for input to the router, type x25 win [*number of packets*]. You could set the window size to 5 and the command would read win 5. Press **Enter**.

8. To set the window out setting, type x25 wout followed by the number of packets, such as x25 wout 5. Press **Enter** to continue. Figure 15.5 shows the commands entered in steps 1–8 as they appear on the router console.

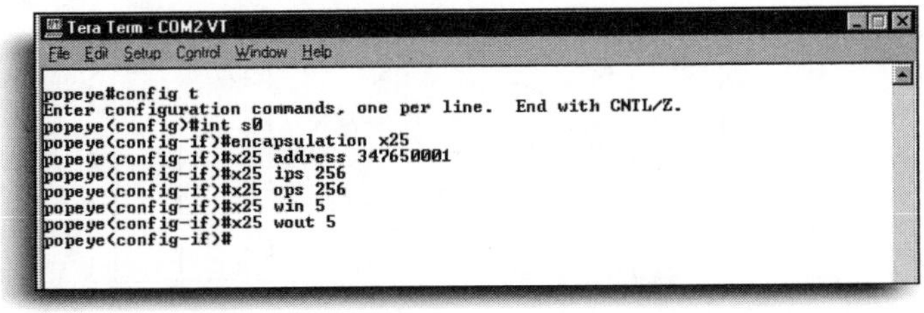

```
Teta Term - COM2 VT
File Edit Setup Control Window Help

popeye#config t
Enter configuration commands, one per line.  End with CNTL/Z.
popeye(config)#int s0
popeye(config-if)#encapsulation x25
popeye(config-if)#x25 address 347650001
popeye(config-if)#x25 ips 256
popeye(config-if)#x25 ops 256
popeye(config-if)#x25 win 5
popeye(config-if)#x25 wout 5
popeye(config-if)#
```

FIGURE 15.5
X.25 encapsulation may require input and output packet sizes and window in and out settings.

9. To end the configuration of the interface, press **Ctrl+Z**.

10. Press **Enter** again to return to the privileged prompt.

You can quickly view your X.25 settings on a serial interface. Type show interface [*serial #*], where the *serial #* specifies the serial interface that you configured for X.25.

SEE ALSO
➤ For an overview of X.25, see page 62.

Configuring Frame Relay

Frame Relay is a packet-switching, Data Link layer protocol that is used to connect DTE (routers) and DCE devices. The DCE devices on Frame Relay networks consist of the carrier-owned switches (see Figure 15.6). The Frame Relay network (a private or public switched telephone network) is typically represented as a cloud.

Frame Relay uses permanent virtual circuits for communication sessions between points on the WAN. These virtual circuits are identified by a *DLCI* (data link connection identifier)—a value provided by the Frame Relay service provider. The DLCI is provided for the connection between the router and the switch (see Figure 15.6) and a DLCI number must be input when configuring Frame Relay on the router.

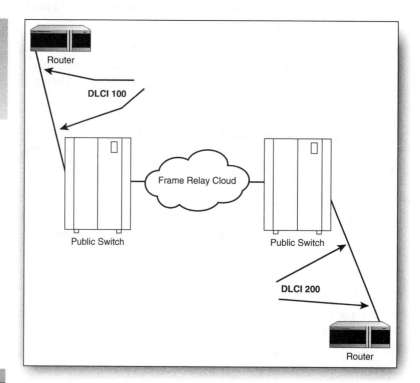

FIGURE 15.6
Frame Relay provides connectivity between routers and public switches.

Another parameter that can be configured for Frame Relay is the *LMI (local Management Interface)*. LMI is the signaling standard used between the router and the Frame Relay switch. Three LMI types are supported by Cisco routers:

- cisco—Cisco, Northern Telecom, DEC, and StrataCom LMI type
- ansi—American National Standards LMI type
- q933a—International Telecommunications standard LMI type

Configuring Frame Relay on the router is similar to configuring the other WAN protocols discussed.

Auto-detect the LMI

Beginning with IOS version 11.2, the router will try to auto-detect the LMI type that is being used on the line between the router and the switch. It will send a request to the Frame Relay switch, which will then respond with the LMI type or types for the line. The router then auto-configures itself using the last LMI type that it receives from the switch (in cases where the switch has sent more than one LMI type response).

Configuring Frame Relay on a serial interface

1. At the Privileged prompt, type `config t`, and then press **Enter**. You are placed in the Global Configuration mode.

2. To configure a particular WAN interface, type the name of the interface at the prompt, such as **interface serial 0**. Then press **Enter**. The prompt changes to the config-if mode.

3. Type `encapsulation frame`, and then press **Enter**.

4. To set the DLCI for the connection between the router and the Frame Relay switch, type `frame-relay interface-dlci [#]`, where the # is the DLCI number provided for the line between the router and the switch. If the DLCI number provided is 100, the command would read `frame-relay interface-dlci 100`. Press **Enter** to continue.

5. The `frame-relay interface-dlci 100` command actually places you at a dlci prompt to configure advanced parameters related to the dlci virtual circuit. To return to the Interface Configuration mode, type `int s0`, and press **Enter**.

6. To configure the LMI (only perform this if you have a version of the IOS older then version 11.2), type `frame-relay lmi-type [LMI type]`, where `LMI type` is cisco, ansi, or q933a. To set ansi as the LMI type, the command would read `frame-relay lmi-type ansi`. Press **Enter** after entering the command (see Figure 15.7).

FIGURE 15.7
Frame Relay can be quickly set up on a router serial interface.

7. To end the configuration of the interface, press **Ctrl+Z**.

8. Press **Enter** again to return to the privileged prompt.

After you have configured your router, you can use the `show interface serial [interface number]` command to view the configuration parameters for Frame Relay. Two other commands that are useful for verifying the Frame Relay configuration on your router are `show frame-relay lmi` and `show frame-relay map`.

The show frame-relay lmi command provides a listing of invalid messages that have been sent or received by the router and also shows the valid LMI messages that have been sent and received. Figure 15.8 shows the result of this command (you can use the command at the User or Privileged prompt).

FIGURE 15.8
The show frame-relay lmi command provides the status of the LMI type chosen for the router.

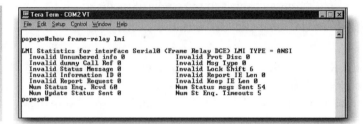

The show frame-relay map command shows how the DLCI number has been mapped to each of the network protocols that have been configured on the router. For example, Figure 15.9 shows the DLCI 100 mapped to IP, IPX, and AppleTalk.

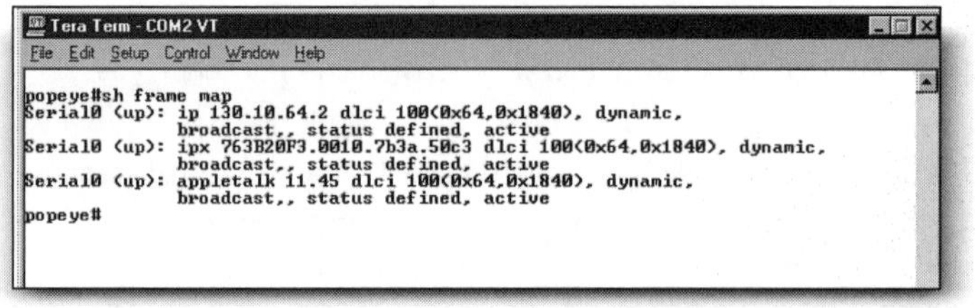

FIGURE 15.9
The show frame-relay map command provides information on the mapping of the DLCI number to the network protocols on the router.

One advanced trick to remember is that a single router interface can be configured for multiple DLCI numbers (virtual circuits) using subinterfaces. For example, after configuring interface serial 0, you can specify at the configuration prompt that you want to configure serial interface serial 0.1, where the 1 is the first subinterface. You would then configure this subinterface with a particular DCLI number.

Configuring ISDN

ISDN (Integrated Services Digital Network) is a digital service that actually functions over the existing phone lines. It comes in two flavors: Basic Rate ISDN (BRI) and Primary Rate ISDN (PRI).

Typically, if you want to configure ISDN on your router, you want to make sure that you have a router with a built-in ISDN interface. Otherwise, you will have to purchase a *terminal adapter* (also known as an ISDN modem) and connect it to one of the router's serial interfaces.

ISDN is a little different than the other WAN protocols that you've looked at in this chapter. ISDN is the physical conveyance of the data as it moves from a router to the Public Switched Telephone network. It isn't the encapsulation type. You still have to specify an encapsulation type such as PPP or Frame-Relay after you configure the router to use ISDN.

Let's take a look at how you would configure Basic Rate ISDN on a router. Remember that BRI consists of two B channels each providing 64K of bandwidth (which can be combined for a throughput of 128K). Each of these channels must be identified by a *SPID (service profile identifier)*. The SPID number authenticates the channel to the switch that connects the ISDN-enabled route to the phone system. Each channel must have a different SPID number.

Another piece of information that you need to configure ISDN is the *switch type*, which is an identifier code that refers to a particular manufacturer's ISDN switch that you connect to. After you have the SPID numbers and the switch type, all you have to do is provide the encapsulation type for the connection (such as PPP or HDLC).

Configuring BRI ISDN on an ISDN interface

1. At the privileged prompt, type `config t`, and then press **Enter**. You are placed in the Global Configuration mode.

2. To set the switch type for your ISDN connection, type `isdn switch type basic-`[*switch identifier*], where the *switch identifier* is the manufacturer ID code for the switch type you will connect to. Then press **Enter**.

3. Now you can configure the ISDN interface. Type `int bri` [*number*], where the *number* is the BRI interface number on the router, such as BRI 0 or BRI 1. Press **Enter**.

4. At the `config-if` prompt enter the encapsulation type (such as `encap ppp`), and then press **Enter**.

Connecting two routers with Frame Relay

If you have the opportunity to connect two routers directly using DTE and DCE V.35 cables (for configuration practice, as you do in the class I teach), you must let the router know that it will serve as a DCE device. During the serial interface configuration, use the command `frame-relay interface-type dce` at the config-if prompt. You will also have to set the clock-rate on the router that you specify as the DCE. To make the router act as a Frame-Relay switch, use the `frame relay switching` command at the global config prompt.

ISDN configuration

ISDN can be configured on a dedicated connection or a dial on demand connection where the router has been configured to dial-up and connect to send and receive data. The router can also be configured to answer incoming calls. Check out the `www.cisco.com` site for more information on configuring ISDN BRI and PRI. Also check out the documentation CD-ROM provided with your Cisco router.

5. To provide the SPID number for the two ISDN B channels at the config-if prompt, type isdn spid1 [*SPID #*], where the *SPID #* is the telephone number provided by your service provider to reach the particular channel (such as 6125551234). Using this example, the full command would be isdn spid1 6125551234. Press **Enter**.

6. To provide the SPID number for the second channel, repeat the isdn spid2 [*SPID #*] command using the SPID number for the second channel. Press **Enter** after typing the command at the config-if prompt.

7. When you have finished entering the outlined information, press **Ctrl+Z** to end the configuration session.

After configuring your ISDN interface you can use the show int bri[*number*] command to view your configuration settings. Make sure that you use the copy running-config startup-config command to save the new configuration settings to the router's NVRAM.

SEE ALSO

➤ *For an overview of ISDN, see page 60.*
➤ *For more about NVRAM, see page 113.*

chapter 16

Configuring the Router with Cisco ConfigMaker

What Is Cisco ConfigMaker?

ConfigMaker is an incredible, basic router configuration tool that Cisco provides for free. You can download it from the Cisco Web site and it comes with newer versions of the Cisco IOS on a separate CD. You can use ConfigMaker to build your router configuration (you can even build the configurations of all the routers on your internetwork) and then load them onto the routers via your network. If your network isn't up and running yet you can load the router configuration from a PC that is running ConfigMaker and is connected to the router via the Console port.

I've saved the discussion of ConfigMaker until late in the book because, although it is extremely easy to use, it isn't a substitute for an understanding and knowledge of the Cisco IOS commands that are used at the command line on a router console. ConfigMaker is a good way to quickly get a new router up and running, but the fine-tuning of the router configuration will have to be made at the command line. ConfigMaker also doesn't provide any of the router monitoring commands (like show, although you can use ping from within ConfigMaker).

One hitch in using ConfigMaker to configure a router is that the router must have Cisco IOS 11.2 or newer installed on it (The Cisco IOS was up to version 12.0 at the time of the writing of this book). To check the IOS version on your router use the show version command on the router console (at the user or privileged prompt).

If you are using one of the IOS versions that supports ConfigMaker, you're all set. If not, you can still use ConfigMaker to create a network diagram. You can also use it to become more familiar with configuring LAN protocols and their addressing systems on router interfaces.

Downloading ConfigMaker

If you didn't receive Cisco ConfigMaker with an IOS upgrade or with your router, and would still like to use it, you can download it from the Cisco Web site. You can download it even if you don't own a Cisco router, but be advised you cannot use it to configure internetworking devices from other manufacturers. When you do download ConfigMaker from the Cisco Web site, you will have to fill out a registration form.

Connect to the Internet and open your Web browser. In the address box on the Web browser type `http://www.cisco.com/warp/public/734/configmkr`. Then press **Enter**.

On the ConfigMaker Web page that opens, click the **To Download Cisco ConfigMaker, Click Here** link. You will be taken to the registration form page. Fill out the form and then click **Submit**. You will then be provided links to several FTP sites that you can download the ConfigMaker installation file. Select an FTP site and complete the download process.

After the download is complete, you will be ready to install ConfigMaker on your computer.

Installing ConfigMaker

Cisco ConfigMaker runs on Microsoft Windows 95/98–, Windows NT 4.0–, and Windows 2000–based computers. The basic system requirements for running the software are as follows:

- 486 or better (Pentium recommended) computer
- 16MB of RAM
- 20MB of free hard drive space
- SVGA monitor at 800×600 with at least 256 colors
- CD-ROM drive (if installing ConfigMaker from a CD)

As stated earlier, you can install ConfigMaker from a CD-ROM (if you received ConfigMaker with your router or an IOS upgrade) or you can install it from the download version of the ConfigMaker installation program.

For a CD-ROM installation, place the CD in your CD-ROM drive. The installation will start automatically. Follow the prompts to install ConfigMaker to a particular drive and folder on your computer.

If you are installing from the downloaded ConfigMaker installation file, locate the file on your computer using Windows Explorer, and then double-click on the filename. The installation process will begin. Follow the prompts provided to complete the installation.

Now that ConfigMaker is installed on your computer, you can use it to create internetwork diagrams and configure the routers you insert onto the diagram.

Designing Your Internetwork with ConfigMaker

ConfigMaker is really a drawing tool where you create a map or diagram of your internetwork. Icons are available for routers, hubs, LANs, Corporate networks, and a variety of other devices. You basically drag a particular device out onto the network diagram area.

When you drag devices, such as Cisco routers, onto the network diagram, you will be asked to name the device and provide passwords for the device (you will be asked to provide the login password for the router and the Privileged password for the router). In the case of routers, you will also be asked to specify the network protocols (IP, IPX, and AppleTalk) that the router will support.

ConfigMaker handles a number of tasks with easy-to-use Wizards. There is an Address Network Wizard that can be used to address the router interfaces on the various routers in the internetwork and there is a Deliver Configuration Wizard, which walks you through the steps of delivering a router configuration to a router.

The first step in designing your own internetwork with ConfigMaker is to start the software. You can start ConfigMaker from the Windows **Start** menu (click **Start**, point at **Programs**, and then click **Cisco ConfigMaker**) or double-click the **ConfigMaker** icon that was placed on the Windows desktop during the ConfigMaker installation.

Whichever method you use, the ConfigMaker application window will open as shown in Figure 16.1. If this is the first time you've started ConfigMaker you will be asked if you want to view the Getting Started Tutorial; for now let's forgo the tutorial by clicking **No**. This clears the tutorial dialog box from the screen.

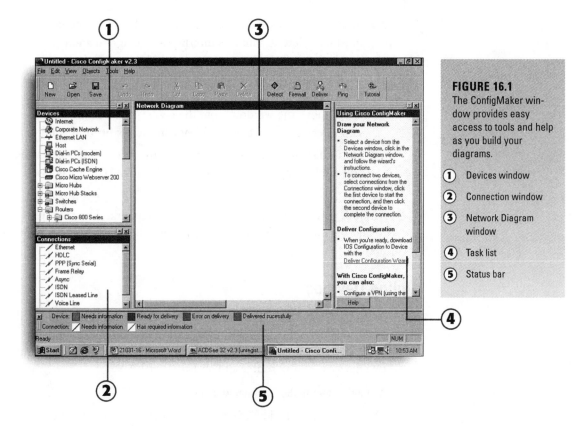

FIGURE 16.1
The ConfigMaker window provides easy access to tools and help as you build your diagrams.

1. Devices window
2. Connection window
3. Network Diagram window
4. Task list
5. Status bar

The ConfigMaker Application window is broken down into several key areas (which are also referred to as windows):

- Devices window—This window provides icons for a number of Cisco devices including routers, hubs, and switches. It also contains the icons for other network devices such as LANs and Corporate Networks.

- Connection window—This window provides the icons for the different types of connections that you can make between the devices that you place in your network diagram. There are LAN connections such as Ethernet and WAN connections such as HDLC and PPP.

- Network Diagram window—This is the space where you build your network diagram using the device icons from the Device window and the various connection icons from the Connection window.

- Task list—This window provides a checklist of all the tasks you must complete to build an internetwork diagram and connect the devices in the diagram. You can hide the Task list to give yourself more room to work in the Diagram window. Click the **View** menu, and then click **Task List** to clear the checkmark and remove the window from the application window (use these same steps to put the window back in the application window).

- Status bar—Provides information on the status of devices when you are loading configurations from ConfigMaker to a device.

Now that you're familiar with the geography of the ConfigMaker window, you can begin to build your internetwork. The first step is to add the devices, such as routers, that will be a part of your internetwork.

Adding Devices

Adding devices to the internetwork diagram is very straightforward. You can add routers (which is of special interest to us, of course) and other devices such as LANs. Let's walk through the steps of adding two devices: a 2505 router and an Ethernet LAN.

Adding routers to the Diagram window

1. First, you will add a 2505 router to the diagram. Scroll down through the Device list until you see the 2505 router folder. Click the **Plus (+)** symbol on the left of the folder to open it. This lists all the routers in the 2500 series family (see Figure 16.2).

2. To add a 2505 router to the diagram, click the **2505** icon and then click in the Diagram window. The Cisco 2505 Router Wizard will appear.

3. In the Device Name box (in the Wizard window), type the name that you want to give to your router (in this case you will use **Popeye**). After typing the name, click **Next**.

4. The next Wizard screen asks you to provide a router password and a Privileged password (see Figure 16.3). Type the passwords you want to use in the appropriate boxes and then click **Next**.

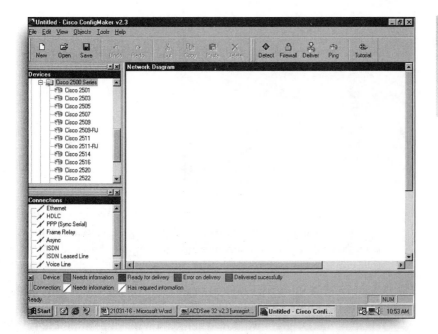

FIGURE 16.2
Router folders are provided that contain the icons for routers that are part of that series.

FIGURE 16.3
The Router Wizard asks you to set the login and privileged passwords for the router.

5. The next screen asks you which network protocols you want to enable on this router. IP is the default, but you can also add IPX and AppleTalk (see Figure 16.4). Click the check boxes for the protocols you want to select, and then click **Next**.

6. The last wizard screen lets you know that your router will be added to the diagram. Click **Finish** to end the process.

FIGURE 16.4
You can quickly select the protocols that you want enabled on the router.

Getting rid of icons

If you select a Device or Connection icon and decide that you've chosen the wrong one, press **Esc** to discard the icon before transferring it to the Diagram window. If you've already placed the device in the window, select the device and press **Delete**.

Your router will appear in the Diagram window. You can change the position of the router in the window by dragging it to a new location. Now that you have a router on the diagram, let's add a LAN that you can connect to the router.

Adding a LAN is very simple. Locate the Ethernet LAN icon in the Devices window. Click the **icon** in the Devices window and then click on the Diagram window where you want to position the LAN icon.

The Ethernet LAN will appear in the Diagram window. Figure 16.5 shows your work so far. You have a router and a LAN in the diagram window. You need to connect them with the appropriate connection type.

Connecting LANs to Routers

Connecting LANs to routers is very straightforward. All you have to do is choose the appropriate connection type from the Connection window and then place it between the router and the LAN. At that point you will also have to supply addressing information such as the IP address for the router interface and the subnet mask. If you chose IPX and AppleTalk as supported protocols when you placed the router on the diagram, you will also have to supply addressing information for each of these protocols.

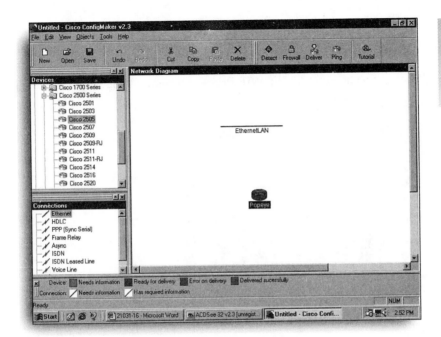

FIGURE 16.5
LANs and routers added to the diagram must be connected.

Connecting a router to a LAN

1. Because you have an Ethernet LAN, the connection between the LAN and the router must be an Ethernet connection. Locate the Ethernet Connection icon in the Connection window. Click on the icon to select it.

2. Click on the router and then click on the Ethernet LAN. This strings the Ethernet connection between the two device icons.

3. As soon as you click on the second icon (the Ethernet LAN), the Ethernet Wizard appears. The wizard helps you set up the connection between an Ethernet LAN and a router Ethernet interface. Click **Next** to begin.

4. You are asked to enter the IP address and subnet mask for the Ethernet interface on Popeye (if you were routing IPX, you would be asked for the IPX network address, for AppleTalk you would be asked the cable range and the zone name). Type the IP address for the router interface in the IP address box (see Figure 16.6).

5. Enter the subnet mask for the interface in the **Subnet Mask** box. You can alternatively enter the number of network bits plus the number of subnet bits used to create your subnets. See Chapter 10, "TCP/IP Primer," to remind you what I'm talking about).

FIGURE 16.6
Enter the IP Address and the Subnet Mask for your router interface.

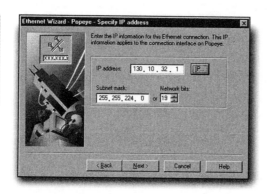

The Ethernet Wizard has an IP calculator

If you click the **IP** button on the Ethernet Wizard screen where you enter the IP address and subnet mask for the router interface, you can see the range of addresses that are available in the subnet that you set and the broadcast and network address for the subnet that you are pulling the current IP address from. When you figure out the ranges of IP addresses in your subnet (see Chapter 10), use the IP calculator in the Ethernet Wizard to check your math.

6. After entering the IP address and the subnet mask, click **Next** to continue.

7. You are told by the last wizard screen that your connection was created successfully. Click **Finish** to close the wizard.

Your connection will appear between the router and the Ethernet LAN. To view the addressing related to the connection (the router interface), click the **View** menu, point at **Attributes**, and then choose either **IP Address**, **IPX Address**, or **AppleTalk Address** (depending on the type of network addressing you are using on the Ethernet LAN and the router). As you know, you can have more than one addressing scheme on the router, so you may want to select more than one option on the **Attributes** submenu.

You can also use the **Attributes** submenu to label the interfaces on the routers that appear in your diagram. Click the **View** menu, point at **Attributes**, and then choose **Port Number**. Figure 16.7 shows the connection that you created between your router and the Ethernet LAN with the router interface labeled with interface number and IP addressing information.

Now that you've seen how to connect a LAN to a router, let's take a look at how you use ConfigMaker to set up serial connections between routers.

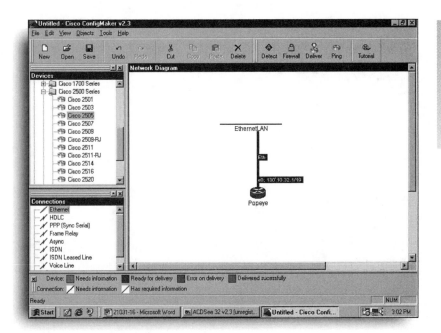

FIGURE 16.7
Use the **View** menu to turn on some of the view attributes such as addressing, to provide address labeling on the diagram.

Connecting Routers to Routers

As you already know, routers can be connected using LAN cabling (you can connect two routers in ConfigMaker using the Ethernet connection) or connected to each other remotely using serial connections and a particular WAN protocol such as PPP or Frame-Relay. ConfigMaker makes it very easy for you to create serial connections between the routers on your diagrams. First, you will add another router (it doesn't matter what kind, you may want to explore some of the high end routers in ConfigMaker, even if your company doesn't use them). I've placed another 2505 router on my diagram (see Figure 16.8) and will connect it to the router that is currently in the diagram (Popeye).

Connecting a router to a router with a WAN protocol

1. With the two routers visible in the Diagram window, click the Wan Protocol connection type (such as PPP) in the Connection window.

2. Click the first router and then click the second router to specify where you want to create the connection.

FIGURE 16.8
Place two routers on the diagram and then you can connect them with a particular WAN technology.

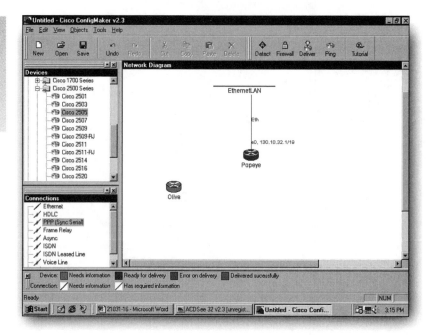

FIGURE 16.8
Place two routers on the diagram and then you can connect them with a particular WAN technology.

3. As soon as you click on the second router icon, the Wizard for the WAN protocol that you selected (such as PPP or HDLC) will open. In the figures shown in subsequent steps you will see that I chose **PPP**.

4. To begin the connection process click **Next**.

5. On the next screen you are asked to select a serial interface (such as Serial 0) to configure for the WAN connection. Use the drop-down arrow on the Wizard screen to select the serial interface you want to use (see Figure 16.9). Then click **Next** to continue.

FIGURE 16.9
Select the serial port you want to configure for the WAN connection to the other router.

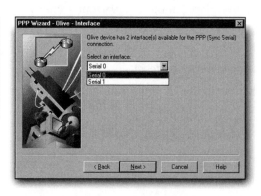

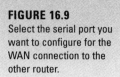

6. On the next screen you are asked to enter the addressing information for the Serial port that you chose (see Figure 16.10). In this case (because I set up the router's to route IP only, you must provide the IP address and subnet mask for the serial interface on Olive. Enter the IP address and Subnet Mask and then click **Next** to continue.

FIGURE 16.10
Provide the addressing information for the selected serial interface, such as the IP address and subnet mask.

7. On the next screen you are asked to select the serial interface on the other router (in this case Popeye) After using the drop-down arrow to select a serial interface, click **Next**.

8. Supply the addressing information (such as IP address and subnet mask) as you did for the other router in step 6. Click **Next** to continue.

9. The next screen asks you if you want to create a backup connection for this WAN connection. In this case, you will go with **No Backup** (the default). Click **Next**.

10. On the last screen you are told that you have successfully created a WAN connection. Click **Finish**.

The connection will be created in the Diagram window (see Figure 16.11). If you have the View Addressing attribute turned on (using the **View** menu), you can see the addressing information for the serial interface on each of the created routers.

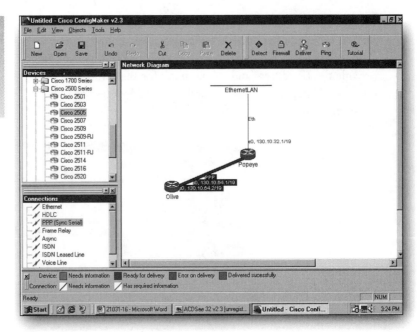

FIGURE 16.11
The new WAN connection will appear between the routers in the Diagram window.

Delivering the Configuration to a Router

You can use ConfigMaker to build an entire internetwork diagram. You can connect LANs and routers, hosts and routers, and connect routers to routers. All the devices that you could possibly need and the various connection types are available in the Device and Connection windows respectively. After you build your internetwork, you can actually use the configuration settings that you provided for your router (or routers) interfaces directly to the router.

You can download a configuration to a router or routers using a PC that is running ConfigMaker and is connected to the same network that the routers are connected to. You must have configured the PC and routers with IP addresses, however, before ConfigMaker can send the configuration over the network. This requires that you "preconfigure" the router using the router console.

An easier method of quickly delivering a configuration to a router that contains no configuration what-so-ever, is to download the configuration from a PC running ConfigMaker that is connected to the router using the console port and console roll-over cable. You would connect the PC to the router as you would connect a PC console.

One thing that you should check before you try to deliver the configuration (as shown in the steps that follow), is that ConfigMaker will deliver the configuration port using the correct serial port on your computer. The default setting is COM port 1.

If you need to change the COM port setting, click the **View** menu, and then select **Options**. In the Options dialog box that appears use the COM port drop-down arrow to select he appropriate COM port and then click **OK**.

Delivering a router configuration using the Console port

1. With the internetwork diagram open in ConfigMaker that contains the router configuration that you want to deliver, select the appropriate router icon (see Figure 16.12). I selected the Popeye configuration).

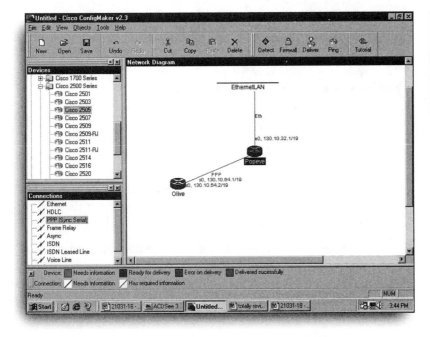

FIGURE 16.12
Select the router icon that will supply the configuration you will deliver to the connected router.

2. Click the **Deliver** button on the ConfigMaker toolbar. The Deliver Configuration Wizard will open, listing the router that you selected in your diagram.

3. Click **Next** to continue. The next screen tells you to make sure that no other programs are using the COM port that will be used to deliver the configuration (if this PC also serves as the router's console, make sure that your terminal emulation software isn't running).

4. When you are ready to deliver the configuration, click **Next**.

That status of the configuration delivery will be displayed on the Wizard screen (see Figure 16.13). The current configuration on the router (if any) will be erased and then the router will be rebooted. The new configuration will then be loaded into the router's NVRAM.

FIGURE 16.13
You can watch the progress of the configuration delivery.

A final wizard screen will appear providing the router name, the delivery method (console) and the time and date that the delivery was completed. Click **Finish** to close the wizard box.

Your router is now configured with the configuration that was downloaded. Use your terminal emulation software and check out the delivered configuration using the show startup-config command. You should see the same settings that you placed in the configuration for the router that appeared in your ConfigMaker diagram.

When you have finished working on a particular internetwork diagram, click the **Save** button on the ConfigMaker toolbar. In the Save As dialog box type a name for the internetwork diagram and use the **Save In** drop-down box to specify a drive and folder for the file. Click **Save** in the dialog box to save your diagram.

To exit ConfigMaker, click the **File** menu, and then click **Exit**. ConfigMaker is a pretty cool piece of software. Use it to learn more about the hardware and software configurations of the various routers and devices that Cisco manufactures. It's not bad at all for free.

SEE ALSO

➤ *For a review of connecting a PC console to the router, see page 115.*

> **Getting help in ConfigMaker**
>
> ConfigMaker is a typical Windows program. Click the **Help** menu, and then click Cisco **ConfigMaker Help Topics** to open the Help dialog box. You can use the **Contents**, **Index**, and **Find** tabs to get help on the various ConfigMaker features.

chapter 17

Using a TFTP Server for Router Configuration Storage

What Is a TFTP Server?

Saving router configurations to a location other than the router's own NVRAM is a way to protect the time and effort that you have put in configuring a particular router. When all is said and done the router configuration becomes the main factor in how the router actually gets its job done. So being able to back up the configuration file is a vital part of building some fault tolerance into your internetworking. You already know that when you reconfigure a router you must use the **Copy** command to move the new configuration parameters from the running configuration to the startup configuration in NVRAM. There is also a way to copy a running configuration or startup configuration to a computer that is on the network.

Trivial File Transfer Protocol (TFTP) is a TCP/IP transport protocol that can be used to move files from the router to a PC running TFTP server software. TFTP is actually very similar to the *File Transfer Protocol (FTP)* that is used for uploading and downloading files on the Internet (your Web browser supports FTP). FTP requires a username and password when you log on to an FTP server.

TFTP doesn't require a username or password (hence the "trivial" notation). All you need to know is the IP address of the computer that is running the TFTP server software and you can copy your configuration file to the server. You can also use TFTP servers to copy a configuration file to your router or upgrade (or change) your router IOS image by copying a new IOS file to the router's flash RAM. Because most routers don't have disk drives, TFTP servers provide you with an alternative location for backup files related to the router (such as a copy of the configuration or alternative configurations). Figure 17.1 depicts the different file manipulations that can take place between a router and a TFTP server.

So, a TFTP server is a PC that is running TFTP server software and is accessible on the network. Because neither login nor password is required, all you need to know to connect to the TFTP server is its IP address.

SEE ALSO

➤ *For information on using the* **Copy** *command with configuration files, see page 154.*

FTP and the Web

You probably have access to FTP sites on the World Wide Web, and have downloaded files from them. And you are probably thinking that you don't remember providing a username and password. Many of the FTP sites available on the Web are anonymous FTP sites. You log in as anonymous with no password (or your IP address or email address sometimes serves as the password). When you log on to a secure FTP site, you have to provide an appropriate username and password.

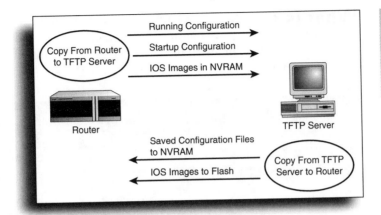

FIGURE 17.1
You can copy files from the router to the TFTP server and vice versa.

Obtaining TFTP Software

Several different TFTP server software packages are available. Cisco provides a free TFTP server application for registered Cisco product users. The TFTP server software can be downloaded from the Cisco site at www.cisco.com.

If you don't have access to the Cisco TFTP server software or would like to try other TFTP server software, you can find it on the Web. Use your favorite search engine and search for the keywords **TFTP server**. One shareware TFTP server is the SolarWinds TFTP server available at http://www.solarwinds.net/. SolarWinds makes a number of add-on tools for Cisco routers. You will find that most of the TFTP server software packages work pretty much the same. You start the server software and then execute the appropriate commands on the router. The TFTP server is pretty passive throughout the entire process but most TFTP server applications will have a window that shows you the status of a copy to or from the server.

If you want to use the Cisco TFTP server software, all you need to do is log on to the Cisco site (www.cisco.com) using your customer username and password (provided to you by the Cisco reseller that sold you your router). Then click the **Software Center** link on the Cisco Home Page.

On the Software Center page, click the link for **Other Software**. You will be taken to the page that provides the link for downloading the Cisco TFTP server (see Figure 17.2). Click the link and then choose an appropriate folder on your computer where the server software can be placed during the download. After the download is complete, you can install the Cisco TFTP server software as outlined in the next section.

FIGURE 17.2
Cisco's TFTP server can be downloaded from the Cisco software center on the Web.

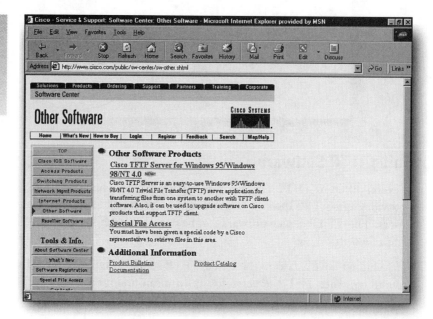

Installing the Cisco TFTP Server Software

You can install the Cisco TFTP server software on a Windows 95/98 workstation that is on the same network as the router (this means that the router is the default gateway for the TFTP server). For example if the router's Ethernet 0 port is configured with the IP number 10.16.0.1, this number should be entered as the workstation's default gateway. The IP address for the workstation also needs to be in the same subnet range as the Ethernet 0 port. Because I've divided a Class A network (you should be able to tell this by the first Octet of the default gateway IP address, if not, go back and take another look at Chapter 11) into 14 subnets, and used the first subnet on the Ethernet network connected to the router's E0 port, the range of IP addresses available would be 10.16.0.1 to 10.32.255.254. Because my workstation serves as the TFTP server, I made sure its IP address was in this range. I chose 10.16.0.4 in the TCP/IP Properties dialog box, as shown in Figure 17.3.

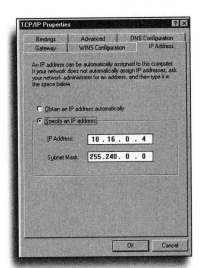

FIGURE 17.3
Make sure the workstation that will serve as the TFTP server is configured with an appropriate IP number.

After you've got the IP addressing squared away, you can set up the TFTP server software on the workstation. The installation process is very straightforward.

Setting up the Cisco TFTP server software

1. Use the Windows Explorer to locate the folder where you downloaded the Cisco TFTP server software.

2. Double-click the **Cisco TFTP** icon. The installation program for the software will load.

3. Click **Next** after reading the opening Installation. You will be asked to choose a location for the installation of the TFTP server software or allow it to be installed to a default folder.

4. Choose a different folder using the **Browse** button or go with the default. Click **Next** to continue.

5. A Default Icons folder will be created for the TFTP program. You can choose to have the icon placed in another folder by selecting the folder list provided on this screen. Click **Next** to continue.

6. The software will be installed. Click **Finish** to complete the process.

DHCP servers automatically assign IP addresses

If you use a DHCP server, such as an NT 4 server with DHCP enabled, IP addresses are automatically assigned to the workstations on the network. You might want to block out an address for the workstation that will serve as the TFTP server and manually assign the address in the TCP/IP properties box (see Figure 17.3).

Now that the software is installed on the workstation that will serve as the TFTP server, you are ready to copy files to and from the router. The next section discusses copying a configuration file to the TFTP server.

Copying to the TFTP Server

As you learned previously, you can copy startup configuration files from NVRAM or the running configuration file from RAM to the TFTP server. For example, let's say that you have a solid startup configuration saved in NVRAM and you want to save it to the TFTP server before you make any changes to it. This would enable you to restore the original startup configuration file to the router from the TFTP server, if your configuration changes turn out to affect network operations negatively.

Copying the startup configuration to the TFTP server

1. Start the TFTP server software on the workstation: select the **Start** menu, choose **Programs**, and then click **Cisco TFTP Server**. The TFTP Server window will open. The window is really just a gray, empty box that displays the IP address of the TFTP server (the computer you are running the software on) on the Title bar.

2. On your router console, enter the Privileged mode using the `enable` command and the enable password.

3. At the router prompt, type `copy startup-config tftp`, and then press **Enter**.

4. You are asked to provide the IP address of the remote host. Enter the IP address of the TFTP server (in this case my IP address was `10.16.0.4`). Then press the **Enter** key.

5. You will be asked to supply the name of the file you would like to write to the server. The default is the router's name followed by config (such as cisco2505-config). Press **Enter** to accept the default or enter the name of the configuration file you want to copy and then press **Enter**.

6. You will be asked to confirm the procedure (see Figure 17.4). Press **Enter** to confirm (if you don't want to confirm, type n for no and you will be returned to the Privileged prompt).

The file will be written to the TFTP server. A prompt reading
Writing router name-config. !! [OK] means that the copy was a success. If you return to the TFTP Server workstation and look at the
server window, you will find that a record of the copy job has been
recorded, as shown in Figure 17.5. The TFTP server window also
confirms that the copy job was a success.

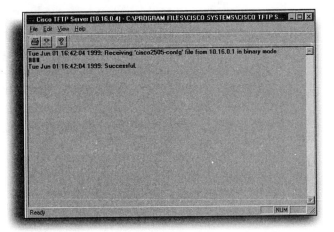

You can also copy the running-config from RAM using the procedure outlined. The only difference is that the command in step 3
would read copy running-config tftp.

Copying from the TFTP Server

The reverse operation—copying a file from the TFTP server to the
router—is as straightforward as the process outlined in the previous
section. You can copy a configuration file from the TFTP server into
the router's NVRAM or you can copy the configuration from the
server directly into RAM as a new running-configuration. If you
copy the file into NVRAM it not only becomes the new running
configuration for the router but it also will be the startup configuration when you reboot the router. Let's take a look at how to copy the

Viewing the copied file

You can take a look at the configuration file that was copied using the Window Explorer on the TFTP server workstation. Right-click the *My Computer* icon and choose *Explore* from the shortcut menu. The default location for the TFTP server folder is C:\Cisco Systems\ Cisco TFTP Server. Check out this folder in Explorer and you should see the copy of the configuration file that was placed there during the copy process.

configuration file from the server into the NVRAM where it becomes the new startup configuration for the router.

Copying the startup configuration to router

1. Start the TFTP server software on the server workstation.

2. On your router console, enter the Privileged mode using the `enable` command and the enable password.

3. At the router prompt, type `copy tftp startup-config`, and then press **Enter**.

4. You are asked to provide the IP address of the remote host. Enter the IP address of the TFTP server (in this case my IP address was 10.16.0.4). Then press the **Enter** key.

5. You are asked to provide the name of the configuration file on the TFTP server you want to copy. Type the name at the prompt (if you use the default name when you copied the file to the server, you don't need to enter a new name). Press **Enter** to continue.

6. You will be asked to confirm the procedure (see Figure 17.6). Press **Enter** to confirm.

FIGURE 17.6

After you've entered the IP address for the server and the filename, press Enter to confirm the process.

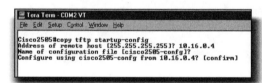

The file will be loaded to the router and will become the active configuration (and will be saved in NVRAM). Again you will receive an [OK] message on the router that the procedure was a success. You can return to the TFTP server where the process will also be confirmed as a success.

Loading a New IOS from the TFTP Server

As you can see, copying to and from the TFTP server is a pretty easy process (when you compare it to creating IP subnets or doing some of the other configuration chores required by the router). You can also use the TFTP server to copy various versions of the IOS to the Flash RAM on the router. This makes it very easy to update the operating system on the router.

Cisco is constantly fine-tuning the IOS available for their routers. A number of different release versions are available. At the time this book was being written a new release, version 12, became available. Of course, as with any new operating system, bugs are found and fixes are programmed so a number of service releases are also made available for new IOS versions. In Cisco's case, upgrade versions of even what would be considered an older IOS such as 11 are still being fine-tuned, as well. You can view all the most recent IOS versions available on the Cisco Web site at www.cisco.com.

To download operating system images (files), you must have the appropriate service agreement with the Cisco reseller who sold you your router. A valid service contract number is required and you must register on the Cisco site to download IOS files. Figure 17.7 shows the Web page that provides the links to the various IOS images. This page also provides a convenient IOS planner that enables you to choose new IOS versions by your router (for example, I would click my Cisco 2505 router and only the IOS images appropriate for that model of router would appear on the Planner page.

To load a new IOS into a router's Flash RAM, download an appropriate IOS image from the Cisco Web site (if you purchased an IOS update from your Cisco reseller, you might also have the IOS files on a CD). Place the IOS file in the TFTP server's root folder. The default for this folder is C:\Cisco Systems\Cisco TFTP Server and you can use the Windows Explorer to copy or move the file to the appropriate folder.

Copy not working?

If the copy doesn't work, it typically means that the TFTP server cannot be found on the network. Make sure that the workstation is connected to the network and that the IP address for the workstation/TFTP server is in the same subnet range as the Ethernet port on the router that serves that particular subnet. If you think you have everything set up correctly, ping the TFTP server. At the router console prompt type `ping IP Address`, and then press **Enter** (where the IP address is that of the server/workstation). If you get a positive result, reinstall the TFTP software and try the process again.

FIGURE 17.7
Cisco provides a conve-
nient IOS Planner page
on the Web that you can
use to identify router IOS
updates available for
your router.

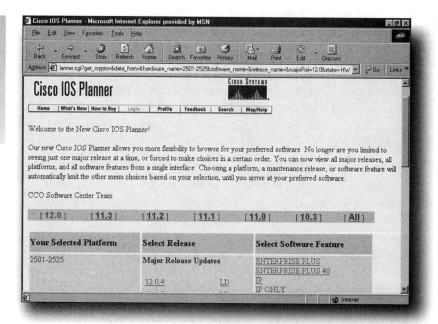

Now you are ready to copy the new IOS into the router's Flash. Be advised that this version of the IOS will replace the previous version. You can choose to not have the Flash RAM erased during the copy process, but that means you will have multiple copies of the IOS in Flash; in the case of the 2505 router with only 8MB of Flash, there is only enough room for one IOS image, anyhow.

After the IOS file is on the TFTP Server, you are ready to begin the process that will move the IOS file onto the router.

Copying a New IOS to the Router's Flash RAM

1. Start the TFTP server software on the server workstation.

2. On your router console, enter the Privileged mode using the `enable` command and the enable password.

3. At the router prompt, type `copy tftp flash`, and then press **Enter**.

4. You are notified that the router will proceed with the copy, but that router functions will be stopped while the IOS image is updated. To proceed, press **Enter**.

5. You are asked to provide the IP address of the remote host. Enter the IP address of the TFTP server (in this case my IP address was 10.16.0.4). Then press the **Enter** key.

6. You are asked to provide the name of the IOS file on the TFTP server you want to copy. Type the name at the prompt. Make sure the file is an IOS Image; in your example I used 80114109.bin, which is the image for IOS 11.2. Press **Enter** to continue.

7. You will then be asked for the destination filename. Go with the default name of the IOS (as entered in step 6). Press **Enter** to continue.

8. You will be asked to confirm that the flash RAM will be erased before the new IOS is written to it. Press **Enter** to confirm. Because Flash contains the current IOS, you will be asked to confirm a second time. Press **Enter** to confirm.

9. You will be asked whether you want to save the modified system configuration. Type yes, and then press **Enter**. Figure 17.8 shows my entries on the 2505 router for the upgrade of the IOS.

10. You will be asked for a final confirmation to proceed with the Flash erase. Type yes and press **Enter**.

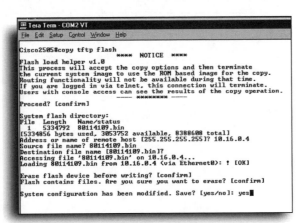

FIGURE 17.8
The writing of a new IOS to Flash RAM requires a number of confirmation steps.

The current IOS image will be erased and replaced by the new IOS image. A series of exclamation points appear on the router as the process takes place. This process may take a couple of minutes because the IOS images can be quite large (the 11.2 IOS is over 6MB). If you take a peek at the Cisco TFTP server window, a series of number symbols (#) repeat across the screen as the process takes place.

The router will reboot after the new IOS file is copied. You can now press **Enter** and enter the console password (if required) to place yourself at the user prompt. To check your new IOS image, type show flash at the prompt, and then press **Enter**. The new IOS image (the filename you entered in step 6) should now reside in the router's Flash.

You can also copy the current IOS image to a TFTP server if you want. This gives you a backup if the Flash RAM on the router goes bad or you just like having a copy of the IOS safely filed away in a secondary location. The command at the Privileged prompt would be copy flash tftp. You then provide the IP address of the server and other information as requested in the steps already discussed.

TFTP servers make an excellent repository for alternative configuration files and IOS updates. They supply you with the backup storage space that the router itself doesn't have.

chapter

18

Basic Router Troubleshooting

Troubleshooting Hardware Problems

Although the subject of troubleshooting your router connections and configurations would certainly fill an entire book (or books), it probably makes sense to finish up a primer book on internetworking and Cisco routers with a basic overview of troubleshooting techniques. Hardware problems that you could face can include a failed router interface controller, making an interface or interfaces inoperable, or a router that has just rolled over and died completely.

Other problems on your internetwork will most likely boil down to two categories such as physical connection problems and router configuration problems. Some physical connection problems you have control over such as a bad router serial cable or a hardware problem with a hub or a stretch of network cabling. Other events such as an out-of-control Jeep Cherokee crashing into the phone company's switching equipment is just a little beyond your control. Some hardware problems you can fix; others you just have to sit and wait (which is difficult when your users can't access the resources that they need to do their jobs).

As far as configuration problems go, some adjustments to a configuration might be necessary if there are radical changes to the network topology (such as a downed connection). In other cases, your original configuration might not be up snuff and you need to edit it to resolve issues that are affecting the internetwork negatively. You will look at configuration issues and the troubleshooting of specific protocols later in this chapter.

Router Problems

Router hardware problems can revolve around interface controllers, RAM modules, the router's processor, and even the router's fan. And although it might sound silly, the first thing you should check on a router that is down is whether the router has been turned off or the power cord has been kicked out of the wall socket.

You learned the basics of router interfaces in Chapter 6, "Understanding Router Interfaces." The various network and WAN interfaces on the router are each connected to a controller. The interface controller is either hardwired to the router's motherboard (as is the case with the 2500 series) or contained on the interface card that you placed in one of the slots available on the router (as is the case with Cisco's higher end routers like the 4500 series).

One way to check a particular interface on the router is using the show interfaces command. If the interface is up and the line protocol is up (as shown in Figure 18.1), you don't have a problem with that interface. If the interface controller no longer functions, the interface won't register as an available interface when you use the show interfaces command. If the interface is up and the line protocol is down, your problem is a configuration issue, not a hardware problem.

FIGURE 18.1
The show interfaces command can be used to quickly check the interface status on a router.

You can also check the controllers on your router. The show controllers command provides statistics for interface controller cards. Figure 18.2 shows the results of the show controller ethernet command.

Another component on the router that is of vital importance is the router's fan (it's one of the cheapest parts but also one of the most important). If the fan doesn't work, the router will overheat (just like a PC with a broken fan). It will reboot. So, if you have a router that seems to reboot after only being on for a short period of time, power up the router and listen carefully to see if the fan is working.

Check LAN and WAN connections

If a particular interface is down, such as a serial interface, the V.35 cable might have become disconnected. Always check the various LAN and WAN connections to the router. Loose cables can make it appear as if there is a hardware problem with the router itself.

(Some of the high-end Cisco routers actually have complex cooling systems and also enable you to monitor the temperature of the device.)

FIGURE 18.2
The show controller command can be used to view statistics related to the controllers installed on the router.

In cases where the router crashes, it can be tough to determine if the problem was hardware- or software-related. You can use the show stacks command to retrieve error messages that were saved by the ROM monitor at the time of the crash. (Cisco technical support representatives can use the show stacks information to pinpoint the software or hardware problem that caused the crash).

Besides the physical failure of router components, you might also run into situations where the router doesn't have enough RAM (or processor speed) to really handle all the traffic that you have flowing through it. You might need to add additional routers to the internetwork to lighten the load or upgrade existing router hardware components (such as RAM). In some cases you might want to upgrade from the existing router to a higher-end router.

One way that network administrators identify bottlenecks on their networks (a *bottleneck* is a device that is slowing network traffic) is to use some type of network management software package that allows the monitoring of devices, protocols, and other aspects of the network and enables you to view the current health of your internetwork. CiscoWorks is an example of a network management software package that provides a number of tools for monitoring and troubleshooting internetworks. On large internetworks some sort of network management software is vital for keeping tabs on the network and its various devices.

Other Hardware Problems

Other hardware problems that will affect the job that your router is doing relate to devices that are directly connected to the router.

On Ethernet networks, hubs are typically attached to an Ethernet port on the router. If the hub goes down, the LAN's connection to the router also goes down, making node addresses on the LAN unavailable to other nodes on the internetwork.

Hubs typically have a power on LED somewhere on the unit that makes it easy for you to determine whether the hub is on or off. If the hub is plugged in and turned on and still provides no indication that the unit has powered up, replace the hub.

If you are having trouble with individual nodes on a LAN, hubs typically have an LED that lights when a particular port on the hub is connected to a node via a twisted-pair cable. If the display light isn't on, you either have a bad cable (see the next section concerning cabling and LAN connections) or the port on the hub is bad.

The same types of problems can be associated with router connections to Token Ring networks. A Token Ring Multi-Station Access Unit will be attached to the router providing the connection between the nodes on the LAN and the router. If the Access Unit goes down, the LAN's connection to the router will be disrupted.

WAN connectivity devices can also pose potential problems to the internetwork. Routers are often connected to CSU/DSUs that provide connectivity to certain WAN technologies such as leased lines and packet-switching network. If the CSU/DSU goes down, the WAN connection between the router and the rest of the internetwork also goes down.

If the hardware problem is related to your service provider's switching equipment there is little that you can do to fix the problem yourself. You have to sit and wait for the connection to come back up. In many cases, network administrators will build fault tolerance into an

> **Approach your troubleshooting systematically**
>
> Whether you are troubleshooting hardware or software problems, approach the problem systematically. First identify the problem, and then gather facts related to the problem. You can use various router commands to help you gather facts. After you have some information to work with, take each parameter that might be the cause of the problem and test it individually until you find the cause of the problem. Changing a lot of different parameters all at once isn't going to let you identify the root cause of a particular problem.

internetwork by providing redundant connections (backup connections) between certain routers. For example, you might have a Frame Relay connection between two routers. As a backup, you configure the router so that it can also connect to the remote router using a dial-up connection over a modem if necessary. The modem line won't give you the speed that the Frame-Relay connection will, but if you have to move time-sensitive data, you at least have a backup route for the packets.

Cabling Problems

Connectivity problems on a LAN related to physical cabling on the LAN can be due to shorts, breaks, and other problems. In cases where physical connections (that you have control over) are suspect, a variety of tools are available for checking cabling ranging from voltmeters to time domain reflectometers (TDR).

A digital *voltmeter* is a simple device that can be connected to a cable and test the cable for a break or a short. Basically, the voltmeter can tell you if the cable is bad or not and whether you are looking at a short or break. If the cable has a short, replace it. If there is a break, you must trace the cable (have fun standing on a ladder with your head stuck up in the drop-ceiling) to find where the break has occurred.

A *TDR* is a more sophisticated device that can diagnose shorts and breaks in a cable but it can also provide you with information on where the short or break exists on the cable. The TDR actually emits short pulses down the cable and is able to use a timing mechanism that estimates the distance that the pulse has traveled.

Network cabling is always suspect. People move furniture and disrupt cable connections, a leaky roof allows cabling in the ceiling to become soaked with water (sometimes leading to shorts)—all sorts of weird things can happen to cables that sever the connection that they were providing. Always check cables first. Then move on to some of the other devices you've discussed.

SEE ALSO

➤ *For a review of network cabling, see page 17.*

A Final Word on Hardware

When troubleshooting hardware problems, don't immediately assume that the connection problem lies with the router's hardware. Make sure that you systematically check the other devices discussed in this section and their connective media to the router. Because routers usually live out their lives powered on (you aren't constantly turning them on and off), the hardware does seem to last forever (as long at the fan doesn't go down or you place it in a closed closet where the temperature is about 100 degrees).

You can protect the router itself against power problems using a couple of different devices. Uninterruptible Power Supplies (*UPS*) will supply power to the router using a battery if the electricity is cut. You can protect the router against power surges using some sort of surge suppressor. The router isn't unlike a computer, so place it in an environment that is favorable to a valuable electronic device.

Troubleshooting LAN Interfaces

Another aspect of troubleshooting the router's connection to LANs is becoming familiar with the output that appears on the router console when you use certain IOS commands to diagnose problems. One of the most powerful diagnostic tools on the router is the show command. You will take a look at the show command and how the information that it provides is related to two popular LAN types: Ethernet and Token Ring.

SEE ALSO

➤ *For a review of Ethernet and Token Ring, see page 25.*

Troubleshooting Ethernet with Show

Ethernet is a passive network architecture that uses Carrier Sense Multiple Access with Collision Detection (CSMA/CD) as its strategy for network access. Problems related to Ethernet can revolve around excess collisions on the network due to cable breaks, cable runs that exceed the maximum length allowed, and malfunctioning network cards that can cause excessive broadcast traffic.

The show interfaces ethernet [*interface number*] command enables you to view statistics related to a particular Ethernet interface. Figure 18.3 shows the results of this command on an Ethernet 0 interface on a Cisco 2505 router.

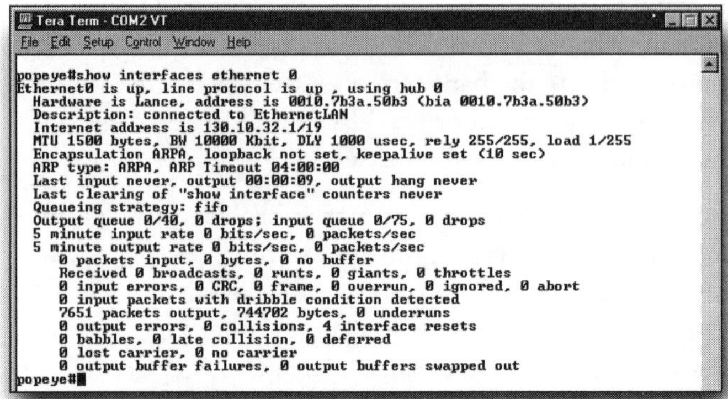

FIGURE 18.3
The show interfaces ethernet command can be used to view statistics related to the Ethernet interfaces installed on the router.

```
Tera Term - COM2 VT
File  Edit  Setup  Control  Window  Help

popeye#show interfaces ethernet 0
Ethernet0 is up, line protocol is up , using hub 0
  Hardware is Lance, address is 0010.7b3a.50b3 (bia 0010.7b3a.50b3)
  Description: connected to EthernetLAN
  Internet address is 130.10.32.1/19
  MTU 1500 bytes, BW 10000 Kbit, DLY 1000 usec, rely 255/255, load 1/255
  Encapsulation ARPA, loopback not set, keepalive set (10 sec)
  ARP type: ARPA, ARP Timeout 04:00:00
  Last input never, output 00:00:09, output hang never
  Last clearing of "show interface" counters never
  Queueing strategy: fifo
  Output queue 0/40, 0 drops; input queue 0/75, 0 drops
  5 minute input rate 0 bits/sec, 0 packets/sec
  5 minute output rate 0 bits/sec, 0 packets/sec
     0 packets input, 0 bytes, 0 no buffer
     Received 0 broadcasts, 0 runts, 0 giants, 0 throttles
     0 input errors, 0 CRC, 0 frame, 0 overrun, 0 ignored, 0 abort
     0 input packets with dribble condition detected
     7651 packets output, 744702 bytes, 0 underruns
     0 output errors, 0 collisions, 4 interface resets
     0 babbles, 0 late collision, 0 deferred
     0 lost carrier, 0 no carrier
     0 output buffer failures, 0 output buffers swapped out
popeye#
```

Although the statistics provided might seem rather cryptic at first examination, they actually provide a great deal of information that can help you troubleshoot problems related to an Ethernet interface. Some of these statistics also provide insight into the use of other hardware resources on the router such as RAM. The list that follows highlights some of the statistics found in response to the show interfaces ethernet [*interface number*] command.

■ Ethernet 0 is Up, Line Protocol is Up—This lets you know that the interface is active and that the Ethernet protocols believe that the line is usable. If the interface is down, check the LAN connection to the interface. You can also try to bring up the interface in the Configuration mode (if the LAN connection is okay). Enter the configuration-if mode for the interface and "bounce" the interface. Use the shut command (to down the interface), and then use the no shut command to up the interface. This might bring the interface back up.

■ Hardware Address—This is the hexadecimal MAC address for the interface.

■ Internet Address—This is the IP address and subnet mask assigned to the interface (you will learn IP addressing in the "Troubleshooting TCP/IP" section).

- MTU—This is the maximum transmission unit for the interface in bytes.

- BW—This is the bandwidth for the interface in kilobits/second.

- Rely—This is a measurement of the reliability of the line with 255/255 being 100 percent reliable. The lower the first number in the reliability measurement, the less reliable the interface connection (due to downed lines or other problems).

- Load—This measures the current load on the interface. The measurement 255/255 would be a totally saturated interface (meaning too much traffic, you might need to add another interface or router to service the network).

- Encapsulation—This is the Ethernet frame type assigned to the interface. ARPA is the default and is the 802.2 Ethernet frame type. If the frame type doesn't match the frame type used on your network (such as an older NetWare network using 802.3 raw frames, you must reset the frame type. Use the arp command at the config-if prompt for the interface and assign the correct Ethernet encapsulation type (such as arpa, or snap).

- Collisions—This shows the number of collisions monitored by the interface. A large number of collisions means that there might be some physical problem on the network such as a break in a cable or a malfunctioning network interface card that is generating a large amount of broadcast traffic. This could also mean that cables are too long on the LAN.

As you can see, this one IOS command provides a lot of information related to the health of a particular interface and the traffic that it is experiencing. And as you also can see, problems with an Ethernet interface might be core problems with the LAN that it is servicing (such as excessive collisions).

Troubleshooting Token Ring with Show

Token Ring uses token passing as its method of access to the LAN. The device with the token can transmit. Other devices must wait until they take possession of the token so that they can transmit. So problems with Token Ring networks don't revolve around packet collision issues as Ethernet does.

The command to view the statistics related to a Token Ring interface is show interfaces tokenring [*interface number*]. And as with the show interfaces command on Ethernet interfaces, this command shows the status of the interface and information on the hardware and protocol addresses of the interface as well as information on the interface's reliability. A number of the parameters shown in the statistics are the same as those shown for an Ethernet port (such as Hardware Address, Internet Address, MTU, BW, and Rely). Other settings have to do with Token Ring LAN functionality such as ring speed.

- Token Ring is Up—This lets you know that the interface is currently active. If the interface is down, you can try to bounce the interface in the configuration-if mode to get it back online.

- Hardware Address—This is the hexadecimal MAC address for the interface.

- Internet Address—This is the IP address and subnet mask assigned to the interface (you will learn IP addressing in the "Troubleshooting TCP/IP" section).

- MTU—This is the maximum transmission unit for the interface in bytes.

- BW—This is the bandwidth for the interface in kilobits/second.

- Rely—This is a measurement of the reliability of the line with 255/255 being 100 percent reliable. This measurement is averaged for the interface over a period of five minutes.

- Load—This measures the current load on the interface. The measurement 255/255 would be a totally saturated interface and again means that you might have too large of a Token Ring LAN being serviced by the one interface on the router.

- Ring Speed—This is setting for the speed of the Token Ring LAN that the router is connected to. All devices on the Token Ring network, including the router, must be using the same ring speed (either 4Mbps or 16Mbps). Any mismatches will result in an interruption in the flow of data. To check the ring speed set on the router use the show running-config command. If you need to reset the ring speed enter the config-if mode on the router console for the interface. Then use the ring-speed command to reset the ring speed.

- Restarts—On Token Ring Interfaces this value should always be 0. If it is other than 0, the interface has been restarted because of some problem on the Token Ring LAN.

Troubleshooting Token Ring interfaces on routers requires a very good understanding of how Token Ring LANs operate. Problems such as congested rings, for example, require that you further segment the Token Ring LAN. And although this section provides some primer information on Token Ring interface settings, you should learn a lot more about Token Ring itself than can be provided in this book. A very good source for Token Ring related information is www.ibm.com. They are the architects of Token Ring and provide a number of white papers and other resources related to Token Ring LANs.

Troubleshooting WAN Interfaces

Basic troubleshooting of WAN interfaces is very similar to troubleshooting LAN interfaces. You can use the show interface serial [interface number] to view the statistics related to a particular interface. However, more precise troubleshooting of WAN interfaces is much more complex than LAN interfaces because of the different WAN protocols (such as PPP or Frame Relay) that you might be using on your serial connection between routers. Also thrown into this mix is the state of your service provider's leased lines or packet switched network connections.

Let's take a look at the show interface serial command and how some of the statistics related to a serial interface can provide insight into potential problems. Figure 18.4 shows the results of the show interface serial 0 command on a 2505 router.

- Serial 0 is Up—This lets you know that the interface is active. If the interface is down, there might be a problem with the connection from the router to the CSU/DSU. Check the cable. Or there might be a problem with the telephone company line that you are connected to (if the CSU/DSU is okay, call your service provider to see if the line is down—first check the status of the router on the other end of the connection). You can also try to bounce the interface to bring it back up (as discussed in the Ethernet section).

```
Tera Term - COM2 VT
File Edit Setup Control Window Help
popeye#show interfaces serial 0
Serial0 is up, line protocol is up
  Hardware is HD64570
  Description: connected to olive
  Internet address is 130.10.64.1/19
  MTU 1500 bytes, BW 2000 Kbit, DLY 20000 usec, rely 255/255, load 1/255
  Encapsulation PPP, loopback not set, keepalive set (10 sec)
  LCP Open
  Open: IPCP, CDP, ATALKCP, IPXCP
  Last input 00:00:00, output 00:00:00, output hang never
  Last clearing of "show interface" counters never
  Input queue: 0/75/0 (size/max/drops); Total output drops: 0
  Queueing strategy: weighted fair
  Output queue: 0/64/0 (size/threshold/drops)
     Conversations  0/1 (active/max active)
     Reserved Conversations 0/0 (allocated/max allocated)
  5 minute input rate 0 bits/sec, 0 packets/sec
  5 minute output rate 0 bits/sec, 0 packets/sec
     17974 packets input, 707978 bytes, 0 no buffer
     Received 0 broadcasts, 0 runts, 0 giants, 0 throttles
     0 input errors, 0 CRC, 0 frame, 0 overrun, 0 ignored, 0 abort
     17981 packets output, 708047 bytes, 0 underruns
     0 output errors, 0 collisions, 6 interface resets
     0 output buffer failures, 0 output buffers swapped out
     0 carrier transitions
     DCD=up  DSR=up  DTR=up  RTS=up  CTS=up
popeye#
```

- Line Protocol is Up—This lets you know that the WAN protocols in use believe that the line is usable. If the line protocol is down, your router might not be configured correctly (use the show running-config command to check this). Or the router that you are attempting to connect to isn't configured with the appropriate protocol (check it too). You might also be experiencing a problem due to the service provider's line or switching equipment.

- Internet Address—This is the IP address and subnet mask assigned to the interface (you will learn IP addressing in the "Troubleshooting TCP/IP" section).

- MTU—This is the maximum transmission unit for the interface in bytes.

- BW—This is the bandwidth for the interface in kilobits/second. This is set for the interface at the config-if prompt using the bandwidth command. The bandwidth must be set to a value that coincides with the speed of the line that the router's serial interface is connected to.

- Rely—This is a measurement of the reliability of the line with 255/255 being 100 percent reliable. The lower the first number in the reliability measurement the less reliable the interface connection (due to downed lines or other problems).

- Load—This measures the current load on the interface. The measurement 255/255 would be a totally saturated interface (meaning too much traffic, you might need to add another interface or router to service the LAN).

- Encapsulation—This is the WAN protocol assigned to the interface. It must match the WAN protocol on the router that is at the other end of the connection. The WAN protocol must also be set for the type of service you are being provided from your service provider (don't set it for PPP if you are connecting to a Frame-Relay switch).

- CRC—This shows the number of cyclical redundancy checks that have failed on incoming packets. This is usually an indication that the line provided by the phone company is experiencing a great deal of noise or that your serial cable from the router to the CSU/DSU is too long.

Again, this is only an overview of the information provided by the show command for a serial interface on a router and how it relates to potential problems. Troubleshooting WAN connection demands that you have a great deal of experience configuring and working with WAN connections on an internetwork. For example, troubleshooting dial-up connections and ISDN connections are really a science unto themselves. As with any discipline, the more time you spend working with WAN issues on internetworks the better you become at diagnosing problems relating to them.

Troubleshooting TCP/IP

TCP/IP is a large routable protocol stack that can present a number of interesting problems to router administrators. You've already seen in Chapter 10 that subnetting IP networks can be a mathematical nightmare in and of itself. And you will find that when you work with IP networks, a number of the problems that you face have to do with improper configurations on a router or node on the network.

Routers configured as a DCE must provide a clock rate

If you have configured your router as a DCE, the router must provide a clock rate for the serial connection. At the config-if prompt for the interface, use the `clock rate` command to set the appropriate clock rate. Legal clock rates range from 1200 to 800,000,000 bits per second. To see if an interface has been configured as a DCE, run the `show controllers serial [interface number]` command. This will show you the clock rate set for the line and the type of cable connected to the interface (DCE or DTE).

A duplicated IP address on a workstation will take that workstation offline and the workstation that also has been configured with the duplicate IP address.

Let's take a look at some of the common IP network–related problems first. Then you will look at the `ping` and `trace` commands and how you can use them to help troubleshoot IP–related problems. The list that follows provides some basic IP related problems and how you would fix them:

- Default Gateway Improperly Configured—When you set up the workstations and servers on a LAN that connects to a router, the default gateway for the LAN (and all the computers on it) is the IP address of the router interface directly connected to the LAN. If a workstation cannot communicate with the network, check the default gateway (or even more basic—check the IP address).

- Routing Not Enabled On One of the Routers—Use the `show ip route` command to see whether the router has been enabled for routing. If the routing table doesn't have any learned entries in it, the router has not been enabled for routing.

- Routing Protocol Has Not Been Enabled—You must enable a routing protocol, if you want the router to build a routing table. Use the `show running-config` command to see whether a routing protocol has been enabled (which should match the routing protocol you are using on the other routers on your network).

- No IP Address Configured on an Interface—You will have problems if the router interface has not been configured with an IP address. Use the `show ip interfaces` command to make sure your interfaces have been configured with an IP address (except in the cases of serial connections which can be configured IP unnumbered).

Watch those Access lists

I discussed standard IP Access lists in Chapter 14, "Routing AppleTalk." Grouping Access lists to router interfaces without a good understanding on how those lists will affect network traffic is a big mistake. Don't use Access Control lists unless you are sure that it will filter traffic that you don't want, not traffic that you require to be passed through the router interface.

Using *ping*

A great tool for checking the physical network connection between two routers on the internetwork (or any two nodes) is the `ping` command. `ping` sends an ICMP echo packet to the noted IP address and if the address received the packet it echoes the packet back to the source. The time that the echo packet takes to go the roundtrip is measured in milliseconds.

To use the `ping` command, type `ping [ip address]`, where you supply the IP address of the destination router interface or node on the network. Figure 18.5 shows the results of a `ping` command between two routers.

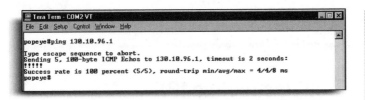

FIGURE 18.5
The show ping command can be used to check the connection between a router and other nodes on the internetwork.

An extended `ping` command also exists that enables you to set the protocol type for the echo packet (`ping` can be used with IPX and AppleTalk), the size of the packet, and the timeout for the response. Type `ping` and then press **Enter**. Supply the information requested by each step in the extended `ping` command, followed by **Enter**, (just press **Enter** to accept the defaults). Figure 18.6 shows the results of an extended `ping` command.

FIGURE 18.6
The extended ping command enables you to set parameters such as protocol type and timeout for the ping packet.

Using *trace*

Another command that you can use to troubleshoot connectivity problems is the `trace` command. It enables you to see the route that the packets take from source to destination. This enables you to determine if routers that would normally participate in the path between a particular router and node or router and router is currently down. To use the trace command, type `trace [ip address]`.

Using ping and trace
`ping` and `trace` can both be used at the user prompt or the privileged prompt.

The results of the `trace` command shown in Figure 18.7 show that the route determined by trace consisted of one directly connected router with the IP address of 130.10.64.2. The trace took four milliseconds.

FIGURE 18.7
The `trace` command can show the route between two routers on the internetwork.

Troubleshooting IPX

Networking with IPX poses some of the same problems that you face when working with IP. Incorrectly entered IPX network numbers on router interfaces can cause problems just as incorrectly configured IP addresses on interfaces do. Let's take a look at some of the basic troubleshooting issues you might face when working with IPX networks:

- Incorrectly Configured Clients—Novell Networks are very server-centric and so the hosts on the network must have their client software configured to correctly communicate with the NetWare server. It is the server that verifies the user to the network, so make sure that you are using the appropriate version of the client software for the version of server software that you are using.

- Too Many Clients—When you install a NetWare server you must provide a disk that shows the server how many licenses you have purchased for client machines. If you try to add more clients than you have licenses for, the server will not let the user on the network. Use the `Load Monitor` command on the NetWare server to check the number of client spots available on the server.

- Problems with Ethernet Encapsulation—NetWare supports several different Ethernet frame types—such as Ethernet 802.2 and Ethernet 802.3 (raw Ethernet) If you inadvertently mismatch the frame type on a router LAN interface with the frame type used by NetWare hosts and servers, the router is going to have problems routing packets. Check the frame type (encapsulation) of all your router interfaces using the `show ipx interface brief` command (the results of this command on a 2505 router appear in Figure 18.8).

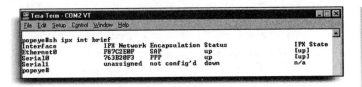

FIGURE 18.8
Quickly check the Encapsulation type of IPX-enabled interfaces on the router.

Obviously, one of the first things that you should do when you experience problems on a router is check your configuration and the settings on the interfaces. Other troubleshooting issues revolve around hardware and cabling issues. Because IPX is typically found on LANs, make sure that the LAN is working correctly before connecting to the router. Then if you have problems you know that they are on the router not the network.

SEE ALSO
➤ *For a review of IPX addressing, see page 214.*

Using extended `ping`

You can use extended `ping` to check nodes on the network (or router interfaces) using their IPX address in the form network number.node number.

Troubleshooting AppleTalk

AppleTalk LANs are typically small (when compared to corporate IP or IPX networks); it is somewhat simpler to deal with physical cabling problems and hardware problems (because you are typically dealing with fewer computers). Dealing with configuration and software problems is another issue.

When Apple Macintosh users looks for a particular service on the AppleTalk network, they employ the Chooser on the Macintosh. If the user can't find a particular service or zone, you've got a problem. And you will find that most of the problems with AppleTalk networks typically revolve around cable ranges and zone names. If a router's configuration doesn't agree with the cable ranges and zone names used on the AppleTalk internetwork that it is connected to, routing problems will occur and Mac clients won't find what they're looking for in the computer's Chooser.

AppleTalk phases

AppleTalk actually exists in two different phases: 1 and 2. Phase 1 didn't allow cable ranges but required a single network address for a network segment. If you are trying to route traffic through an AppleTalk internetwork where both AppleTalk Phase 1 and Phase 2 are in use, you might experience routing problems. It is a good idea to upgrade routers and other devices to support AppleTalk Phase 2.

Another thing to keep in mind, because the administrator assigns cable ranges, is that you don't want to inadvertently configure two LAN segments with the same network number or cable range. This will obviously cause routing problems.

Two router commands that are useful for troubleshooting in AppleTalk environments are `ping` and the `debug appletalk routing` command. `ping`, as you know, enables you to check the connection to a particular node on the network or check whether or not a router interface is up. The `debug` command enables you to view advertisements of routes on the AppleTalk internetwork and reports of conflicting network numbers on the network.

To use the `ping` command for AppleTalk addresses, type `ping appletalk [network number.node address]`. For example, on my router I want to ping the Ethernet 0 port on another router that has been configured for AppleTalk. The command is `ping appletalk 12.176` (you can also use the extended `ping` command for AppleTalk). Figure 18.9 shows the result of this command.

FIGURE 18.9
Check the status of a node on the AppleTalk network using the `ping` command.

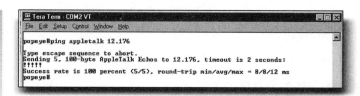

The `debug` command (a Privileged command) is simple to use, but it requires a lot of the router's resources, such as memory, so you don't want to leave it on forever (use `no debug all`, to quickly turn it off). The command is entered as `debug apple routing`. Figure 18.10 shows some of the information that the command provides.

A Final Word on Troubleshooting

In this chapter you have taken a look at some of the basic troubleshooting techniques for hardware, network architectures (such as Ethernet), and network protocols (such as IP). One thing that I haven't talked about is a network map. Any network administrator worth his salt will be sure to have an up-to-date map of the entire network including the addressing scheme and the location of devices such as routers, bridges, and servers.

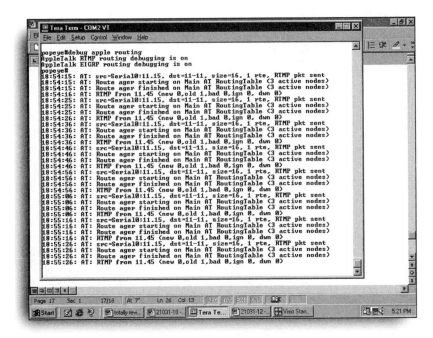

FIGURE 18.10
Use debug to monitor AppleTalk routing updates.

A map (or diagram if you want) of your internetwork can be used to find node addresses when you need them for commands like Ping or Telnet. The map also provides you with a complete overview of the topology of the network. You really can't run the network efficiently without a map.

And creating a network map is easy. Network diagramming tools such as Visio Standard (from Visio Corporation) make it easy to build simple and complex network diagrams. Other versions of Visio such as the Enterprise version supply all the icons that you need for just about every networking device manufactured, enabling you to create diagrams that can be understood by any network administrator.

Even if you don't use a network-diagramming tool, use some sort of graphics package and get a network map on to your computer, so that you can upgrade it as the network topology changes or grows. You won't be sorry that you have it when trouble rears its ugly head. Good luck!

part

V

APPENDIXES

Basic Router Command Summary

Cisco IOS Command Summary

This appendix provides a summary of the Cisco IOS commands covered in this book. The commands are broken down into tables; each table contains a list of associated commands. Commands in each table are listed alphabetically. For example, router examination commands are contained in Table A.1. This resource is best used after you have completed reading the entire book. You will then understand the context of each command and its use.

Because some root commands overlap—for example, show is used as a general examination command and as a troubleshooting command—you might find variations of the same command in more than one table. The fact that commands are grouped by their typical usage, however, should make the tables an easy way to reference a particular group of related commands.

For example, you can go to a particular table category, such as IP-related commands or AppleTalk-related commands, and find the specific IP or AppleTalk IOS command you are looking for. It is understood that each command is executed by typing the command at the appropriate prompt (noted in the results of the command) and then pressing **Enter**.

Router Examination Commands

Router examination commands enable you to quickly check the status of the router's interfaces and other parameters. Table A.1 summarizes these commands. These commands can be used at both the user and privileged prompts unless otherwise noted.

Table A.1 Router Examination Commands

Command	Results
show CDP Neighbor	Shows the routers that are directly connected to your router by LAN or serial connections.
show clock	Shows the time and date settings for the router.
show flash	Shows the IOS file or files contained in the router's Flash RAM and the amount of total Flash RAM and used Flash RAM.

Command	Results
show history	Shows a list of your last 10 commands.
show hub	Shows information on the status of the hub ports of a 2505 router.
show interface ethernet [*interface number*]	Shows the current configuration of a specified Ethernet interface.
show interface serial [*interface number*]	Shows the current configuration of a specified serial interface.
show interfaces	Lists all the interfaces on the router and statistics related to the interface such as their current configuration and encapsulation. Also tells you if the interface is active.
show processes	Shows CPU utilization information.
show protocol	Lists the routing protocols configured on the router.
show version	Shows the version of the IOS currently running on the router.

Router Memory Commands

Router memory commands enable you to check information such as the current running configuration or the startup-configuration stored in NVRAM. These commands also enable you to copy or erase configuration files from the router's memory. Commands for saving and retrieving router configurations or IOS files to and from an FTP server are also included in this list. These commands can be used at the user and privileged prompt unless otherwise noted (see Table A.2).

Table A.2 Router Memory–Related Commands

Command	Results
copy flash tftp	Privileged command to copy an IOS file from Flash to the TFTP server
copy running-config startup-config	Copies the currently running configuration to the router's NVRAM.

continues...

Table A.2 Continued

Command	Results
copy startup-config tftp	Privileged command to copy the startup configuration from NVRAM to a TFTP server.
copy tftp flash	Privileged command to copy an IOS file from a TFTP server to the router's Flash RAM.
copy tftp startup-config	Privileged command to copy a startup configuration file from a TFTP server to the router's NVRAM.
erase startup-config	Erases the startup-configuration from the router's NVRAM.
show running-config	Privileged command that shows the router configuration currently running in RAM.
show startup-config	Privileged command that shows the router configuration stored in the router's NVRAM. Loaded by the router when the router is rebooted.

Password and Router Name Configuration Commands

Password and router name commands enable you to change the various passwords on the router including the router login password and the secret enable password for the Privileged mode (see Table A.3). This list also contains the command for changing the router's name. Each of these commands is used in the Configuration mode.

Table A.3 Password and Router Name Commands

Command	Results
enable secret password [password]	Global configuration command that enables you to change the secret Privileged mode password on the router.
hostname [name]	Global configuration command that changes the name of the router.

Command	Results
`line console 0`	Enables you to enter the Line Configuration mode to set the login password for the router.
`line vty 0 4`	Enables you to enter the virtual terminal Configuration mode to set the virtual terminal password for the router.
`password [password]`	Used in the line console 0 Configuration mode to set the login password for the router; also used in the line vty 0 4 Configuration mode to set the virtual terminal password for the router.

SEE ALSO

➤ *For help recovering forgotten passwords, see page 137.*

Interface Configuration Commands

Interface configuration commands relate to configuring interfaces on the router (see Table A.4). The general configuration command, `con-fig` (the Privileged command to enter the configuration mode), is included among the commands. For interface configuration related to a specific network or WAN protocol, see the appropriate table (such as WAN-Related Commands).

Table A.4 Interface Configuration Commands

Command	Results
`config`	Privileged command that enables you to enter the Global Configuration mode.
Ctrl+Z	While not an actual interface configuration command, it is the command used to end a router configuration session.
`enable cdp`	Enables a particular interface (you must be in the config-if Configuration mode) to show connected neighbor routers (you can then use the show cdp neighbor command on the router).

continues...

Table A.4 Continued

Command	Results
encapsulation [encapsulation type]	Interface-specific configuration command that enables you to set the encapsulation type for a LAN or serial interface on the router.
interface ethernet [interface number]	Global Configuration command that enables you to configure parameters related to a particular Ethernet interface.
interface serial [interface number]	Global configuration command that enables you to configure parameters related to a particular serial interface.

IP-Related Commands

IP commands are related to configuring IP addressing on interfaces and enabling IP routing on the router (see Table A.5). Commands related to RIP and IGRP are also included.

Table A.5 IP-Related Commands

Command	Results
access-list [list #] permit or deny [ip address] [wildcard mask]	Global configuration command for creating an IP Access list. The network or node address that will be permitted or denied must be included and the wildcard mask must be provided. Repeat this command for each line that will appear in the Access list. The list # range for IP lists is 1–99.
debug ip igrp transaction	Privileged command that enables you to view statistics related to IGRP update messages on the router.
debug ip rip	Privileged command that enables you to view the RIP update messages sent and received by the router.

Command	Results
ip access-group [*list number*] out or in	Interface configuration command where you group a particular IP Access list to an interface. The out or in parameter is used to filter traffic going either out or in the specified interface.
ip address [*ip address*] [*subnet mask*]	Used in the config-if mode to assign an IP address to a router interface. The *ip address* command is followed by the *ip address* and *subnet* you are assigning to the interface.
ip routing	Global configuration command that enables IP routing on the router.
ip unnumbered [*interface or logical interface*]	Config-if prompt command enables you to designate a serial interface as not having its own IP address. The interface or logical interface parameter must designate a router interface (such as an Ethernet port) on the router that does have an IP address.
network [*major network number*]	Used with the router rip and router igrp commands to specify the major IP networks that the router is directly connected to.
no debug all	Turns off debugging (Privileged mode command).
no ip routing	Global configuration command that disables IP routing on the router.
router igrp [*autonomous system number*]	Global configuration command that turns on IGRP routing. The autonomous number is the AS number for the routing domain that the router belongs to (if an AS exists).
router rip	Global configuration command the turns on RIP routing.
show access-list [*list number*]	Enables you to view a particular Access list. The list number is the number you assigned to the list when you created it.

continues...

329

Table A.5 Continued

Command	Results
show ip interface [*interface type and number*]	Command enables you to view the IP related configuration settings for a particular router interface.
show ip protocol	Provides information related to the routing protocol updates sent and received by the router (such as RIP broadcasts).
show ip route	Shows the RIP or IGRP routing table for the router.
telnet [*ip address*]	A user and Privileged command that enables you to log in to a router remotely.

IPX-Related Commands

These commands are related to the configuration of IPX addressing on interfaces and enabling IPX routing on the router (see Table A.6). Commands related to IPX RIP also included.

Table A.6 IPX-Related Commands

Command	Results
access list [*list #*] permit or deny [*source network address*] [*destination network address*].	Access list creation command (a Global Configuration command) that enables you to create IPX Access lists. The list numbers available for IPX are 800 to 899.
access-list [*list #*] permit or deny -1 -1	IPX Access list creation statement that enables you to permit or deny all networks and nodes not specified in other statements in the Access list.
debug ipx routing activity	Privileged command that enables you to view the IPX routing updates coming in and going out of the router.
ipx access-group [*list #*] in or out	Config-if configuration command that enables you to group an IPX access list to a router interface. in or out the interface must be specified.

Command	Results
ipx network : ipx network [*network number*] *encapsulation* [*frame type*]	Interface configuration command (config-if prompt) that enables you to set the IPX network address for a router Ethernet interface and set the Ethernet frame type for the interface.
ipx routing	Global configuration command that enables IPX routing on the router.
no debug ipx routing activity	Turns off IPX debugging.
show access-list [*list #*]	View an IPX or other type of Access list.
show ipx interface	View the settings for IPX enabled router interfaces (a User and Privileged command).
show ipx route	View the IPX routing table on a router.
show ipx traffic	View statistics related to the IPX packets sent and received.

AppleTalk-Related Commands

These commands are related to the configuration of AppleTalk and the viewing of AppleTalk configuration settings (see Table A.7).

Table A.7 AppleTalk-Related Commands

Command	Results
access-list [*list #*] deny or permit zone [*zone name*]	Global configuration command that enables you to build Access list lines based on zone names. AppleTalk Access lists can have a list number range of 600 to 699.
access-list [*list #*] permit or deny cable-range [*cable range*]	Global configuration command that enables you to build an AppleTalk Access list.
appletalk access-group [*list #*]	Config-if command that groups an AppleTalk Access list to a specified router interface.

continues...

Table A.7 Continued

Command	Results
appletalk cable-range [cable-range number]	Interface configuration command where you set the AppleTalk cable-range for a selected interface.
appletalk routing	Global configuration command that enables AppleTalk routing.
appletalk zone [zone name]	Interface configuration command that enables you to set the AppleTalk zone name for a particular interface.
show appletalk global	Provides information on the number of networks and zone available on the internetwork and the time interval for ZIP queries and RTMP updates.
show appletalk interface	Provides more detailed information on the router interfaces and their AppleTalk configurations.
show appletalk interface brief	Provides a short summary of all the interfaces on the router and their AppleTalk configurations.
show appletalk interface e0	Enables you to view detailed AppleTalk configuration information for a specified router interface.
show appletalk zone	Provides zone and network information for the zone available on the internetwork.

WAN-Related Commands

These commands are related to the configuration of WAN protocols on router serial interfaces (see Table A.8). Command for configuring Frame-Relay and X.25 on a router are included in this list.

Table A.8 WAN-Related Commands

Command	Results
bandwidth [*bandwidth*]	A config-if command for setting the bandwidth of a serial interface.
clock rate [*clockrate*]	config-if command used to set the clock rate on a serial interface when the router is used as a DCE device.
encapsulation [*WAN protocol*]	config-if command for setting the WAN encapsulation type for a serial interface (such as PPP, HDLC, and so on).
frame-relay interface-dlci [*dlci #*]	config-if command to set the DLCI number for a Frame-Relay configured interface.
frame-relay lmi-type [*LMI type*]	config-if command to set the LMI type for a Frame-Relay configured interface.
isdn spid[*spid channel designation*] [*SPID #*]	Global configuration command for entering the unique SPID number for each ISDN channel.
isdn switch type basic-[*switch identifier*]	Global configuration command that sets the ISDN switch type that your router is connected to.
show frame-relay lmi	Shows invalid messages sent or received via the router's Frame-Relay connection.
show frame-relay map	Shows the DLCI mapping to the router's interfaces.
x25 address [*data link address*]	config-if command used to set the data link address for X.25, when X.25 is set as the encapsulation type.
x25 ips [*bits*]	config-if command used to set the input packet size for an X.25 interface.
x25 ops [*bits*]	config-if command used to set the output packet size for an X.25 interface.
x25 win [*number of packets*]	config-if command to set the input window size for an X.25 interface.
x25 wout [*number of packets*]	config-if command to set the output window size for an X.25 interface.

Troubleshooting Commands

The commands in this table are related to troubleshooting the router (see Table A.9). The `ping` and `trace` command are included in this list.

Table A.9 Troubleshooting Commands

Command	Results
ping [*node address*]	Used to check the connection between two different router's (`ping` followed by the IP address or AppleTalk node address) on the remote router's interface. This command can also be used to check the connection between nodes on the network.
show controller	Lets you take a look at the status of interface controllers on the router.
show interface [*interface type*] [*interface number*]	An excellent command for viewing all the parameters related to a specific interface on the router.
show stacks	Provides error messages related to the crashing of a router when the router is restarted.
trace [*ip address*]	Shows the path between your router and another router or node on the internetwork. This command can also be used with AppleTalk addresses.

Miscellaneous Commands

This table contains some miscellaneous router commands such as the banner creation command and the command for setting the time and date on the router (see Table A.10).

Table A.10 Miscellaneous IOS Commands

Command	Results
banner motd [*banner end character*]	Global configuration command that enables you to create a banner for the router login screen. The banner end character is any non-alphanumeric

Command	Results
	character that tells the configuration mode that you are signaling the end of the banner text.
Ctrl+Z	While not an actual interface configuration command it is the command used to end a router configuration session.
disable	Exits the Privileged mode and returns to the User mode.
enable	Enter the Privileged mode. You must supply the Privileged password to enter the Privileged mode using this command.
quit	User and Privileged command that enables you to exit the router.
reload	Privileged command that reboots the router.
set clock	Privileged command that enables you to set the time and the date on the router.

Appendix

B

Selected Cisco Router Specifications

Router Selection

When planning any enterprisewide internetwork (or even a campus network that is only a portion of the enterprise), the hardware that will be implemented as part of the plan must be capable of performing its intended function and imparting some scalability and flexibility to the network in case of future growth or the possible need for topology changes. Scalability and flexibility have really become industry buzzwords and in the final analysis really boil down to purchasing hardware. In this case, routers must not only serve the current situation but also enable you to upgrade or reconfigure the equipment if necessary without throwing everything out and starting over.

Cisco 7500 Routers

The Cisco 7500 routers are high-end routers that typically serve as border routers (also called *core routers*) and provide the routing of packets between routing domains. The 7513 router shown in Figure B.1 serves as a border router between the corporate network and the Internet (notice also that a firewall is installed between the internetwork and the border router).

The 7513 comes with 11 slots that are hot-swappable (interface cards can be swapped or inserted even while the router is running). The 7513 can provide several different interfaces including Ethernet, Fast-Ethernet, Token Ring, FDDI, T-1, Synchronous serial, and primary ISDN.

The 7513 router can also be configured with dual redundant power supplies and dual route switch processors. Table B.1 summarizes the hardware configuration for a basic 7513.

Table B.1   Cisco 7513 Specifications

Power supplies	2
Flash RAM	16MB standard, expandable to 220MB
Standard RAM	32MB, expandable to 128MB
Interface slots	11
Processor slots and type	2 slots/MIPS RISC processor
Weight	75 pounds

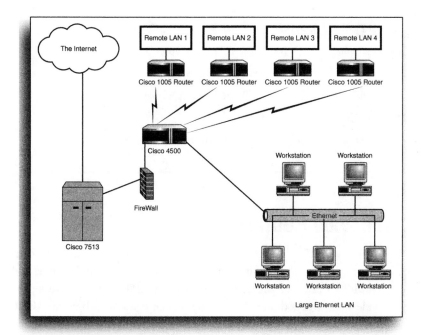

FIGURE B.1
This internetwork uses several different types of Cisco routers to connect various LANs.

Cisco 4500 Routers

The Cisco 4500 routers are considered distribution-level routers and are used as the central connection point for small LANs and remote sites on the internetwork. Notice in Figure B.1 the 4500 router is used as a sort of central distribution point for the remote offices (which are connected to the 4500 by access routers) and the main LAN (which is directly connected to the 4500 via a LAN interface).

The Cisco 4500 routers are modular, so their interface slots can be customized with particular types of interface cards with varying numbers of ports. The Cisco 4500 router, although considered a medium-capacity router, has a broad range of interface cards available and can support Ethernet, Fast-Ethernet, Token-Ring, FDDI, serial, and ISDN to name a few.

The 4500 series does not support hot swappable interface cards (like the 7000 series) nor do they have the capacity for redundant power supplies. Table B.2 shows the basic specifications for a 4500 router.

Why include the router weight?

I included weight as a specification to give you an idea of how the different router families differ in size. A 7513 router weighs 75 pounds while one of the Series 2500 routers weighing in at only 10 pounds can be carried under your arm like a notebook.

Table B.2 Cisco 4500 Specifications

Power supplies	1 internal power supply
Flash RAM	4MB standard expandable to 16
Standard RAM	4MB standard expandable to 16
Interface slots	3 slots
Processor slots and type	1 slot 100-MHz IDT Orion RISC
Weight	14 pounds

Cisco 2500 Routers

The Cisco 2500 series routers are inexpensive routers and are considered access-level routers. Figure B.2 shows the 2505 router, and Table B.3 explains the 2505 specifications. 2500 series routers provide more ports than other branch-office routers such as the 1000 series. They support synchronous and asynchronous serial interfaces, Ethernet interface, Token Ring interfaces, and ISDN interfaces.

FIGURE B.2
Over a million 2500 series routers have been sold by Cisco, making it the most popular router in the world.

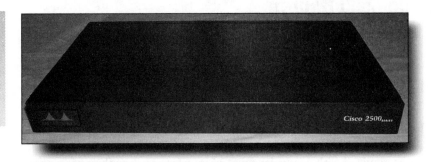

Table B.3 Cisco 2505 Specifications

Power supplies	1 internal power supply
Flash RAM	8MB
Standard RAM	4MB expandable to 16
Interface slots	No slots/2 serial interfaces, 1 Ethernet interface in the form of an 8-port hub
Processor slots and type	1 processor 20MHz 68030
Weight	10 pounds

Cisco 1000 Routers

The Cisco 1000 series routers are small routers designed to connect remote LANs to the overall WAN (or internetwork). In Figure B.1, Cisco 1005 routers are used by remote sites to connect to the 4500 distribution router. The 1005 routers would be connected to the 4500 using a serial interface and a particular WAN technology. Because the primary job of the 1000 series is accessing the internetwork, these routers are often referred to as access-class routers.

The Cisco 1005 router only comes with one serial interface (with a 60-pin serial port, which is typical of Cisco routers—see Figure B.3). This serial interface supports both synchronous and asynchronous communication, so several different WAN protocols could be used to connect to the 4500 router including PPP, Frame Relay, or HDLC.

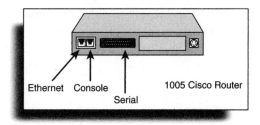

Ethernet   Console   1005 Cisco Router
                 Serial

FIGURE B.3
The Cisco 1005 router supplies one Ethernet and one serial interface.

Because the Cisco 1005 is designed to support a remote site, it contains only one Ethernet port, which can be hooked to the hub that connects the Ethernet workstations to the network. Table B.4 details some of the specifications of the 1005 router.

Table B.4   Cisco 1005 Specifications

Power supplies	1 external power supply
Flash RAM	None, PCMCIA slot provides option of a Flash card
Standard RAM	8MB
Interface slots	No slots/2 interfaces
Processor slots and type	1 processor MC68360
Weight	6 pounds

A Final Note

Probably the most amazing thing about all these routers is that, although they differ a great deal in processor power and the number of interfaces they provide, each of these routers uses the same operating system—the Cisco IOS. This makes it extremely easy for a network administrator to configure several different router types without really missing a beat. The fact that the command set is consistent across the routers means you must learn only one operating system to work with many different internetworking devices.

As a final word of advice, you should definitely make the time to explore Cisco's Web site at www.cisco.com. It not only provides specifications for all of Cisco's products, but it also provides white papers, manuals, and even free software that you can download. Although you might find the site somewhat difficult to navigate at first, you will find that it provides a real wealth of knowledge related to internetworking technologies.

GLOSSARY

AARP (AppleTalk Address Resolution Protocol)   A Network layer protocol that resolves AppleTalk network addresses to hardware addresses. AARP sends broadcasts to all stations on the network to match hardware addresses to logical destination addresses for packets.

AARP broadcast   Broadcasts to all stations on an AppleTalk network to match hardware addresses to logical destination addresses for packets.

Access list   A list of conditions called `permit` and `deny` statements that help regulate traffic flow into and out of a router.

agents   Software watchdogs used by SNMP to keep an eye on network processes. See also *SNMP*

anding   A method used by the router in which it compares or "ands" an IP address with its subnet mask to determine the network address.

AppleTalk   A routable networking architecture developed by Apple that provides network services to Apple Macintosh computers.

area   A subset of an internetwork containing several member routers. When several areas are grouped into a higher-level subset this organizational level is called a routing domain.

ARP (Address Resolution Protocol)   A TCP/IP protocol used to map IP addresses to node hardware addresses.

asynchronous communication   Serial data transfer connections that rely on start and stop bits to make sure that the data is completely received by the destination device.

ATM (Asynchronous Transfer Mode)   An advanced packet-switching protocol that uses fixed packet sizes (53 bytes) called cells to increase the throughput of the data transfer. Typically run over high-speed fiber optic networks. See also *cells* and *SONET*

attenuation   The degradation of the data signal over the run of the cable.

343

autonomous system   In cases where link-state routing protocols are used that require greater memory and processing capabilities from the routers on the network, it isn't uncommon to divide the internetwork into routing domains. In IP networks, a routing domain is referred to as an autonomous system. See also *border router*

bandwidth   The capacity of a medium to conduct data.

banner   A message that appears on the login screen of a router on a router console or virtual terminal.

baseband   A transmission that uses a single bit stream over the entire bandwidth available.

beaconing   A Token Ring fault tolerance strategy where nodes on the ring can determine the state of the network in cases where cable failure has taken place or there is a problem with a down stream neighbor on the ring.

BGP (Border Gateway Protocol) A commonly used routing protocol for interdomain routing. It is the standard EGP for the Internet. BGP handles the routing between two or more routers that serve as the border routers for particular autonomous systems.

border router   A high-end router used to connect autonomous systems. Also known as core routers.

bottleneck   A device that is slowing network traffic.

breakout box   A device used to determine whether you are getting a signal from the CSU/DSU connected to a router.

BRI   See *ISDN*

bridges   Internetworking devices that operate at the Data Link layer of the OSI model. Bridges are used to segment networks that have grown to a point where the amount of data traffic on the network media is slowing the overall transfer of information.

broadcast storms   A condition caused when broadcast traffic from devices on an Ethernet network overwhelms it with messages bringing down the network.

bus network   A network topology characterized by a main trunk or backbone line with the networked computers attached at intervals along the line.

cable range   A network designation for an AppleTalk network segment assigned by the network administrator. Cable ranges can consist of a single number designating one network on the network wire or it can be a range of network numbers specifying a number of networks on the same wire.

campus   A portion of an internetwork that is made up of several connected LANs as one location. See also *internetwork*

CDP (Cisco Discovery Protocol) A Cisco proprietary protocol that provides you with the ability to access information related to neighboring routers. See also *Neighbors*

cells   Packets of fixed size used by Asynchronous Transfer Mode. See also *ATM*

circuit switching   A connectivity strategy where a dedicated connection is established between the sender and receiver on a switched network (such as the Public Switched Telephone Network). Data moves from the source to the destination along the circuit (the lines) that has been established for the particular session.

Class A   Large IP networks that supply over 16 million node addresses for the network.

Class B   Large- to medium-sized IP networks that supply over 65,000 node addresses.

Class C   Small IP networks that only provide 254 node addresses.

Class D   A class of IP network addresses used by multicast groups receiving data an internetwork from a particular application or server service. An example of a multicast use of Class D addresses is

Microsoft NetShow, which can broadcast the same content to a group of users at one time.

Class E   IP addresses that belong to an experimental class and are unavailable for general use.

CLI (Command-Line Interface) The interface provided by the Cisco IOS on a router console or virtual terminal that allows you to enter the various IOS commands.

clients   A computer on the network that is logged in by and receives services from (such as printing or file access) a server computer.

clock ticks   A metric used by the IPX Routing Information protocol. A tick is 1/18 of a second.

Configuration mode   The router mode that enables you to configure the router configuration using global commands and specific interface-related commands.

convergence   The time it takes for all the routers on the network to be up-to-date in terms of the changes that have taken place in the network topology. The longer it takes for all the routers on the internetwork to converge the greater the possibility that packets will be routed to routes that are no longer available on the network.

CRC (Cyclical Redundancy Check)   The Data Link layer makes sure that frames sent over the physical link are received error free.

345

Protocols operating at this layer will add a trailer on each frame called a CRC check. Basically this is a mathematical calculation that takes place on the sending computer and then on the receiving computer. If the two CRCs match up then the frame was received in total and its integrity was maintained during transfer.

CSMA/CA (Carrier Sense Multiple Access with Collision Avoidance)   A network access strategy used by AppleTalk. A device that is ready to send data out onto the network will notify the other network nodes of its intention to place data on the network.

CSMA/CD (Carrier Sense Multiple Access with Collision Detection)   A network access strategy used by Ethernet networks. If a node sending data detects that there has been a collision, it will wait to resend the data until the line is determined to be free of other data.

CSU/DSU (Channel Service Unit/Digital Service Unit)   A device that connects LAN equipment such as a router to digital phone lines.

data link broadcasts   Broadcast messages used by CDP to discover neighboring Cisco routers that are also running CDP. See also *CDP*

datagrams   Grouping of information in the data bit stream, datagrams are also referred to as packets or frames.

DCE (Data Circuit Terminating Equipment)   Equipment that provides a connection between the network and the switched network. The DCE often provides clocking information to synchronize the communication between the network termination equipment (such as a DTE) and the switched network. See also *DTE* and *PDN*

DDP (Datagram Delivery Protocol)   An AppleTalk Network layer protocol that provides a connectionless datagram delivery system (similar to UDP in the TCP/IP stack).

DDS Digital Data Service   Leased digital lines used for data communications. DDS lines include the T-Carrier system, which provides a range of line types and data transfer rates.

DECnet   A network protocol stack developed by the Digital Equipment Corporation.

default gateway   The address of the router interface to which a particular LAN is connected. Every device on the LAN uses that connected router interface address as its default gateway.

delay   The amount of time it takes to move a packet from the interface to the intended destination. Delay is measured in microseconds.

deny statements   Statements in an Access list that deny traffic from certain networks or nodes to enter or exit a particular router interface.

dial-up connection   The simplest and least expensive type of data transfer connection uses a modem to connect two computers or other devices over a regular analog voice-grade telephone line.

distance-vector routing algorithms Routing algorithms that require the router to pass their entire routing table to their nearest router neighbors (routers that they are directly connected to). This basically sets up an update system that reacts to a change in the network like a line of dominos falling.

DLCI (Data Link Connection Identifier)   A reference or pointing device that makes sure that packets sent over a switched network, such as Frame Relay, end up at the proper destination. This is done by mapping the logical addresses (IP addresses, for example) of the sending and receiving routers to the DLCI of the virtual circuit that they use to communicate. See also *Frame Relay*

DOD model   When TCP/IP was developed, the Department of Defense (DOD) developed their own conceptual model—the DOD model—(also known as the DARPA model) for how the various protocols in the TCP/IP stack operate.

DTE (Digital Terminal Device) The termination device for a data network and connects to DCE device, which provides a connection to a switched network. See also *DCE* and *PDN*

dynamic algorithms   Routing tables that are built dynamically by a routing protocol.

EGP (Exterior Gateway Protocol) A routing protocol that provides the mechanism for the routing of data between routing domains. Border Gateway Protocol (BGP) is an example of an EGP. See also *BGP*

encapsulation   The packaging of data in a particular protocol header. For example Ethernet data is encapsulated in an Ethernet header before being placed on the network.

Ethernet   The most commonly deployed network architecture; it provides access to the network using CSMA/CD (carrier sense multiple access with collision detection).

Exec   The Cisco IOS uses a command interpreter to execute your commands (it interprets the command and then executes it). The User mode and the Privileged mode are considered different levels of the Exec.

extended segment   An AppleTalk network segment that has been assigned a range of network numbers.

347

FDDI (Fiber Distributed Data Interface)   An architecture that provides high-speed network backbones that can be used to connect a number of different network types. FDDI uses fiber-optic cable, wired in a ring topology, using token passing as its media access method, operating at a data rate of at least 100Mbps and allowing long cable distances.

Flash RAM   A special kind of ROM that you can erase and reprogram. Flash is used to store the Cisco IOS that runs on your router. You can also store alternative versions of the Cisco IOS on the Flash (such as an upgrade of your current IOS), which makes it very easy for you to upgrade the router.

Frame Relay   A packet-switching WAN protocol that uses permanent virtual circuits for communication sessions between points on the WAN. These virtual circuits are identified by a DLCI (Data Link connection identifier)—a value provided by the frame relay service provider. See also *DLCI*

FTP (File Transfer Protocol)   TCP/IP Application protocol that provides the ability to transfer files between two computers.

gateways   Used to connect networks that don't embrace the same network protocol and so protocol translation is necessary between the two disparate networks. For example,

a gateway can be used as the connection between an IBM AS400 miniframe and a PC-based LAN.

global commands   Self-contained, one-line configuration commands that affect the overall global configuration of the router. Examples are hostname and enable secret.

HDLC (High Level Data Link Control)   A synchronous Layer 2 WAN transport protocol. The HDLC used on Cisco routers is a Cisco proprietary version.

high-order bits   The first four bits in any octet of an IP address (on the far left of the octet) are referred to as the high-order bits.

hop count   A metric used by RIP. A hop is the movement of the packets from one router to another router. See also *RIP*

hub   A centralized connectivity device, especially in a star topology. The computers on the network connect to the hub.

hubs   Devices operating at the Physical layer of the OSI model that provide the central connection point for networks arranged in a star topology.

ICMP (Internet Control Message Protocol)   A message service provider and management protocol used by routers to send messages to host computers that are sending data that must be routed.

IGP (Interior Gateway Protocol)
A routing protocol that provides the mechanisms for the routing of packets within the routing domain. IGPs such as RIP or IGRP would be configured on each of the routers in the router domain. See also *RIP*, *IGRP*, and *OSPF*

IGRP (Interior Gateway Routing Protocol)   A distance-vector routing protocol developed by Cisco in the 1980s. IGRP uses a composite metric that takes into account several variables; it also overcomes certain limitations of RIP, such as the hop count metric and the inability of RIP to route packets on networks that require more than 15 hops.

Interface   The physical connection between the router and a particular network medium type; interfaces are also referred to as ports.

International Data Numbers   See X.121

internetwork   When several LANs are connected. This is really a network of networks (this type of network can also be referred to as a campus).

intranet   A corporate network that is internal to the enterprise (not connected to the global Internet) but uses Internet protocols such as Simple Mail Transport Protocol and Hypertext Transport Protocol (the protocol used by Web Browsers) to share information among corporate users.

IOS (Internetworking Operating System)   The Cisco proprietary operating system software that provides the router hardware with the ability to route packets on an internetwork. The IOS provides the command sets and software functionality that you use to monitor and configure the router.

IP unnumbered   Serial interfaces on a router configured without IP addresses (they will still route IP packets even though they are designated as IP unnumbered).

IPX (Internet Package Exchange Protocol)   A connectionless oriented transport protocol that provides the addressing system for the IPX/SPX stack. Operating at the Network and Transport layers of the OSI model, IPX directs the movement of packets on the internetwork using information that it gains from the IPX Routing Information Protocol (RIP).

IPX network number   The first part of the IPX address, which can be up to 16 hexadecimal characters in length (this part of the network.node address is 32-bits. The remaining 12 hexadecimal digits in the address make up the node address (which makes up the remaining 48 bits of the address).

IPX RIP (Routing Information Protocol)   A routing protocol that uses two metrics: clock ticks (1/18 of a second) and hop count—to route packets through an IPX internetwork.

IPX/SPX (Internetwork Packet Exchange/Sequenced Packet Exchange)   The NetWare proprietary network protocol stack for LAN connectivity. IPX is similar to TCP/IP in that the protocols that make up the IPX/SPX stack don't directly map to the layers of the OSI model. IPX/SPX gained a strong foothold in early local area networking because IPX/SPX was strong on performance and didn't require the overhead that is needed to run TCP/IP.

IRQ (Interrupt ReQuest)   A unique request line that allows a device to alert the computer's processor that the device connected to that IRQ requires processing services.

ISDN (Integrated Services Digital Network)   Is digital connectivity technology used over regular phone lines. A device called an ISDN modem is used to connect a device to the telephone network. ISDN is available in Basic Rate ISDN (BRI) and primary Rate ISDN (PRI).

ISDN modem   See *terminal adapter*

ISO (International Standards Organization)   This global standard organization develops sets of rules and models for everything from technical standards for networking to how companies do business in the new global market. They are responsible for the OSI conceptual model of networking. See also *OSI*

keepalives   Messages sent by network devices to let other network devices know that a link between them exists

LAN (Local Area Network)   A server-based network of computers that is limited to a fairly small geographical area, such as a particular building.

LAN interface   A router interface providing a connection port for a particular LAN architecture such as Ethernet or Token Ring.

leading bits   The first three bits in an IP network address. Rules have been established for the leading bits in the first octet of each of the classes (A, B, and C). Class A addresses must have 0 as the first bit. In Class B addresses the first bit of the first octet is set to 1, and the second bit is set to 0. In Class C addresses the first two bits of the first octet are set to 1 and the third bit is set to 0.

lease lines   Dedicated phone providing a full-time connection between two networks through the PSTN or another service provider. Leased lines are typically digital lines.

LLC (Logical Link Control)   A sublayer of the Data Link layer that establishes and maintains the link between the sending and receiving computer as data moves across the network's physical media.

LMI (Local Management Interface)   The signaling standard used between a router and a Frame Relay switch. Cisco routers support three LMI types: Cisco, ANSI, and q933a.

Load   The current amount of data traffic on a particular interface. Load is measured dynamically and is represented as a fraction of 255, with 255/255 showing the saturation point.

LocalTalk   The cabling system used to connect Macintosh computers (it uses shielded twisted-pair cables with a special Macintosh adapter).

logical interface   A software-only interface that is created using the router's IOS. Logical interfaces are also referred to as virtual interfaces. See also *loopback interface, null interface*, and *tunnel interface*

loopback interface   A software-only interface that emulates an actual physical interface and can be used to keep data traffic local that is intended for a hardware interface that is non-functioning. See also *logical interface*

lower-order bits   The first four bits in any octet (counting from right to left) are referred to as the lower-order bits.

MAC (Addresses Media Access Control)   MAC addresses are burned on to ROM chips on network interface cards, giving each of them a unique address.

MAU (Multistation Access Unit)   Token Ring networks are wired in a star configuration with a MAU providing the central connection for the nodes. The MAU itself also provides the logical ring that the network operates on.

mesh topology   A network design where devices use redundant connections as a fault tolerance strategy.

metric   The method routing algorithms use to determine the suitability of one path over another. The metric can be a number of different things such as the path length, the actual cost of sending the packets over a certain route, or the reliability of a particular route between the sending and receiving computers.

NADN (Nearest Downstream Neighbor)   On a Token Ring network, a NADN would be the active node directly downstream from a particular node. See also *NAUN*

NAUN (Nearest Upstream Neighbor) In Token Ring network a computer that passes the token to the next computer on the logical ring would be called the nearest active upstream neighbor or NAUN.

NBP (Name Binding Protocol) A Transport layer protocol that maps lower-layer addresses to AppleTalk names that identify a particular network resource such as a printer server that is accessible over the internetwork.

NCP (Netware Core Protocol) An IPX/SPX protocol that handles network functions at the Application, Presentation, and Session layers of the OSI model.

neighbors Routers that are directly connected to a particular router by LAN or WAN connections.

NetBEUI (NetBIOS Extended User Interface) A simple and fast network protocol that was designed to be used with Microsoft's and IBM's NetBIOS (Network Basic Input Output System) protocol in small networks.

network A group of computers and related hardware that are joined together so that they can communicate.

NIC (Network Interface Card) A hardware device that provides the connection between a computer and the physical media of a network. The NIC provides the translation of data into a bit; sometimes referred to as an adapter.

NLSP (NetWare Link Services Protocol) A Novell developed link-state routing protocol that can be used to replace RIP as the configured routing protocol for IPX routing.

node Any device on the network (such as a computer, router, or server).

nonextended segment An AppleTalk network segment that is assigned only one network number.

NOS (Network Operating System) Any number of server-based software products, such as Windows NT, Novell NetWare, and AppleTalk, that provides the software functionality for LAN connectivity.

NT domain A network managed by an NT server called the Primary Domain Controller.

null interface A software only interface that drops all packets that it receives. See also *logical interface*

NVRAM Nonvolatile RAM RAM that can be used to store the startup configuration file for the router. NVRAM can be erased and you can copy the running configuration on the router to NVRAM. NVRAM does not lose its contents when the router is rebooted.

octet   Eight bits of information; one portion of the four octet IP address used on IP networks.

OSI (Open Systems Interconnection Model)   A conceptual model for networking developed in the late 1970s by the International Standards Organization (ISO). In 1984 the model became the international standard for network communications. It provides a conceptual framework (based upon seven layers called protocol stacks) that helps explain how data gets from one place to another on a network.

OSPF (Open Shortest Path First)   A link state protocol developed by the Internet Engineering Task Force (IETF) as a replacement for RIP. Basically, OSPF uses a shortest-path-first algorithm that allows it to compute the shortest path from source to destination when it determines the route for a specific group of packets. See also *IGP*

packet switching   A Wide Area Networking strategy where the bit stream of data is divided into packets. Each packet has its own control information and is switched through the network independently.

PDN (Public Data Network or Private Data Network)   A packet switching network operated by a service provider. PDNs provide WAN connectivity avenues for the connecting of LANs at remote sites.

peer-to-peer network   A local area network that operates without a server but allows connected computers to access shared resources such as files and printers.

permit statements   Statements in an Access list that permit traffic from certain networks or nodes to enter or exit a particular router interface.

Ping (Packet InterNet Groper)   An IP protocol used to test the connection between two or more nodes on a network. These nodes can be host computers, servers, or routers.

port commands   A set of commands that enable you to specify a particular interface or controller for configuration; these commands must be followed by subcommands that provide additional configuration information. See also *subcommands*

Port   See *interface*

PPP (Point-to-Point Protocol)   A synchronous and asynchronous protocol that can provide WAN connections over a number of different connection types.

PRI   See *ISDN*

privileged mode   A complete access level to the router that enables you to view, save and erase router configuration parameters and enter the Configuration mode for the router. See also *Configuration mode*

Protocols   The software-based rules that define how networked computers send and receive data.

PSTN (Public Switched Telephone Network)   The telephone communication infrastructure provided by the Baby Bells.

RAM (Random Access Memory) Similar to the dynamic memory you use on your PC, RAM provides the temporary storage of information (packets are held in RAM when their addressing information is examined by the router) and holds information such as the current routing table.

reliability   The ratio of expected-to-received keepalives. See also *keepalives*

repeaters   Physical devices that take the signal received from network devices and regenerates the signal so that it maintains its integrity along a longer media run than is normally possible. Repeaters are also referred to as concentrators.

ring topology   Networked computers connected one after the other on the wire in a physical circle. Ring topology moves information on the wire in one direction with each networked computer actually resending the information it receives onto the next computer in the ring.

RIP (Routing Information Protocol)   A distance-vector routing protocol that uses hop count as its metric. RIP summarizes the information in the routing table by IP network numbers (also referred to as major network numbers).

roll-over cable   The cable used to connect the console computer and the router.

ROM (Read Only Memory) Memory chips that contain burned-in software instructions. Router ROM contains the Power-on Self-Test (POST) and the bootstrap program for the router.

routable protocol   A networking protocol that provides the necessary Layer 3 protocols for the routing of packets.

router   An internetworking device used to connect LANs via LAN and WAN connections. The router uses a combination of software and hardware to route packets between networks.

router console   The computer serving as the router's dumb terminal. Used to view and enter configuration settings on the router.

routers   Internetworking devices that operate at the Network layer (Layer 3) of the OSI model. Using a combination of hardware and software (Cisco Routers use the Cisco IOS—Internetwork Operating System), routers are used to connect networks.

routing protocol   Protocols that provide the mechanism for a router to build a routing table and share the routing information with other connected routers.

RTMP (Routing Table Maintenance Protocol)   A Transport layer protocol that is responsible for establishing and maintaining routing tables on routers that have been enabled to route AppleTalk.

running configuration   The router configuration currently running in the router's RAM.

SAP (Service Access Point)   The LLC sublayer provides these reference points so that a computer sending data can refer to the SAPs when communicating with the upper-layer protocols of the OSI stack on a receiving node.

SAP (Service Advertisement Protocol)   A protocol that advertises the availability of various resources on the NetWare network.

serial adapters   Adapters provided with the router used to connect the rollover cable to the COM port on a computer.

serial interfaces   A router interface providing a connection port for various WAN technologies. A router port would typically be attached to a cable such as a V.35 cable that then attaches to a WAN DCE device. See also *DCE*

server   The provider of data communications resources to client machines on the network.

server-based network   A network where client computers are authenticated on the network by a server computer. The server provides centralized file storage and other centralized services such as printing and other resources.

session   A transaction between networked nodes.

share-level security   Typically used in Peer-to-Peer networks, each shared resource requires a password for access. See also *peer-to-peer network*

SMTP (Simple Mail Transport Protocol)   TCP/IP Application layer protocol that provides mail delivery between two computers.

SNMP (Simple Network Management Protocol)   A TCP/IP Application layer protocol that can be used to monitor the health of an internetwork. SNMP uses software agents that report back on a particular measured parameter related to the network.

SONET (Synchronous Optical Network)   a Fiber Optic network developed by Bell Communications Research that provides voice, data, and video at high speeds.

SPID (Service Profile Identifier)
A number used to authenticate an ISDN channel to the switch that connects the ISDN–enabled device to the phone system. Each channel must have a different SPID number.

SPX (Sequence Packet Exchange)
A connection–oriented transport protocol in the IPX/SPX stack that provides the upper layer protocols with a direct connection between the sending and receiving machines.

star topology A network design where all the computers connect together at a central hub, each with its own cable.

static algorithms Internetwork mapping information that a network administrator enters into the router's routing table.

static routing Routing where the routing tables have been entered and updated manually by the network administrator.

subcommands Commands that provide specific configuration information for the interface or controller that you specify with a particular port command. See also *port commands*

subnet mask A four-octet mask that is used to determine which bits in the IP address refer to the network address, which bits in the IP address refer to the subnet address, and which bits in the IP address refer to the node address.

switches A Layer 2 internetworking device that can be used to preserve the bandwidth on your network using segmentation. Switches are used to forward packets to a particular segment using MAC hardware addressing (the same as bridges). Because switches are hardware-based, they can actually switch packets faster than a bridge.

switching The routing of packets on a router from an incoming interface to an outgoing interface.

synchronous communication Serial connections that use a clocking device that provides the precise timing of the data as it moves from sending to receiving computer across a serial connection.

TCP (Transport Control Protocol) A connection-oriented protocol that provides a virtual circuit between user applications on the sending and receiving machines on a TCP/IP network.

TCP/IP (Transmission Control Protocol/Internet Protocol) A routable protocol stack that can be run on a number of different software platforms (Windows, UNIX, and so on) and is embraced by most network operating systems as the default network protocol.

TDR (Time Domain Reflectometer) A device that can diagnose shorts and breaks in a cable and can also provide information on where the short or break exists on the cable.

Telnet   A terminal emulation protocol (part of the TCP/IP stack) that enables you to connect a local computer with a remote computer (or other device such as a router).

terminal adapter   Also known as an ISDN modem, used to connect a node configured for ISDN to the phone system. See also *ISDN*

TFTP server   A computer running TFTP software that can be used for the saving of router configuration files. Files can be copied from the router to the TFTP server, or from the TFTP server to the router.

TFTP (Trivial File Transfer Protocol)   A stripped-down version of FTP that provides a way to move files without any type of authentication (meaning no username or password).

Token Ring   A network architecture developed by IBM that is arranged in a logical ring and uses a token passing strategy for network access. Token Ring can run at 4 or 16Mbps. IBM developed and supports token-passing LANs.

topology   Networks have a physical layout or topology that will reflect, for instance, the cable type used and the actual architecture of the network (such as ring, bus, mesh, or star topology).

tunnel interface   A logical interface that can be used to move packets of a particular network architecture type over a connection that doesn't typically support these types of packets. See also *logical interface*

UDP (User Datagram Protocol) A connectionless-oriented TCP/IP stack transport protocol that provides a connection between application layer protocols that don't require the acknowledgements and synchronization provided by TCP. See also *TCP*

UPS (Uninterruptible Power Supply)   A device that will supply power to a computer device such as a router using a battery if the electricity is cut.

User mode   The basic access level to the router, User mode commands allow you to examine the router's configuration but don't allow you to change any configuration parameters. See also *Privileged mode* and *Configuration mode*

virtual circuit   A defined route established across a WAN cloud so that all the data packets move to the destination along the same route. The use of virtual circuits in packet switching networks can improve the overall performance of data transfers.

virtual interfaces   See *logical interface*

virtual terminal   A computer or router that uses Telnet to access another router.

VLMs (Virtual Loadable Modules Netware)   Software modules that establish and maintain network sessions between the client and server on an IPX/SPX network.

voltmeter   A device that can be connected to a cable to test the cable for a break or a short.

WAN (Wide Area Network)   A group of connected campuses or internetworks that span large geographical areas.

WAN interfaces   Serial interfaces or special interfaces such as ISDN interfaces that are used for WAN connectivity. See also *serial interfaces*

wildcard mask   32-bit mask used with IP addresses to determine which portion of the IP address should be ignored in Access list `deny` and `permit` statements.

X.121   A telephone standards addressing scheme (also known as International Data Numbers) used by the X.25 WAN protocol that is comprised of one to 14 decimal digits. This number identifies the local X.121 address for your serial interface and must be configured on the router that is being enabled for X.25.

XNS (Xerox Network Systems) In the 1960s a bunch of geniuses at the Xerox Palo Alto Research Center developed the XNS (Xerox Network Systems) network operating system. NetWare is based heavily on this early networking protocol stack.

ZIP (Zone Information Protocol) A Network and Transport layer protocol that is used to assign logical network addresses to nodes on the network.

Zone   A logical grouping of different AppleTalk physical network segments. Zones are logical groupings of users (similar to the concept of workgroups in Microsoft peer-to-peer networking).

INDEX

Symbols

56K modems, 56

A

Access lists, 244
AppleTalk Access lists, 256-258
building, 246-247, 252-253
deleting, 254
deny statements, 244-247
grouping to an interface, 253-254
IP Access lists, 247-254, 314
IPX Access lists, 254-256
operation of, 244-246
permit statements, 244-247
wildcard masks, 248-252

access-list [list #] deny or permit zone [zone name] command, 331

access-list [list #] permit or deny -1 -1 command, 330

access-list [list #] permit or deny cable-range [cable range] command, 331

access-list [list #] permit or deny [ip address] [wildcard mask] command, 328

access-list [list #] permit or deny [source network address] [destination network address] command, 330

active hubs, 72

Address Resolution Protocol (ARP), 47, 172

addresses
AppleTalk, 229-232
hardware addresses, 45
IP addresses, 47, 174
classes, 175-177
cost, 176
DHCP servers, 293
obtaining, 176
purpose of, 174-175
router interfaces, 196-201
subnet masks, 178-181
subnetting, 180-194
TFTP servers, 290
written forms, 174, 177-179
IPX addresses, 214-216
MAC addresses, 45
finding, 43
router LAN interfaces, 104
routing, 175
major network addresses, 192
network addresses, 192

administration of peer-to-peer networks, 10

algorithms for routing, 87
distance vector, 88-90
dynamic, 88-89
link state, 88-89
metrics, 89-91
static, 87, 89

American Registry for Internet Numbers, 176

Apple Macintosh networks
AppleTalk, 30-31, 228
addressing, 229-232
as a routable protocol, 85
configuring, 232-236
monitoring, 237-240
network interface cards, 228
phases, 230, 318
protocols, 49-51, 228-229
resources, 232
troubleshooting, 317-319
zones, 232-233
LocalTalk, 30

AppleTalk, 30-31, 228
addressing, 229-232
as a routable protocol, 85
configuring, 232-235
LAN interfaces, 235-236
WAN interfaces, 236
monitoring, 237-240
network interface cards, 228
phases, 230, 318
protocols, 49-51, 228-229
AARP, 50, 228
AFP, 50
AppleShare, 50
ATP, 50
DDP, 51, 228
NBP, 50, 229
RTMP, 229
ZIP, 50, 228
resources, 232
troubleshooting, 317-319
zones, 232-233

K-L

Get **FREE** books and more...when you register this book online for our Personal Bookshelf Program

http://register.quecorp.com/

 Register online and you can sign up for our *FREE Personal Bookshelf Program*...unlimited access to the electronic version of more than 200 complete computer books—immediately! That means you'll have 100,000 pages of valuable information onscreen, at your fingertips!

 Plus, you can access product support, including complimentary downloads, technical support files, book-focused links, companion Web sites, author sites, and more!

 And you'll be automatically registered to receive a *FREE subscription to a weekly email newsletter* to help you stay current with news, announcements, sample book chapters, and special events, including sweepstakes, contests, and various product giveaways!

 We value your comments! Best of all, the entire registration process takes only a few minutes to complete, so go online and get the greatest value going—absolutely FREE!

Don't Miss Out On This Great Opportunity!

QUE® is a brand of Macmillan Computer Publishing USA.

For more information, please visit *www.mcp.com*

Other Related Titles

Practical Windows Peer Networking
Jerry Ford
ISBN: 0-7897-2233-X
$29.99 US/
$44.95 CAN

Practical Network Cabling
Frank Derfler and Les Freed
ISBN: 0-7897-2247-X
$29.99 US/$44.95 CAN

Upgrading and Repairing PCs, Eleventh Edition
Scott Mueller
ISBN: 0-7897-1903-7
$59.99 US/$89.95 CAN

Terabit Networks: The Next Infrastructure
Marcus Goncalves
ISBN: 0-7897-2139-2
$39.99 US/$59.95 CAN

Deploying and Supporting Internetworking Services in Windows 2000
James Ramsey
ISBN: 0-7897-2230-5
$39.99 US/$59.95 CAN

Upgrading and Repairing Networks, Second Edition
Terry Ogletree
ISBN: 0-7897-2034-5
$49.99 US/$74.95 CAN

Practical Microsoft Windows 2000 Professional
Ed Bott
ISBN: 0-7897-2124-4
$24.99 US/
$37.95 CAN

Practical Microsoft Windows 2000 Server
Robert Reinstein
ISBN: 0-7897-2141-4
$29.99 US/
$44.95 CAN

www.quecorp.com

All prices are subject to change.